Teaching Mathe
through Problem

Prekindergarten–Grade 6

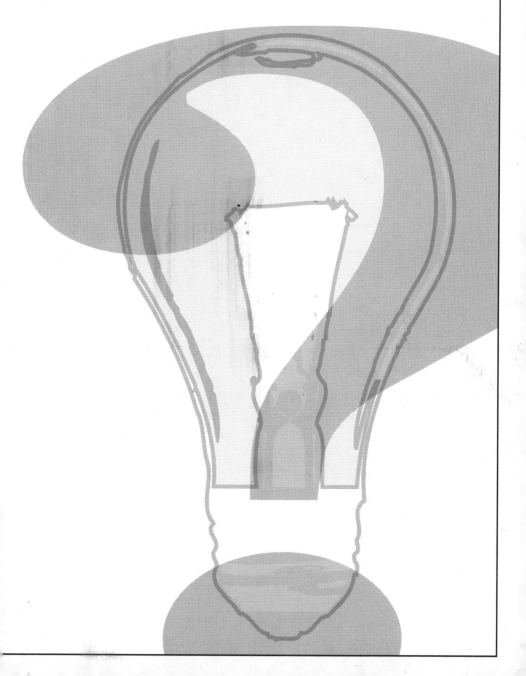

Teaching Mathematics through Problem Solving

Prekindergarten–Grade 6

Frank K. Lester Jr.
Volume Editor

Indiana University
Bloomington, Indiana

Randall I. Charles
Series Editor

Carmel, California

NATIONAL COUNCIL OF
TEACHERS OF MATHEMATICS

Library of Congress Cataloging-in-Publication Data

Teaching mathematics through problem solving : prekindergarten-grade 6 /
Frank K. Lester, Jr., volume editor.
    p. cm.
Includes bibliographical references.
  ISBN 0-87353-540-5 (pbk.)
  1. Mathematics--Study and teaching (Elementary)--United States. 2.
Mathematics--Study and teaching (Early childhood)--United States. 3.
Problem-based learning. I. Lester, Frank K.
  QA13.T4315 2003
  372.7--dc22
                              2003021744

The National Council of Teachers of Mathematics is a public voice of
mathematics education, providing vision, leadership, and professional
development to support teachers in ensuringmathematics learning of
the highest quality for all students.

Printed in the United States of America

Contents

Preface

Recommendation 1: Problem solving must be the focus of school mathematics in the 1980s.

—An Agenda for Action: Recommendations for
School Mathematics of the 1980s

Problem solving . . . can serve as a vehicle for learning new mathematical ideas and skills. . . . A problem-centered approach to teaching mathematics uses interesting and well-selected problems to launch mathematical lessons and engage students. In this way, new ideas, techniques, and mathematical relationships emerge and become the focus of discussion. Good problems can inspire the exploration of important mathematical ideas, nurture persistence, and reinforce the need to understand and use various strategies, mathematical properties, and relationships.

—Principles and Standards for
School Mathematics

THE TWO statements above, made twenty years apart by the National Council of Teachers of Mathematics (1980, p. 2; 2000, p. 182), serve as evidence of a long-term commitment of the Council to making problem solving a central theme of school mathematics instruction. The first statement was made at a time when the NCTM was just beginning to assert itself as a leader in efforts to change the nature of mathematics teaching in our schools. The second statement demonstrates that after two decades of curriculum development, research, and considerable reflection, the Council has developed a mature position about the role that problem solving should play in mathematics instruction.

The second statement also captures the essence of what this volume and its companion for grades 6–12 are about, namely, that the role of problem solving in mathematics instruction should change from being an activity that children engage in after they have studied various concepts and skills to being a means for acquiring new mathematical knowledge. But to suggest, as do the authors of *Principles and Standards,* that problem solving "can serve as a vehicle for learning new mathematical ideas and skills" (NCTM 2000, p. 182) is one thing; to provide the sort of coherence and clear direction that teachers need is another matter. These volumes represent a serious attempt to provide this coherence and direction.

In conceptualizing these volumes, the Editorial Panel was guided by what it saw as a central message of all four NCTM *Standards* documents (1989, 1991, 1995, 2000), namely, their emphasis on the importance of viewing classroom mathematics teaching as a system. According to Hiebert and his colleagues (1997), the five dimensions of this system are (1) the nature of classroom tasks, (2) the role of the teacher, (3) the social culture of the classroom, (4) mathematical tools as learning supports, and (5) equity and accessibility. Changing any of the elements of this system requires parallel changes in each of the other dimensions.

The system of mathematics classroom instruction that has characterized U.S. schools for at least the entire past century can be characterized in terms of the foregoing dimensions roughly as follows. Classroom tasks come mainly from the worked examples and homework exercises in the textbook. These are predominantly short, out of context, and symbolic, with emphasis on mastering and maintaining procedural skills. The teacher's role is to work examples for the students using direct teaching with the expectation that students will listen and learn to apply the same procedures that the teacher demonstrates. Students then practice those procedures through individual classwork and homework in which they try many more exercises that are very similar to those the teacher just demonstrated. If any applications of these procedures to real-world problems are included, they are briefly stated and straightforward "word problems" presented immediately after the procedures that students are expected to use to solve the problems.

The social culture of the traditional classroom includes the agreement that the teacher and the answer key in the textbook are the sole mathematical authorities. Students who develop proficiency in using the procedural strategies given in the textbook and demonstrated by the teacher are rewarded with praise and high grades. The nature of the students' thinking and the strategies, both mathematically valid and invalid, that they may have tried for solving problems are generally of much less interest than getting the right answer using the method shown in the textbook.

The most unfortunate consequence of instruction of the sort just described is that too often students leave school with at best a command of a set of facts, procedures, and formulas that are understood in a superficial or disconnected way. Even worse perhaps, they have little or no notion of how they might use what they have learned as they pursue their lives outside of school.

The chapters of this book together describe in some detail the characteristics of a classroom system called "teaching mathematics through problem solving" in which the main goal is for students to develop a deep understanding of mathematical concepts and methods. The key to fostering understanding is engaging students in trying to make sense of problematic tasks in which the mathematics to be learned is embedded. In addition to the mathematics that is the residue of work on the tasks, the kind of sense making and problem solving in which students engage involves doing mathematics. As students attempt to solve rich problem tasks, they come to understand the mathematical concepts and methods, become more adept at mathematical problem solving, and develop mathematical habits of mind that are useful ways to think about any mathematical situation.

This approach to classroom instruction involves much more than finding and using a collection of "fun" problems. First and foremost, the problematic tasks that are chosen must have embedded in them the mathematics that is to be learned. Second, the tasks must be accessible and engaging to the students, building on what they know and can do. Third, the teacher's role is very important in ensuring that the classroom norms are supportive of students' learning in this way and in pressing students to think deeply about their solution methods and those of their classmates and, most important, about the mathematics they are learning. Teachers also have a role in ensuring that students have access to appropriate technological and intellectual tools for learning, including facility with important paper-and-pencil procedures. A final challenge for teachers and curriculum developers is to find ways to ensure that the understanding that comes from learning mathematics through problem solving is accessible to all students.

This volume focuses on mathematics in prekindergarten through grade 6, and its companion volume deals with the secondary grades. The issues and the organization of the two volumes are similar, a reflection of the overlap of teaching issues across all grade levels.

This volume consists of three main sections—"Issues and Perspectives," "In the Classroom," and "The Role of Technology"— and a final chapter that presents a research perspective on teaching mathematics through problem solving. No single section addresses the entire set of issues concerning teaching mathematics through problem solving, but the volume as a whole presents much of what we mathematics educators as a profession know and have experienced about the topic.

The chapters in section 1 raise issues and points of view about teaching mathematics through problem solving that anyone who teaches mathematics to young children should carefully consider. In chapter 1, Diana Lambdin suggests several benefits of teaching through problem solving. In a nutshell, she argues that a close relationship exists between problem solving and understanding and that tremendous benefits result from learning mathematics with understanding. She brings her chapter to a close by showing how learning through problem solving promotes deep, rich understanding of mathematical concepts and processes.

Chapter 2, written by E. Paul Goldenberg, Nina Shteingold, and Nannette Feurzeig, focuses "not only on how mathematics reflects important ways of thinking that we believe *all* subjects should support and *all* children can and should acquire but also on the special role that mathematics plays in honing, refining, and extending these ways of thinking" (p. 16). The authors discuss five "habits of mind" that are especially relevant in prekindergarten through sixth grade and provide some concrete suggestions about how these habits of mind fit into teaching that emphasizes problem solving.

In the next chapter, Beatriz D'Ambrosio takes us on a trip from ancient to modern times to look at how conceptions of problem solving and the role it plays in the mathematics curriculum have changed over time. She notes that problem solving has been an important component of the school mathematics curriculum for at least 150 years and argues that teaching mathematics through problem solving emerged rather slowly and has recently begun to appear in some school mathematics textbooks.

Section 2, comprising chapters 4–12, focuses on how teaching mathematics through problem solving might play out in the classroom. Taken as a whole, these chapters serve to describe how the five dimensions of the classroom teaching system discussed previously might be thought of when problem solving becomes the means through which understanding of important mathematics is attained. A chapter by James Hiebert opens this section, and in it he identifies several "signposts" that can guide teachers in giving students opportunities to develop deep understanding of important mathematics. He notes, "Just as signposts along the road can highlight for travelers important information for reaching their destination, so signposts for the classroom can highlight for teachers essential features for helping students achieve the intended learning goals" (p. 54).

In chapter 5, John Van de Walle points out that adopting a problem-solving stance toward instruction requires the teacher to pay special attention to those tasks or problems that are at the heart of this approach. He addresses three fundamental questions: How do we choose good tasks? What do they look like? and How can we make them accessible to every child so that all children can learn?

Susan Jo Russell, Rebeka Eston, Jan Rook, Malia Scott, and Liz Sweeney, the authors of chapter 6, pose the question "What does it mean to have a mathematics curriculum that focuses on problem solving?" (p. 85). They point out that they have moved from viewing problem solving as separate from the rest of the mathematics curriculum to regarding the use of problems as a mechanism for focusing on the "coherent development of important mathematical ideas that are core to the curriculum" (p. 85).

An essential ingredient of teaching mathematics through problem solving is "listening" to students as they do mathematics. For Erna Yackel, the author of chapter 7, listening includes paying attention to what children do as well as to what they say. In general, listening to children in the mathematics classroom involves attempting to figure out how children make sense of and solve the problems they are given in mathematics class. She challenges teachers to think about how to use listening to move children forward in their thinking and enhance learning for all.

In chapter 8, Frances Curcio and Alice Artzt "explore the parallels between the process of teaching a mathematics lesson that leads to deep understanding and the process of solving a mathematics problem" (p. 137). Specifically, they discuss teaching mathematical problem solving within a teaching-as-problem-solving framework, and they show how teachers' knowledge, beliefs, goals, and problem-solving behaviors can be transferred to their students in ways that develop the students' understanding of important mathematics.

Because teaching mathematics through problem solving involves substantive changes in the nature of classroom activity and discussion, as well as changes in what is expected of both students and teachers, teachers should establish and sustain a risk-free classroom environment in which students' reasoning, not just answers, is valued. In chapter 9, Michelle Stephan and Joy Whitenack use examples from a first-grade classroom to illustrate how the teacher and the students can create a classroom environment conducive to rich problem solving as they establish both social and sociomathematical norms in the classroom.

Carmel Diezmann, Carol Thornton, and James Watters assert that teachers should pay particular attention to the needs of exceptional students if they intend to provide worthwhile problem-solving experiences for all the students in their classrooms. In chapter 10, the authors suggest ways to tailor mathematics instruction to meet the needs of students with learning difficulties as well as those with special talents in mathematics. They note that for both groups of students, their potential for learning is extended when they are challenged to engage in real problem solving.

In chapter 11, Lyn English points out that "[p]roblem posing—like its companion, problem solving—should be an integral component of the mathematics curriculum across all content domains" (p. 197). She suggests that problem posing tends not to be given the attention it deserves in mathematics class, even though it occurs naturally in everyday life. She discusses the fundamental importance of building inquiry-oriented classroom environments that foster problem posing and engage students in constructive dialogue and debate about their mathematical conjectures and constructions.

In the final chapter of this section, Yoshinori Shimizu gives an overview of the Japanese approach to teaching mathematics through problem solving and describes a typical organization of mathematics lessons in Japanese elementary schools. He also presents a specific problem that is typically found in Japanese textbooks and the related anticipated students' solutions to it to show how students share their solutions during the whole-class discussion. He ends his chapter by offering teachers some practical ideas that he has picked up from his work with Japanese teachers.

Section 3 contains chapters by Warren Crown (chapter 13) and Michael Battista (chapter 14). Crown discusses the role that technology can and cannot play in helping teachers use a problem-based approach in their mathematics teaching. He identifies various kinds of technology available for use in elementary classrooms and points out their strengths and weaknesses in supporting teaching through problem solving. Battista illustrates how special computer software can be used to support problem-based learning of geometry. He gives examples of sequences of problems that guide students' construction of geometric concepts and illustrates the nature of students' reasoning and learning as they work on these problems.

In chapter 15, Jinfa Cai summarizes what research tells us regarding four questions frequently asked about teaching through problem solving: (1) Are young children really able to explore problems on their own and arrive at sensible solutions? (2) How can teachers learn to teach through problem solving? (3) What are students' beliefs about teaching through problem solving? (4) Will students sacrifice basic skills if they are taught mathematics through problem solving? Cai concludes that some aspects of teaching mathematics through problem solving have considerable support from empirical research, but some important issues need additional research.

A special feature of this volume is the inclusion of a collection of Teacher Stories that amplify the perspectives and suggestions offered by the chapter authors. These stories, written by teachers involved in professional development seminars, serve to illustrate many of the ideas about teaching mathematics through problem solving discussed in those chapters.[1] The teachers were asked to choose classroom episodes that interested, intrigued, puzzled, or surprised them. They wrote to reflect on their own practice and to articulate questions or concerns that they wanted to share with the other teachers in the group. These stories, therefore, were not created to illustrate exemplary practice, to explain what works, or to tell other teachers how to carry out a specific activity or implement a teaching technique. Rather, they are attempts to capture episodes of mathematical activity in real classrooms, accompanied by the authors' own thoughts. In a sense, the stories bring to life many of the ideas about teaching mathematics through problem solving presented in the other chapters. The stories represent a wide range of classroom settings—large cities, small urban centers, and suburban towns. We are grateful to these teachers for sharing their practice with us. We hope their stories will serve to spark other

[1] The development of the teacher stories was supported in part by grant number ESI-9050210 from the National Science Foundation to TERC, Cambridge, Massachusetts, and grant number ESI-9731064 from the National Science Foundation to Education Development Center, Newton, Massachusetts. The teacher stories are used here with permission. The opinions expressed are those of the authors and not necessarily those of the Foundation. Pseudonyms are used for students' names in the teacher stories.

teachers' thinking about how to begin to teach mathematics through problem solving. Furthermore, we also hope that this collection of teachers' stories and perspectives offered by the other authors will provide both the coherence and the clear direction concerning teaching through problem solving that teachers have been seeking.

Finally, the conceptualization and preparation of this volume was undertaken by a small team of mathematics educators who thought long and hard about what it might mean to use problem solving "as a vehicle for learning new mathematical ideas and skills" (NCTM, 2000, p. 182). Without their very able assistance, this volume would have never been completed. Not only did each of them write a chapter and review drafts of chapters, but they each also gave us invaluable feedback whenever we asked for it. We wish to extend our sincerest thanks to these dedicated individuals, the members of the Editorial Panel:

> Diana V. Lambdin, Indiana University,
> Bloomington, Indiana
>
> Susan Jo Russell, Education Research Collaborative,
> Boston, Massachusetts
>
> John Van de Walle, Virginia Commonwealth University,
> Richmond, Virginia

Frank K. Lester Jr.
Volume Editor

Randall I. Charles
Series Editor

Section 1

Issues and Perspectives

CHAPTER 1

Benefits of Teaching through Problem Solving

Diana V. Lambdin

S TUDENTS in a fifth-grade class discuss their ideas about the following problem:

> Suppose 39 students want to share 5 candy bars fairly. How much can each student get?[1]

Leo: That's 5 divided by 39, and we decided last year that you can't divide a bigger number into a smaller number.

Anthony: I think that 39 ÷ 5 will be 7 remainder 4, but I think that 5 ÷ 39 will make a decimal number.

Jackson: I think that you will end up with a fraction of a number because, well, because 5 and 39—you can't divide 5 by 39 equally. I think it's going to be a number below 0.

After some further discussion about which notation (39 ÷ 5 or 5 ÷ 39) actually represents the situation in this problem and what sorts of numbers might be possible answers (e.g., fractions, decimals, remainders, "smaller numbers"), Mitchell chooses the correct notation and proposes that the answer will be pieces of candy bars.

Mitchell: So if each kid was going to get equal shares, they would have to cut the five candy bars into little equal pieces.

Teacher (MaryAnn): Can you name those equal pieces?

Mitchell: They might be candy bars.

---

[1] This scenario is adapted, with permission, from *Making Meaning for Operations* (Schifter, Bastable, and Russell 1999, pp. 77–82).

Teacher: Can you name the fraction that they might be?

Mitchell: [After a long pause] They wouldn't be able to do it.

The teacher stops to take a class poll.

Teacher: How many people think that you can do the problem 5 ÷ 39? How many think no, you can't?

The results are yes, 13; no, 15.

After a pause, Leo says that he wants to change his no to a yes. On the board, he draws five rectangles for the five candy bars and shows that partitioning two candy bars into sevenths will yield fourteen pieces. Then, without making lines, he indicates that partitioning four candy bars will produce twenty-eight pieces. He pauses when he realizes that the fifth candy bar will give him a total of thirty-five pieces. He then draws in lines to show that he has cut the last bar into eleven pieces. Now he is satisfied because he has a total of thirty-nine pieces. (See fig. 1.1.)

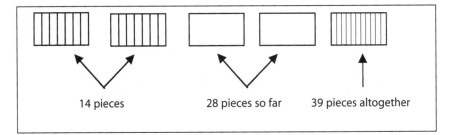

Fig. 1.1 Leo's solution to the candy-bar problem

Cynthia quickly responds that Leo's representation cannot be correct because it does not yield equal shares. She seems sure of her statement. Four rectangles are divided into sevenths and only one is divided into elevenths. "That's a problem," she says. Eventually, Laila makes a suggestion.

Laila: If I cut each of the five candy bars into thirty-nine pieces and then give each kid one piece from each candy bar, you could have each kid have five-thirty-ninths of a candy bar.

After further discussion, most of the class seems convinced that Laila has proposed a valid solution to the problem, although, as will be seen subsequently, the discussion begins again when Leo and Cynthia propose an entirely different way of thinking about dividing the candy bars.

As this extended discussion of the candy-bar problem in MaryAnn's class illustrates, engaging children in problem-solving situations can give them opportunities for exploring, discussing, experimenting with, and attempting to make sense of mathematical ideas. MaryAnn did not tell her students how to solve the candy-bar problem, choosing instead to support them in figuring it out on their own. In the process, her students revealed and worked through a number of confusions and misconceptions about division and fractions. Several days after the problem had first been posed and solved, the students were still debating and discussing mathematical ideas that would, no doubt, reappear again and again and be dealt with in more and more depth in the weeks and months to come. I revisit this vignette later in this chapter because it serves as a useful example of teaching mathematics through problem solving.

What Does Understanding Mathematical Ideas Mean?

One can think about a model of learning mathematics in which understanding is represented by an increasingly connected and complex web of mathematical knowledge. According to this model, students develop understanding when they figure out how each new idea is related to other things they already know (Brownell 1947; Hiebert and Carpenter 1992). Understanding grows as a student's own personal web of connections becomes more and more complex. Indeed, the web might be imagined as a "hammock-like structure in which knots are joined to other knots in an intricate webbing. Even if one knot comes undone, the structure does not collapse, but still bears weight—as opposed to what might happen if each individual rope was strung only from one point to another, with no interweaving" (Russell 1999, p. 4).

As an illustration of how mathematical ideas are connected in complex, weblike ways, consider figure 1.2, which shows a concept map about fractions made by two fourth-grade boys. As I sat watching them construct their map, the boys took turns thinking about what else they knew about fractions, adding nodes to their map, and drawing lines to link each new node with other nodes. Their map reveals many of the connections between fractions and decimals and whole-number operations that make sense to them.

I quizzed the boys about the meaning of the node that says "go further" and its connection with the node "complex [fraction]" and was surprised by the depth of understanding revealed by their response. As one boy explained, "Well, you know that you can change any fraction to other [equivalent] fractions by multiplying or dividing the top and bottom by the same thing, right? Like 4/6

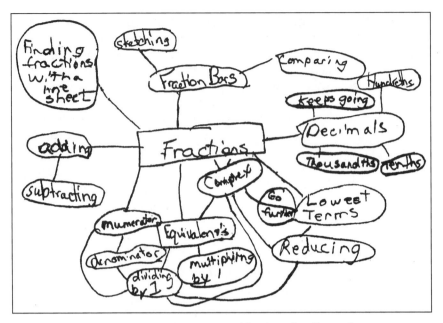

Fig. 1.2. Fractions concept map prepared by two fourth graders

can be 8/12 or 2/3?" I agreed, so he continued his explanation. "What's really neat is that you could go *further* with multiplying or dividing, if you wanted to. Like, you could divide by 2 over and over, like 4/6, then 2/3, and then 1 over 1 1/2, then 1/2 over 3/4, and so on. And the fractions might get messier and messier. They're called *complex fractions* because it's a fraction over another fraction. Isn't that neat?" I readily agreed that the idea of an infinite family of messier and messier equivalent fractions was certainly "neat." I was impressed not only with the enthusiasm these boys showed for thinking about fractions but also with their ability to communicate about the connections they recognized among many different mathematical ideas.

Problem Solving and Understanding– Mutual Support Systems

This book's authors believe that the primary goals of mathematics learning are understanding and problem solving, and that these goals are inextricably related because learning mathematics with understanding is best supported by engaging in problem solving.

The connection between solving problems and deepening understanding is symbiotic. Teachers want students to be able to solve problems—in mathematics and in the real world. After all, if they cannot solve problems with the mathematics they learn, what good is it? To be able to solve problems, one must have deep, conceptual understanding of the mathematics involved; otherwise, one will be able to solve only routine problems. So to become a good problem solver, a student must truly understand the inherent concepts. Thus, *understanding enhances problem solving.*

A problem is, by definition, a situation that causes disequilibrium and perplexity. A primary tenet of teaching through problem solving is that individuals confronted with honest-to-goodness problems are forced into a state of needing to connect what they know with the problem at hand. Therefore, *learning through problem solving develops understanding.* Students' mental webs of ideas grow more complex and more robust when the students solve problems that force them to think deeply and to connect, extend, and elaborate on their prior knowledge.

The next section of this chapter discusses the benefits of learning with understanding. This section could just as well be called "The Benefits of Learning through Problem Solving" because these two activities go hand in hand. To validate this link, after reading through this section, read through it again, substituting *problem solving* wherever the word *understanding* appears. Does the text still make sense?

Benefits of Learning with Understanding

Learning with understanding—making sense of new ideas by connecting them with existing knowledge in coherent ways—is, admittedly, often harder to accomplish and takes more time than simply memorizing or mimicking, yet the benefits of learning with understanding outweigh the challenges. Hiebert (this volume) discusses several reasons why understanding is essential, but much more can be said. Indeed, mathematics educators have identified at least six reasons why students should learn mathematics with understanding (Hiebert and Carpenter 1992; Van de Walle 2001).

Understanding Is Motivating

Nothing is more rewarding than the confident feeling that ideas make sense; and nothing is more frustrating than not understanding. Students who do not understand an idea often feel so discouraged and defeated that they give up even trying to learn. Such students must be motivated to learn by outside rewards (e.g., threat of a test, money for good grades, a gold star on a classroom chart, or desire to please a parent or teacher). By contrast, to understand something is a very motivating and intellectually satisfying feeling. When ideas make sense to students, they are prompted to learn by their desire for even deeper understanding. They want to learn more because feeling successful in connecting new ideas with old is an exhilarating experience. As Hiebert and his colleagues (1997) so aptly stated, "Understanding breeds confidence and engagement; not understanding leads to disillusionment and disengagement" (p. 2).

Understanding Promotes More Understanding

Another important benefit of understanding is that it promotes even more understanding. People make sense of their world by trying to use whatever ideas or procedures they have available to them. When confronted with unfamiliar mathematical problems, they attempt to use ideas or computational methods that they have used before. If those ideas or methods are poorly understood, they may be inappropriate for the situation at hand or may be incorrectly applied; thus, wrong answers are likely to result. However, this outcome is less likely to occur if students have made sense of the mathematics they have learned instead of having learned it without meaning. For example, Cauley (1988) observed that third graders often incorrectly perform multidigit subtraction by subtracting the top, smaller digit from the bottom, larger digit. However, he also found that such errors were more likely to be committed by students who lacked conceptual understanding of the multidigit subtraction procedure. When subtraction truly makes sense to students, they are more likely to recognize the nonsense answers that result from incorrect subtraction methods. Another research study, with fourth graders, revealed that those who had learned to connect decimal numerals with physical representations of decimal quantities were more likely to invent appropriate procedures for dealing with problems they had not encountered before, such as ordering decimals by size and converting between decimal and common fraction forms, than were those who had not previously made these connections (Wearne and Hiebert 1988).

In other words, when students' attempts to solve novel problems grow out of well-connected networks of mathematics understanding, the resulting mathematics is more likely to make sense and to be productive. "Inventions that operate on understandings can generate new understandings, suggesting a kind of snowball effect. As networks grow and become more structured, they increase the potential for invention" (Hiebert and Carpenter 1992, p. 74).

Understanding Helps Memory

When ideas are disconnected, they are hard to remember. Most adults can recall memorizing seemingly endless lists of disconnected facts in school—in various school subjects, not just mathematics. Those same adults often admit that many of the items on those lists were quickly forgotten after the class or the test was over. By contrast, when individual ideas make sense because they are connected with one another in the solver's web of understanding, much less information needs to be remembered. For example, memorizing different rules for the placement of the decimal point in addition, subtraction, multiplication, and division problems involving decimals is unnecessary if a solver simply understands one concept: how place value is represented in decimal notation. By using a fundamental understanding of place value, the solver can easily figure out where the decimal point belongs in any answer. A single big concept—which is actually a richly connected network of smaller concepts—is easier to remember than many small, unrelated concepts.

Understanding Enhances Transfer

Transfer is perhaps the single biggest challenge in all of education. It is one thing to be able to perform well on a test after having learned that very same test material in recent school lessons. It is another thing to be able to apply that learning in new, unanticipated situations, in or out of school. Yet, obviously, transfer should be the goal of education, because school prepares students for a world outside the classroom, for solving future problems that one may not even imagine today.

Many teachers have heard the plaintive cry of students who, faced with a mathematics word problem, plead, "Just tell me what to do (Add? Subtract? Multiply? Divide?), and then I'll be able to solve it just fine." These students have learned certain mathematical ideas or procedures without making sense of them and thus have difficulty transferring these ideas to the novel situation of a problem in context. By contrast, ideas or procedures that make sense to students are much more easily extended and applied.

For example, many of the concepts that students find very difficult when learning to work with fractions are actually just extensions of fundamental concepts of whole-number arithmetic. On the one hand, the process of adding fractions, which may require finding common denominators so that like quantities can be combined, can be better understood if students already recognize that adding whole numbers involves combining like quantities—adding hundreds to hundreds, tens to tens, and ones to ones (which is why we line up the digits according to place value in the standard algorithm before beginning to add). On the other hand, multiplying fractions does not require first obtaining common denominators, for much the same reason that we generally do not need to line up the decimal points before multiplying decimal numerals.

Understanding Influences Attitudes and Beliefs

Understanding leads students to see mathematics in a positive light—as a subject that makes sense because it is logical and connected. When students appreciate the underlying structures of mathematics, they see it as a reasonable, approachable subject; as a result, their self-confidence with mathematics soars and they are generally more willing to tackle challenging problems. By contrast, students who have learned mathematics without understanding are often successful only with solving problems similar to those they have already seen. Unable to see how mathematical ideas are related or useful, these students often see the subject itself in a negative light, viewing it as arbitrary and mysterious—a subject that only "geniuses" can master.

Understanding Promotes the Development of Autonomous Learners

A major goal of school mathematics instructional programs must be to support students in becoming autonomous learners. As described in *Everybody Counts,* "to understand what they learn, [students] must enact for themselves verbs that permeate the mathematics curriculum: examine, represent, transform, solve, apply, prove, communicate" (National Research Council 1989, pp. 58–59). Students learn more and better when they are helped to take control of their own learning by defining learning goals and monitoring their own progress in achieving them.

Children engage in problem solving and sense making quite naturally when they are very young. Preschoolers often drive their parents crazy asking "Why . . .?" as they take things apart, try to put them back together, and just generally attempt to make sense of the world around them. Unfortunately, traditional United States teaching practices often encourage children to suspend their curiosity and to turn off their intuitive ways of thinking, prompting them instead to move—at least in school—toward just trying to imitate whatever the teacher or the textbook tells them to do. Students of all ages bring many ideas with them to school. These ideas include both informal intuitions about the world around them and prior school-based knowledge, and all these ideas can potentially be connected in logical ways with new ideas. Since new learning is most robustly built on prior learning, teachers should make a serious commitment to figuring out what students already know so that they can challenge the students with problems that help build understanding (Simon 1995).

When challenged with appropriately chosen tasks, students become confident about tackling difficult problems, eager to figure things out on their own, flexible in exploring mathematical ideas and trying alternative solution paths, and willing to persevere when tasks are challenging. Effective learners realize the importance of monitoring and reflecting on their own thinking and of learning from their mistakes. Students from classrooms in which problem solving is an everyday expectation view making sense of mathematics as a challenge rather than see difficult problems as a signal to give up and consider oneself a failure. When students successfully solve a difficult problem or finally understand a complex idea, they experience a very special feeling of accomplishment, and they recognize that learning mathematics through problem solving is engaging and rewarding.

Teaching through Problem Solving Promotes Understanding

A teacher's goal must be to help students understand mathematics; yet understanding is not something that one can teach directly. No matter how kindly, clearly, patiently, or slowly teachers explain, they cannot *make* students understand. Understanding takes place in the students' minds as they connect new information with previously developed ideas, and teaching through problem solving is a powerful way to promote this kind of thinking. Teachers can help and guide their students, but understanding occurs as a by-product of solving problems and reflecting on the thinking that went into those problem solutions. For that reason, this book is all about teaching and learning mathematics through problem solving. By solving problems, students learn to make connections among mathematical ideas.

The vignette that introduced this chapter illustrates the power of problems to engage students in making sense of mathematical concepts, in this example, the concept of dividing a number by a larger number. MaryAnn could simply have explained to her class how to perform the division and how to write the answer ("39 doesn't go into 5, so we say it goes 0 times with 5 left over, and we can write either '0 R 5' or '0 and 5/39'"). But this sort of instruction does nothing to help connect the concept of the fraction 5/39 with the process of dividing a number by a larger one. Nor does it help students understand why 5/39 represents each child's fair share of the candy, or even how much 5/39 is. These ideas came up quite naturally in MaryAnn's class several days after the candy-bar problem was initially discussed.

Two students, Leo and Cynthia, proposed to the class an alternative way of dividing five candy bars among thirty-nine people (refer to fig. 1.3). Jackson looked at Leo and Cynthia's diagram and asked what 40 fortieths has to do with 5 ÷ 39. This approach to the problem raised many more questions from members of the class:

> "What is the last piece called? Is it 1/8 or 1/40?" "What's the whole?" "What happens if the last piece is divided into 39 even smaller pieces?" "Do we know what 5/39 means?" "Is 'slightly more than 1/8' a better answer than 5/39 because it's clearer, even though it's less exact?" "What about 1/8 and 1/39 of 1/8? Or should it be 1/8 and 1/39 of 1/40?" "When we say it's 1/8, it's 1/8 of what? And when we say it's 1/40, it's 1/40 of what?" "If we cut the last piece into fortieths, each person gets 1/8 plus 1/40 of 1/8. What happens to the extra fortieth? Do we keep on dividing it?" [The class proceeds to talk about "pieces," "slivers," and "crumbs."] (Schifter, Bastable, and Russell 1999, p. 82)

In the course of solving this problem, Leo, Cynthia, Jackson, and their classmates debated many of the most important—and difficult—aspects of understanding fractional parts and division. For example, their curiosity about whether the "last piece" should be called 1/8 or 1/40 led to a discussion about the importance of clearly identifying the "unit," or whole, whenever looking at a fraction. Indeed, in this problem, as in many fraction problems, the "unit" changes, depending on where one is in the problem solution. To start, the whole is thought of as a collection of five candy bars. To share these bars among thirty-nine students, one could simply say that each student gets one thirty-ninth, that is, 1/39 of the entire stock of five candy bars, if the unit is five bars. To specify how much of each candy bar each student gets, however, one needs to view each candy bar as a unit rather than think of five bars as the unit. Hence, each student gets 5/39 of each candy bar. Leo and Cynthia proposed another way of dividing the bars, suggesting that each student could get 1/8 of a candy bar plus 1/39 of the final, leftover 1/8. For their solution, we need to re-focus our attention to see that final 1/8 as a new unit and to pic-

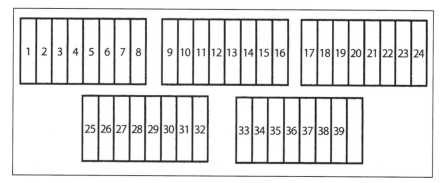

Fig. 1.3. Leo and Cynthia's alternative way to divide the candy bars

ture dividing it into thirty-nine parts. The lengthy discussion in which MaryAnn's students engaged over several days was useful in helping them develop and solidify their understanding both of the relationship between division and fractions and of the importance of recognizing units when working with fractions. These fundamental mathematical ideas arose naturally from the problem-solving experience, not simply from explanations by the teacher.

Students mature mathematically during the prekindergarten through high school years through active engagement with mathematical problems. Learning with understanding is enhanced by classroom interactions as students debate mathematical ideas and conjectures, explain and defend their own ideas, and develop mathematical reasoning skills. Procedural fluency, conceptual understanding, and ability to engage in mathematical debate and argument grow and deepen as students connect new and old ideas through appropriately challenging problem-solving experiences.

CHAPTER 2

Mathematical Habits of Mind for Young Children

E. Paul Goldenberg
Nina Shteingold
Nannette Feurzeig

ELEMENTARY school teachers have the challenging job of managing just about everything that goes on in the classroom. They often try to integrate their activities, finding ways to draw mathematics lessons from literature, science, art, or lunch-money collection; finding ways to draw language lessons from science or mathematics contexts; and so on. "Wouldn't it be nice," they say, "if what we do at reading time, or in the morning calendar activity, or in our study of chicks helped the children use and practice what they are learning in mathematics? And wouldn't it be nice if mathematics lessons gave the children new and useful vocabulary and practice with their reading and writing?"

This way of thinking leads educators beyond thinking about the particulars of each subject and leads us to consider what children really need to gain from all the contexts that we, in schools, can control—mathematical, scientific, linguistic, artistic, and so on. For example, people need to be able to communicate clearly, not only feelings and story plots but also procedures and instructions, and logical, relational, quantitative, and spatial information.

But even though some of what students learn in mathematics is, appropriately, neither unique to that subject nor even especially mathematical, teachers must avoid one subtle risk of "integration": losing what truly is unique about mathematics. This

The writing of this chapter was supported, in part, by the National Science Foundation, grant number ESI-0099093. The opinions expressed are those of the authors and not necessarily those of the Foundation.

15

chapter focuses not only on how mathematics reflects important ways of thinking that we believe *all* subjects should support and *all* children can and should acquire but also on the special role that mathematics plays in honing, refining, and extending these ways of thinking. This dual focus attempts to answer why teachers should, and how they can, teach mathematics that truly serves all students. The "why" is easy enough: A "mathematics for all" curriculum must include the facts and basic skills that everyone uses, and it must teach them well enough that people are mathematically enabled, not disabled. It must support and refine the kinds of reasoning that all people need, regardless of their eventual choice of career or lifestyle. And it must lay a foundation that allows anyone to choose pursuits that require more advanced mathematical ideas than the vast majority of students will ever use explicitly. Without these ingredients, the curriculum either does not really involve mathematics or is not for everyone. "How" to teach mathematics for all becomes clearer when one realizes that mathematics is both a body of facts accumulated over the millennia and a body of ways of thinking that has enabled people to discover or invent these facts. In our view, teaching these ways of thinking, or mathematical habits of mind, is a vital part of mathematics instruction at every level.

In this chapter, we discuss five habits of mind that are especially relevant in kindergarten through sixth grade and are particularly important to teaching mathematics through problem solving. After discussing these habits of mind, we offer concrete suggestions on how they fit into everyday teaching and learning.

Some Habits of Mind for Elementary-Grades Children

The sections that follow describe five habits of mind, their roles outside mathematics, and how mathematics extends, specializes, or sharpens each of them. Because the language arts curriculum is a very important part of elementary schooling, and because communication is a good example of a broadly important skill that mathematics can help develop, we focus much attention on communication-related habits of mind. Our hope is to help you—as teachers—step beyond the examples we give so that you can apply the principles throughout your teaching.

Habit of Mind 1: Thinking about Word Meanings

The process of creating, testing, adjusting, and working with definitions is a major part of mathematics. Although children rarely need to create formal definitions, all the skills involved are part of expressing oneself clearly. A good definition—especially outside mathematics—is hard to write because it must include all cases of the thing to be defined but not allow any extraneous ones. Consider, for example, trying to define *chair*. Young children might just describe its utility: "You can sit on it." But pillows, tables, horses, and the floor also fit that description. Placing the item in a category, such as "a piece of furniture," is also insufficient. Combining the two descriptions, or saying not just that one can sit on it but that "its primary purpose is as a seat," may be more precise. Trying to make definitions helps children and the rest of us see why they can be so difficult to understand. How often has a child looked up a word such as *extinguish* in the dictionary, perhaps even copied the definition faithfully, and then written something like "At night, we extinguish [put out] the cat."

Becoming attuned to the ways words are used, whether for the logical reasoning that mathematics requires or just for the sake of expressing themselves clearly, is a valuable skill for children to acquire. Mathematics provides many opportunities for thinking about, and playing with, the way words are used. Consider the meanings of the words *circle* and *on* in these two contexts:

- Cut out a circle. Place one dot anywhere on that circle.

- Draw a circle. Place one dot in the circle, and one dot on it.

In the first case, "circle" seems to refer to the disk of paper that remains after cutting along the circular rim, and "on" seems to suggest *anywhere* on that disk. In the second case, the word "on" clarifies any ambiguity in the meaning of "circle" and assures us that "circle" refers to the line one drew, and not the area contained within it.

A definition creates a category, and categories may be related. Many authors of mathematics curricula and high-stakes tests expect children in the elementary grades to know the hierarchy of the categories

polygon ⊃ quadrilateral ⊃ parallelogram ⊃ rectangle ⊃ square

as in the problem in figure 2.1, adapted from a teacher-made fourth-grade assessment test. (The ⊃ sign means "includes." As with the > sign, it opens up to the "larger," more inclusive category preceding the sign. So, things that we would call polygons— roughly speaking, closed shapes that have only straight sides— include all the things that we would call quadrilaterals [four-sided polygons], and so on. At this point, English begins to be a bit con-

Look at these pictures.	
List all polygons.	all but E
List all triangles.	only I
List all quadrilaterals.	all but E, H, and I
List all parallelograms.	all but E, H, I, and F
List all rectangles.	A, B, C, D, and K
List all squares.	D and K

Fig. 2.1. Item from a teacher-made fourth-grade assessment test

fusing. It is correct, in English, to say, "Squares are rectangles," but "are" clearly does not mean "=," because rectangles are not necessarily squares. A comparable statement outside mathematics is "Bears are animals": *animals ⊃ bears*.)

Three of the words in this problem—*polygon, quadrilateral,* and *parallelogram*—are frankly of little use to most people outside the school setting, but two worthy ideas emerge from exercises such as this. One is that *hierarchies of categories* exist. This concept is hard for children to grasp, and not just in a mathematics context. Faced with six toy cows and four toy horses, young children regularly trip over such questions as "Which is more, the number of cows or the number of animals?" The difficulty is not with counting. Asked how many animals they see, children will get the right answer. With very young children, calling a set of creatures "cows" seems to exclude those creatures from other categories. Does this tendency mean that young children need specific lessons on quadrilaterals to improve their understanding of hierarchies? No! They will eventually begin to understand multiple levels of classification anyway. But experience at a developmentally appropriate level helps to advance this understanding.

A second useful idea is that *the way categories are used depends on the context.* When we ask students to mark all the rectangles on an examination, we expect them to include the squares. But when we ask students to draw a rectangle and they draw a square, we may well think the students have misunderstood or have even been a bit obstreperous. The category "rectangle" has not changed from the examination context to the drawing context, but the way we use it has changed. The examination item checks whether students understand that the general category "rectangle" includes the special case "square." The request to draw a rectangle—whether in mathematics class or in casual conversation—calls for a picture that suggests the general category, not the special case. Children need to understand "rectangle" used both ways. Context determines which shape is appropriate.

Children need to develop their sensitivity to contexts and to the generality, inclusivity, and specificity appropriate to each. Their nonmathematical writing often suffers because they use words, such as thing or went, that are not specific enough to make their writing interesting or, at times, even understandable. At other times, they err on the side of overspecifying something that is already obvious to the reader, as in "a triangle with three sides." Studying mathematics is not the only way to appreciate the significance of context. Other subjects, especially and obviously language arts, are equally good or better venues. But contexts and categories in mathematics are not as "messy" as in other areas, so they are easier for children to play with. As long as tests and many curricula emphasize vocabulary—which, from a purely mathematical point of view, is an unwarranted and misleading emphasis—we can seize the opportunity to teach good thinking.

Another important concept regarding categories is that they should be both useful and testable.

Usefulness

In some contexts and for some practical purposes, different objects can sensibly be treated as if they are the same. If enough such contexts exist, we define and name a category. The shapes △, ◹, ◺, ◿, and ◺ are all different, yet they have so much in common, so much can be said about all of them, that they are worth treating as a group, even, for some purposes, as if they were all the same. Here are their common attributes:

- The area of each figure can be computed by multiplying the length of its horizontal side by the height of the figure and then dividing by 2.

- The angle sum in each of these figures is the same.

- If you draw any other closed figure with sides the same length as one of these, the new figure will exactly match the old one, angle for angle.

The category "triangles" is useful, so it warrants a name. But except for enabling students to pass tests, a category does not warrant a name until one has something worth saying about it. On the one hand, if students can say little about a rhombus or quadrilateral beyond identifying it, then learning the term gains them no more than a test answer.[1]

How inclusive or exclusive should a definition be? For example, why is a square included in the family of rectangles? And why is 1 excluded from the family of primes? The reason that definitions are built to be neither too exclusive nor too inclusive is to make the categories useful.

Rectangles are often described as if the length of the sides must differ, but they should not be defined that way. Saying that the sides of a rectangle "do not have to be equal" is not the same as saying that they "must differ." (This is an important concept; algebra beginners often misinterpret $a + b$ as necessarily meaning a sum of *different* numbers.) Except for an added restriction (i.e., all four sides must be equal), the square shares all the properties of a rectangle, and everything that can be said about a rectangle (e.g., area formulas) also applies to a square. Therefore, defining rectangles in a way that includes squares is useful.

Likewise, 1 is defined not to be prime because the notion "prime" becomes less useful if it includes 1. For example, nonprime whole numbers can be expressed as the product of a unique set of primes. This statement could not be made if 1 were considered prime: the prime factors of 12 would still be {2, 2, 3} (because $2 \times 2 \times 3 = 12$), but they would also be {1, 2, 2, 3}, {1, 1, 2, 2, 3}, and so on. This inclusion complicates the whole concept of "prime" and makes it less useful.

Testability

A good definition should make it easy to test whether a particular object fits the definition. Sometimes, trying to invent a test helps us understand the category more clearly. Here is a non-mathematical example: A noun can be defined as "a person, place, or thing (or idea)," but a good test to see whether a particular word is a noun might be to see whether one can put *the* or *our* before

---

[1]On the other hand, the word *quadrilateral* can be a great exercise in spelling and etymology for young children—a good use for the lesson if one must teach the term anyway. The origin of word *does* interest many elementary school children. Drawing connections between the technical vocabulary of mathematics and everyday (or, at least, nonmathematical) vocabulary can help both the learning of the specialized mathematical terms and also general vocabulary-building purposes. Quadrilateral, for example, is built from *quadri-* (four) and *lateral* (side). Number-word parts like *quadri* show up in many English words: *quadrant, quadrangle, quadruped, quadruple,* and even in *quarter, quart, square,* and dozens of other words. Children who know "four" in Spanish (*cuatro*) can connect the new technical root *quadri-* with their own special knowledge.

the word or *is* after the word. If one can say "the *x*" or "*x* is," then *x* is acting like a noun. A verb is often described as "an action word," but *is* or *thought* or *can* or even *sat* hardly strike children as involving much action. One can test to see whether a particular word is a verb by trying to put *she* or *they* before it. If one can say "she *x*" or "they *x*," then *x* is acting like a verb. Similarly, if we can say "the *x* cat," *x* is acting like an adjective.

Inventing definitions that are concise, that capture all correct instances, that exclude all others, and that are testable gives students useful practice in clarity of thought and expression. In mathematics, this exercise also helps students understand the concept more deeply than when they merely use definitions.

Do all categories have independent definitions? No. If one looks up any word, such as *chair*, in a dictionary, then looks up all the words used in its definition, one eventually either runs out of words completely or must create a "loop," reusing words that have already been looked up. . . .

To keep mathematical statements unambiguous, we restrict ourselves to using only words that are already defined or ones that we agree we all know. Why is it impossible to use only defined words? When asked this question, a student would probably be able to provide a convincing proof, maybe by contradiction. Perhaps it would be something like "What would the definition of the first word consist of?"

Habit of Mind 2: Justifying Claims and Proving Conjectures

Without some version of proof, much of what children learn remains unexamined and unexplained, a set of memorized facts and patterns, little black boxes that keep mathematics a mystery; but this outcome need not occur. As the authors of *Principles and Standards for School Mathematics* (NCTM 2000) note, age-appropriate proof can—we believe, *should*—exist throughout the elementary school curriculum. Second graders can not only notice (conjecture) that the sum of any two odd numbers seems to be even but can even come up with excellent explanations—true proofs despite the lack of formal appearance—of why this must be so even for pairs of odd numbers they have not tried. Some say (in second grader style) that an even number is just a bunch of pairs, whereas an odd number is a bunch of pairs and one left over. Adding two odd numbers yields a bunch of pairs and two left over, which make a pair, so the result is really "just a bunch of pairs." Others may try to illustrate this concept using concrete materials.

When children begin to think about skip counting by three, they are ready for a fancier experiment, in which investigation, practice, and logical reasoning all come together. Consider the following activity.

Column A	Column B	Column C
0	1	2
3	4	5
6	7	8
9	10	11
12	13	14
15	16	17
18	19	20
21	22	23
24	25	26
27	28	29
30	31	32

1. Write all the whole numbers through 32 in three columns, as shown. What is the same about all the numbers in any one column? Pick any two numbers in column A and add them. Which column contains the answer? Try it for a different pair from column A. What pattern do you see in your results? How might you explain that pattern?

2. Do the same experiment on column B. Pick two numbers in column B and add them. Which column contains the answer? Why is it always that column?

3. Where do you find the answer if you add a number from column B to one from column C?

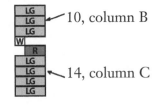

Sum = 24, column A

Long before students have formal algebra to answer these questions, they can use equally generalizable logic, with Cuisenaire rods as a kind of "notation." They might, for example, show that all numbers in column A can be constructed using only light-green (LG) rods (whose lengths are 3 units); that numbers in column B require one additional white (W) rod (whose length is 1 unit); and that numbers in C require a red (R) rod (whose length is 2 units). The answer to problem 3, then, could be given for any particular example with a construction or picture like the one shown here for 10 + 14 = 24; the students can see that any other example would work the same way.

Very few students would find or construct this kind of explanation without help or prior experience, but most students can learn to do so. Giving them such experiences in class helps them develop the habit of looking for patterns, the skills to find them, and the expectation that patterns have explanations. In a similar way, by fourth grade, many students can explain why a product like 109872388 × 3598109 must be even—if they are asked, and if they have had chances to think about questions like this before. Questions like this *should* be asked, as part of a strategy for building the expectation that conjectures and their proofs are part of the mathematics game.

One group of third graders we know loves a set of logic puzzles about two families: the Liars, who can never tell the truth, not even by accident, and the Truthtellers, who cannot lie, even in error. For example, "You meet Dale and Dana. Dale says 'We're both Liars.' What family is Dale from? What about Dana?" Solving logic puzzles like this gives students experience with looking for contradictions (Could Dale be telling the truth?), tracking logical consequences, and trying all the cases, being systematic enough to know what all the cases are. Many students are amused when considering what to make of the statement "I am a Liar." (Adam Case's [1991] *Who Tells the Truth?* has a nice set of these Liar-Truthteller puzzles. This kind of puzzle, famous in mathematics, is found in many recreational mathematics books.)

Here is another example. Fifth grader Naomi proudly proclaims that she has discovered a new mathematics rule: that whenever the perimeter of a rectangle increases, its area also increases. She uses a chart to demonstrate her rule:

	Rectangle 1	Rectangle 2	Rectangle 3	Rectangle 4
length	4 units	6 units	8 units	10 units
width	2 units	3 units	4 units	5 units
perimeter	12 units	18 units	24 units	30 units
area	8 square units	18 square units	32 square units	50 square units

Her rule seems to make sense; it looks like it might be true. Students might start by trying to find other rectangles to prove her rule. But if they are systematic and planful in their choice of examples, or even by mistake, they are likely to find rectangles that contradict Naomi's rule. *A proof by counterexample* is a truly powerful justification and need not be a defeat for Naomi. Students can be taught to pursue the original idea anyway, and ask under what conditions her rule is true, perhaps leading them to think about shape—a good foreshadowing of ideas of geometric similarity.

Children love finding patterns, as long as they present some new or surprising element or challenge, and enjoy explaining why things are the way they are. And when the proofs and proof styles are developmentally appropriate, children can often learn to invent them very well. The curiosity to know what and also why and the skill to pursue these questions are important to foster and develop in children, not just as a precursor to proof in high school geometry but because these traits are valuable outside mathematics as well as within. Whether one becomes an investigative journalist, a mechanic (auto diagnostician), a doctor (human diagnostician), or a scientist, these same inclinations and skills are essential.

Proof within mathematics depends entirely on logic applied to previously agreed-on truths, whereas proof outside mathematics often accepts data (evidence), likelihood, and precedents as factors. Even so, the fact that the same word is used for both styles of thinking suggests that these two kinds of "proof" have something in common. Mathematics should not replace the kind of logic children otherwise use but should surely augment it, especially starting at a time when children naturally begin to think in this way. As students learn mathematical proof, they should consistently see how it relies on—and builds on and refines—their own good sense.

Students do not need to know the names of different kinds of proofs or any such formalities. They do need to recognize the difference among a guess, a conjecture, and a proven assertion. And they need to develop the inclination to wonder why things are as they are, to expect reasons, and—when possible—even to provide a logical chain of reasons as the explanation. They also need to experience a variety of proof styles expressed in developmentally appropriate ways. These might include any of the styles illustrated here: the constructive build-a-model approach with the Cuisenaire rods to investigate the skip-counting-by-three experiment; the raw logic (or exhaustive testing) that works on the Liar-Truthteller puzzles; and the healthy skepticism that leads students to find a counterexample in the perimeter-and-area problem.

Habit of Mind 3: Distinguishing between Agreement and Logical Necessity

Life outside mathematics involves rules: for example, the rule of not interrupting a person who is talking. This rule is purely a social convention, a given. It can even be broken without causing any trouble at all when friends are close and conversation is casual—that is, when all parties agree. The source of authority is *social agreement.*

Mathematics also involves rules. For example, in late elementary school, many curricula teach what is called "the order of operations." Without any instruction to do otherwise, one might expect to perform the arithmetic in an expression like $3 + 4 \times 5 + 1$, from left to right, adding 3 and 4, then multiplying by 5, and finally adding 1 to get 36 as a result. By agreement, however, we do not work strictly from left to right; we perform multiplication and division before addition and subtraction. In this case, the agreement is that 4×5 is done first, leaving us with $3 + 20 + 1$, or 24, as a result. Why this rule is chosen is pure convention, designed, like definitions, to serve only one master: usefulness. The source of authority is social agreement for the sake of clear communication and useful results.

Next consider another mathematical rule, the rule that two lengths may be added only if they are expressed in the same units. Three feet plus 24 inches is not 27 of anything; it is either 5 feet or 60 inches (or 1.666... yards, and so on). Likewise, three nickels and two dimes cannot be added until the units are the same: they can be jointly regarded as coins, in which case the sum is "5 coins," or they can jointly be regarded as cents, in which case the sum is "35 cents." This rule is not based on social agreement; it is logically necessary—addition, as an operation, would make no sense without it—and therefore it applies across the board to addition.

Fractions also must follow this rule: one-half and one-third cannot be added until they are converted to the same units. One such common unit is sixths: three-sixths plus two-sixths is five-sixths. The same rule applies with the standard algorithm for adding two multidigit numbers. Lining up the columns is not an arbitrary practice; it ensures that one adds only things that are expressed in the same units. The following sum of 120 and 43 is wrong because the alignment of the problem requires one to add a 2 and a 3 (and a 1 and a 4) that represent different things. The 2 is tens, or dimes; the 3 is ones, or pennies. The source of authority for all these addition rules is logical necessity: one cannot add apples and oranges!

$$\begin{array}{r} 120 \\ +\,43 \\ \hline \end{array}$$
Oops! 550

Why is it so important to recognize the source of authority—convention or logic—for each mathematical idea? One goal of school mathematics is to support the development of children's reasoning. If all rules are arbitrary or if no distinction is made, rules become divorced from, or even the enemy of, common sense. How often do we see people use, or cave in to, data and graphs, even when the "mathematics" does not really support the argument!

Conventions, such as people's names, addresses, and telephone numbers, may have patterns and reasons and history, but not logical necessity. Mathematics provides a beautiful counterpoint, an opportunity to see that some truths—such as the fact that the sum of two odd numbers must be even—are ones that students can reason out for themselves. Mathematics gives students a chance to practice that kind of reasoning. And only in mathematics is this appeal to logic alone possible.

Students commonly ask, in any subject, "Did I do it right?" "Is my answer correct?" Mathematics often lets students answer such questions themselves, helping them build a certain independence of learning and a confidence that can have benefits far beyond the mathematics lesson. The student can say, "I can figure this out by myself, I don't need books or authority figures. I can be the authority." Recognizing when they can be the authority also helps them learn to recognize when they can *not* be. Convention, cultural legacy, data from history or the physical world, and so on require the authority of reliable outside sources (books, people, or experiments).

Habit of Mind 4: Analyzing Answers, Problems, and Methods

Checking and analyzing answers

For many of us, when we were children, checking meant only doing the problem again or working backward from the answer—checking a subtraction problem with addition, for example. Checking has another, richer meaning—reviewing an answer for reasonableness. We as teachers can tell that students are trying to make sense when we hear such chains of thought as these:

- I added two whole numbers, but my answer is less than either one of them, so something must be wrong.

- My answer is three-and-a-third buses. That makes no sense!

- The area of rectangle A is 24 square inches, and I got 50 square inches for rectangle B's area. This looks OK because B looks much bigger. Oh, and if I place A here on top of B, there is about enough space for another copy of A next to it, so B is about twice as big as A. My answer seems correct.

Students must see that even when computations are required, common sense remains central.

Tinkering with the problem

When students have found, justified, and made sense of an answer, they need to step back and see how the whole problem—statement, solution, and answer—fits in a bigger picture. Can other problems be solved using the same method? How can the answer to this problem be applied elsewhere? Can this problem be extended or generalized to address new situations? This analysis, in turn, leads to one of the most powerful ideas of all: that even (in fact, especially!) in mathematics, one can ask what-if questions. The what-if has to be taken seriously to see what its consequences really are. But only as children see that asking what-if questions is a genuine part of the "mathematics game" can they feel completely free to suggest such questions themselves (see Brown and Walter [1990]; Goldenberg and Walter [2003]).

Creating and analyzing algorithms

Whether children should be learning standard algorithms or making up their own is a hotly debated issue these days. We are inclined to think that the reason the debate rages on is that wisdom is evident on both sides: neither method is sufficient by itself. On the one hand, a standard algorithm[2] gives students a general method for solving certain kinds of problems. On the other hand, the process of inventing personal approaches involves students in analyzing the problems and answers and in developing the kinds of ideas—generally quite algebraic, although without the specialized notation—that may help them understand and appreciate a general algorithm. In fact, creating a good algorithm necessitates

---

[2] Algorithms vary from society to society, and some are more efficient than the ones we call *standard*. For example, the addition algorithm we typically call standard in the United States works from right to left and is reliable and efficient on large columns of multidigit numbers. If only two or three multidigit numbers are to be summed—the much more usual situation—a left-to-right approach is equally efficient, makes mental computation easier, and ties in more closely with other mathematical ideas and curricular goals, such as estimation and rounding off.

reflecting on the steps required for solving a problem, then generalizing these steps in a way that can solve a class of similar problems. Each approach contributes important learning.

These reasons for standard and student-generated algorithms are given from the teacher's perspective. From a student's perspective, another important message is that even routine computations can be done in more than one way, and the method for doing them may come from the student's own logical thinking as well as from the teacher or the book.

Habit of Mind 5: Seeking and Using Heuristics to Solve Problems

Students need ways to approach problems, even when the problems are unfamiliar and the students have no prescribed method for solving them. Such techniques as try some cases, think of a similar problem, and look for a pattern can give insight and move one closer to a solution, but they are not guaranteed methods (i.e., algorithms) for solving the problem. *Heuristics* is a word often used for techniques such as these. Learning some heuristics and using them can build confidence, which makes students more willing to engage in problem solving, which gives them practice and makes them better problem solvers, thus leading them to seek and acquire yet more heuristics!

We will not add to the vast amount that has been written about the value of having a repertoire of mathematical problem-solving techniques that can be used flexibly and appropriately. Some of our favorite books on this subject—for example, Pólya (1945) and Brown and Walter (1990, 1993)—have wonderfully useful lists. Instead, we want to make one point about the learning of heuristics. Because teachers are adults with long experience solving problems inside and outside mathematics, and because they are engaged not only in solving problems but in teaching others how to solve them, they might benefit from focusing specifically on, and learning a collection of, heuristics. But this approach makes less sense for students. If students are not *doing* the problem solving, knowing heuristics will not help them; if they are solving problems, they will develop heuristics by applying them in context. Simply put, the way to learn problem solving is by solving problems.

This statement does not mean that teachers have no role in helping students learn how to solve problems. A teacher's first contribution is to give students frequent opportunities to solve nonstandard problems of adequate difficulty. (Problems should be nonstandard in the sense that the students do not already know a routine method for solving them. Of course, "of adequate difficulty" means challenging enough to be a real problem but still possible for them to solve with effort.) This practice gives students successful experiences with problem solving. A teacher's next contribution is to provide occasional hints to help students who are stuck. Sometimes a single remark, such as "Would a table help?" "Try a simpler case," or "How did you solve the other problem?" not only helps students solve the problem but also solidifies their use of a particular technique so that they are more ready to use it to solve other problems. By introducing a heuristic just when students are stuck, teachers optimize its value to them.

One student's write-up on a problem said, "Once discovering this pattern, we were first at a loss as of what to do with this information. Just as we were in the depths of despair, the beautiful angel of mathematics [their teacher] came and said unto us, 'Try a chart!' We were inspired by this new angle on such a problem and quickly followed her suggestion. . . ." Most probably these students will remember the technique of making a chart forever.

Taking the Habits-of-Mind Perspective When Teaching

Our purpose in focusing on what we call "habits of mind" is to strengthen the connection between common sense and the teaching of mathematics. Moreover, this focus is at the core of what it means to teach mathematics through problem solving—an approach that places high value on students' making sense of what they are learning. (Lambdin, in her chapter in this volume, discusses the benefits of instruction that emphasizes sense making.) Making mathematics support, extend, and refine common sense—not replace it or even supplement it with a set of clever but "magical" tricks and methods—helps develop students' critical thinking and their skills both in mathematics and in other areas. Just as we place importance on students' expecting reasons behind mathematical patterns and facts, we place importance on teachers' expecting reason and sense behind claims made about mathematics teaching. We hope, therefore, that we have provided sufficiently reasonable support for the claims we have made about what is important for students and for teaching. *Thinking,* we think, must be at the core of all school learning. This concept is perhaps so basic to us that it is like a postulate, something accepted without reasons. Mathematics is certainly a discipline whose principal component is thinking.

Drawing Geoblocks

Melissa Hartemink, second-grade teacher

In their discussion of habits of mind, Goldenberg and his colleagues (chapter 2) tell us that "[b]ecoming attuned to the ways words are used, whether for the logical reasoning that mathematics requires or just for the sake of expressing themselves clearly, is a valuable skill for children to acquire" (p. 17). Too often the study of geometry is reduced to learning terms—for example, "this is a cube," "these are parallel lines." How do we make learning about shapes problematic, so that from an early age students are actively engaged in examining and analyzing them and developing language to describe their features? In Melissa Hartemink's second grade class, the students are learning about three-dimensional shapes. She wants her students to observe the features of shapes carefully, describe them in their own language, and begin to learn some useful mathematical vocabulary. The problem she poses here is to develop a good description that distinguishes one three-dimensional block from the rest of the blocks in the set. She asks questions that help her students focus on essential attributes of the blocks and on how to describe those attributes so that the students can distinguish one shape from another. By asking her students to be increasingly precise and thorough as they attempt to create a good description, she is helping them become well acquainted with the parts of these shapes and how the parts come together to make a whole. Melissa Hartemink reminds us that having adequate time for reconsidering and revising is essential to the problem-solving process.

—Frank Lester and Susan Jo Russell

31

R ECENTLY I started our work with 3-D shapes by working with geoblocks. I wanted my students to notice features of the 3-D shapes so that they could compare and contrast the shapes, and I wanted them to begin developing language for describing and comparing shapes. To focus their attention on the features of the geoblock shapes, I planned to have each student choose one block to describe and draw. Then each student would take a turn describing his block to the class and showing his drawing. Other children would try to guess which block matched the description and drawing. I planned the kinds of questions I would ask the students to help them describe their blocks:

- What do you notice about your block?

- What are the important things to say about this block so that others will know it is different from other blocks?

- What did you notice about the size of your block? This face? Etc.

- Are there other blocks with . . . (e.g., 2 square faces and 4 rectangular faces)?

- What helped you guess that person's block?

After the students had spent some time trying to draw their blocks, I met with the whole class. I told them that next they were going to write down at least three things to describe their blocks, thinking about the faces and the uniqueness of their individual blocks. We discussed a couple of blocks as examples. This discussion allowed me a chance to introduce the word *face*. First, I held up the second-largest cube in the geoblock collection.

Teacher: How could we describe this block?
Helen: It's like a cube. All the sides are squares.
Teacher: How do you know how many faces there are? Remember, these sides [pointing] are called faces.
Marie: There are six.
Teacher: Where are they?
Marie: There's one on the top and bottom. That makes two. There's two on the sides and two on the other sides. That makes six.
Teacher: How would we know this cube is different from the other cubes in our geoblock collection?
Belize: It's medium-sized.
Jani: It's the next biggest. There's two medium-sized cubes.

We looked at the four sizes of cubes and noticed that this one was the second biggest. We also looked together at another block, a right-triangular prism. In addition to discussing the faces, the overall shape, and the size of the block, several children compared it with everyday objects—a "squished" carrot, an arrow, and a ramp.

The children went to work on descriptions of their own blocks. They wrote a wide variety of responses, but many were not specific enough to identify one particular block from a pile of blocks. I decided to use one example to help students think about how they could improve their descriptions. Annette volunteered to share her description.

> *Annette:* It has a triangle. It looks like a ramp on the sides. It has a rectangular shape on the bottom. It reminds me of a seesaw.
>
> *Teacher:* Which shapes do we know it can't be? [We took out all the shapes without any triangular faces.] What else do we need to know to identify her block? Who wants to ask Annette a question?
>
> *Belize:* Is it small or big?
>
> *Annette:* Medium.

[I helped students figure out which ones we could definitely take out of the pile. We decided that only the "tiny" triangular prisms could be removed.]

> *Teacher:* Who wants to ask a question about faces?
>
> *Pantu:* [to Annette] What faces does it have?
>
> *Annette:* It has a triangle.
>
> *Pantu:* How many?
>
> *Annette:* Two.
>
> *Pantu:* What are the other faces?
>
> *Annette:* Two squares. [She ignored the base rectangle, which was unseen at the moment.]

At this point many students had their hands raised and were ready to guess which block it was. Diane picked out the correct one. Then we talked about the fact that it actually had an additional face on the "bottom," which was a rectangle. We also talked about how helpful the additional information was in identifying Annette's block. I asked the class to reflect on their own writing and drawing by asking, "Who thinks they'd like to add more information to their drawing or writing? Who thinks they don't need to? Who isn't sure?" We talked about possibilities for adding to the writing—comparing the shape with an everyday object, describing faces, size, and so on.

The students returned to their tables with confidence and enthusiasm. I met with them as they worked, asking them about what they changed or added to their drawings or writing. Annette added to her written description to make it more complete: "It has a triagel. It looks like a ramp on the sides. It remis me of a seasa. Two skwars. One reacktagel on the bottom. Two wide teriales on the sides." [It has a triangle. It looks like a ramp on the sides. It reminds me of a seesaw. Two squares. One rectangle on the bottom. Two wide triangles on the sides.]

Mark had great difficulty making his drawing look three-dimensional. On his second try, he decided to draw a rectangle with "4X" (meaning there are four faces with that shape) and a square with "2X." This seemed quite liberating to him. He wrote, "4 rectangels, 2 sqars, 4 corners, 6 faces, rectanger cube." Pam made her drawings from different points of view. We talked about how things change when you go from seeing only one point of view to seeing two. She also knew that a strong connection existed between what she wrote and what she drew, that somehow neither description was sufficient, but together they completed the picture. Her description of her square pyramid was "4 triangles 1 square, a tilted shape, 5 corners, triangles are LONG."

When we returned to the rug for block-identification time, the children were much more confident about their descriptions, guesses, and language. Most of the descriptions and drawings were complete enough for the children to identify the other students' blocks. When we could not be sure, we talked about which blocks were possible and what other clues we needed. At the end of this discussion, we created a list of what we should consider when describing a shape:

- Lots of detail
- Size
- Tell what it's not.
- What faces are in it
- How many faces
- Where the faces are
- How many points
- If the faces are tilted or not

- Describe what real-world object it looks like.
- Tell its name if you know it.

I was glad that we took the time to revise our writing and drawing after discussion and reflection, and I was pleased with how this revision positively affected the students' work. They really saw their own learning and growth. I do not often leave enough time for reflection and revision in mathematics. I think that taking the time to think about what would help someone else try to guess the block helped each child focus on the important features of these three-dimensional shapes.

Teaching Mathematics through Problem Solving: A Historical Perspective

Beatriz S. D'Ambrosio

> In the following work, the object has been to furnish an elementary treatise, commencing with the first principles, and leading the pupil, by gradual and easy steps, to a knowledge of the elements of the science. . . . For this purpose, every rule is demonstrated, and every principle analyzed, in order that the mind of the pupil may be disciplined and strengthened so as to prepare him, either for pursuing the study of Mathematics intelligently, or more successfully attending to any pursuit in life. (Ray 1848, p. 3)

THIS statement, found in the preface of *Ray's Algebra,* was written by one of the nineteenth century's most prolific authors of United States mathematics textbooks, Joseph Ray. It captures a perspective toward mathematics learning and teaching that was prevalent in mathematics education in the United States during the nineteenth century. It also suggests a specific role for problems in the mathematics curriculum.

Educators in the mid- to late 1800s believed that effective teaching involved showing students mathematical procedures, followed by students' application (i.e., use of the procedure to solve word problems) and practice of those procedures. Educators believed that such practice would strengthen the mind, as Ray indicates above. In fact, all the word problems posed throughout Ray's many books give students opportunities to apply the skills and rules presented in the books. Ray emphasizes in the preface to one of his arithmetic books that "the pupil is never required to perform any operation until the principle on which it is founded has first been explained" (Ray 1857, p. 3). Indeed, this view of problem solving, as the application of "principles" that have been taught—that is, explained by the teacher or presented in the textbook—has dominated the mathematics curriculum and many teachers' views of mathematics teaching and learning for at least 150 years.

As might be expected, conceptions of problem solving and the role it plays in the mathematics curriculum have undergone major changes since the time of Joseph Ray. In this chapter, I review some of these conceptions and argue that the position espoused in this volume—using problem solving as the backbone of mathematics instruction—emerged slowly and has recently begun to be reflected in some school mathematics textbooks.

Conceptions of Problem Solving from Ancient to Modern Times

In their seminal article tracing the history of problem solving in the mathematics curriculum, George Stanic and Jeremy Kilpatrick (1988) describe the role of mathematical problem solving from early civilization until the latter part of the twentieth century. They suggest that early Egyptian (e.g., the Ahmes Papyrus), Chinese, and Greek writings laid the foundation for the nineteenth- and early-twentieth-century views of problem solving reflected in mathematics textbooks of the times. Using examples taken from textbooks by Brooks (1871), Milne (1897), Wentworth (1899, 1900), Siefert (1902), and Upton (1939), Stanic and Kilpatrick illustrate the underlying belief of the authors of this period that "studying mathematics would improve one's ability to think, to reason, to solve problems that one will confront in the real world" (p. 9). This view was based on mental discipline theory, which, among other things, posited that learning mathematics was the primary vehicle for developing reasoning.

Late in the nineteenth century, new viewpoints on learning began to develop that ran counter to mental discipline theory. In particular, studies published by Edward L. Thorndike about the turn of the twentieth century discredited the concepts of mental discipline and transfer of training. As the results of Thorndike's studies became more widely accepted, mental discipline theory slowly fell out of favor and was replaced by Thorndike's "connectionism" (for further discussion see Thorndike [1922]). However, vestiges of mental discipline theory remain even today in the enduring belief that abstract subjects, such as mathematics, are valuable because they sharpen the mind.

Also at the turn of the twentieth century, mathematics education was coming to be considered a legitimate field of study at the college and university level throughout the United States, with such mathematics educators as David Eugene Smith and J. W. A. Young arguing that mathematics is an appropriate area of study for all students. They also argued that mathematics is an indispensable tool for developing students' power of reasoning. However, Stanic and Kilpatrick (1988) note, "It is ironic that as the number of professional mathematics educators at colleges and universities around the country began to grow, the place of mathematics in the school curriculum came under attack" (p. 12). The controversy revolved around the role of applications in the school mathematics curriculum. Interestingly, such mathematicians as Felix Klein in Germany, John Perry in England, and E. H. Moore in the United States argued in favor of a greater role for applications, but mathematics educators, led by Smith, insisted that to replace the study of pure mathematics with applied problems would be wrong minded. Obviously, the place of problems and problem solving in the school mathematics curriculum has been a controversial topic for quite a long time.

With this quick glimpse into the history of the role of problem solving in school mathematics as a backdrop, Stanic and Kilpatrick (1988, pp. 13–20) go on to discuss various themes that have characterized this role. Their discussion is included here, with permission, in its entirety because these themes can help to illuminate what is special and different about teaching mathematics through problem solving.

PROBLEM-SOLVING THEMES

Three general themes have characterized the role of problem solving in the school mathematics curriculum: problem solving as context, problem solving as skill, and problem solving as art.

Problem Solving as Context

The context theme has at least five subthemes, all of which are based on the idea that problems and the solving of problems are means to achieve other valuable ends.

Problem solving as justification. Historically, problem solving has been included in the mathematics curriculum in part because the problems provide justification for teaching mathematics at all. Presumably, at least some problems related in

(Continued on page 40)

some way to real-world experiences were included in the curriculum to convince students and teachers of the value of mathematics.

Problem solving as motivation. The subtheme of motivation is related to that of justification in that the problems justify the mathematics being taught. However, in the case of motivation, the connection is much more specific, and the aim of gaining student interest is sought. For example, a specific problem involving addition with regrouping might be used to introduce a series of lessons leading to learning the most efficient algorithm for adding the numbers.

Problem solving as recreation. The subtheme of recreation is related to that of motivation because student interest is involved, but in the case of recreation, problems are provided not so much to motivate students to learn as to allow them to have some fun with the mathematics they have already learned. Presumably, such problems fulfill a natural interest human beings have in exploring unusual situations. The problem shown earlier from the Ahmes papyrus is a good illustration. The recreation subtheme also differs from the first two in that puzzles, or problems without any necessary real-world connections, are perfectly appropriate.

Problem solving as vehicle. Problems are often provided not simply to motivate students to be interested in direct instruction on a topic but as a vehicle through which a new concept or skill might be learned. Discovery techniques in part reflect the idea that problem solving can be a vehicle for learning new concepts and skills. And when the mathematics curriculum consisted exclusively of problems, the problems obviously served as vehicles.

Problem solving as practice. Of the five subthemes, problem solving as practice has had the largest influence on the mathematics curriculum. In this subtheme, problems do not provide justification, motivation, recreation, or vehicles as much as necessary practice to reinforce skills and concepts taught directly. A page from an 1854 text by Nelson M. Holbrook entitled *The Child's First Book in Arithmetic* shows a good example of this subtheme. Notice that the "mental exercises" on division follow work on the division table (see Figure 13).

Problem Solving as Skill

Problem solving is often seen as one of a number of skills to be taught in the school curriculum. According to this view, problem solving is not necessarily a unitary skill, but there is a clear skill orientation.

Although problem solving as context remains a strong and persistent theme, the problem-solving-as-skill theme has become dominant for those who see problem solving as a valuable curriculum end deserving special attention, rather than as simply a means to achieve other ends or an inevitable outcome of the study of mathematics.

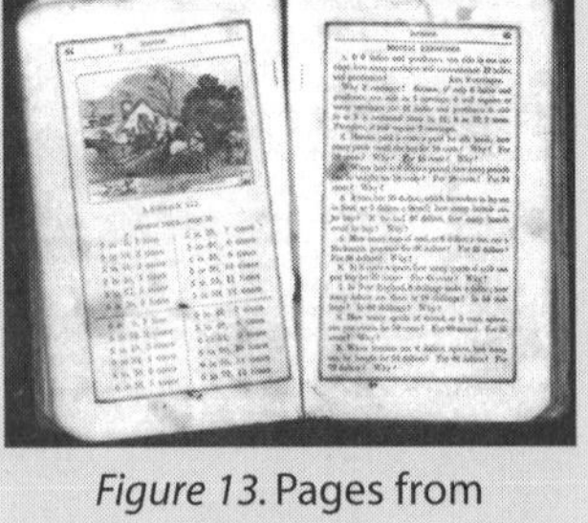

The skill theme is clearly related to the changes that took place near the turn of the century, although not all advocates of this point of view would claim an association with, for example, the work of Thorndike. Nonetheless,

Figure 13. Pages from Nelson M. Holbrooks' *The Child's First Book in Arithmetic* (Holbrook, 1854)

(Continued)

(Stanic and Kilpatrick excerpt continued)

largely because of Thorndike's influence (as well as the other changes discussed earlier), most educators no longer assumed that the study of mathematics improved one's thinking and made one a better solver of real-world problems. Especially because many of our professional forebears were reluctant to give up their claims about mathematics and to include more applied problems in the curriculum, they essentially allowed educational psychologists like Thorndike to define the new view of problem solving.

Putting problem solving in a hierarchy of skills to be acquired by students leads to certain consequences for the role of problem solving in the curriculum. One consequence is that within the general skill of problem solving, hierarchical distinctions are made between solving routine and nonroutine problems. That is, nonroutine problem solving is characterized as a higher level skill to be acquired after skill at solving routine problems (which, in turn, is to be acquired after students learn basic mathematical concepts and skills). This view postpones attention to nonroutine problem solving, and, as a result, only certain students, because they have accomplished the prerequisites, are ever exposed to such problems. Nonroutine problem solving becomes, then, an activity for the especially capable students rather than for all students.

Problem Solving as Art

A deeper, more comprehensive view of problem solving in the school mathematics curriculum—a view of problem solving as *art*—emerged from the work of George Polya, who revived in our time the idea of heuristic (the art of discovery). Mathematicians as far back as Euclid and Pappus, and including Descartes, Leibnitz, and Bolzano, had discussed methods and rules for discovery and invention in mathematics, but their ideas never made their way into the school curriculum. It remained for Polya to reformulate, extend, and illustrate various ideas about mathematical discovery in a way that teachers could understand and use.

Polya's experience in learning and teaching mathematics led him to ask how mathematics came to be—how did people make mathematical discoveries? Won't students understand mathematics better if they see how it was created in the first place and if they can get some taste of mathematical discovery themselves? Polya's experience as a mathematician led him to conclude that the finished face of mathematics presented deductively in mathematical journals and in textbooks does not do justice to the subject. Finished mathematics requires demonstrative reasoning, whereas mathematics in the making requires plausible reasoning. If students are to use plausible reasoning, they need to be taught how.

Like our professional forebears Smith and Young, Polya argued that a major aim of education is the development of intelligence—to teach young people to think. In the primary school, children should be taught to do their arithmetic insightfully rather than mechanically because although insightful performance is a more ambitious aim, it actually has a better chance of success. It yields faster, more permanent results. In the secondary school, mathematics should offer something to those who will, and those who will not, use mathematics in their later studies or careers. The same mathematics should be taught to all students because no one can know in advance which students will eventually use mathematics professionally.

> If the teaching of mathematics gives only a one-sided, stunted idea of the mathematician's thinking, if it totally suppresses

(Continued on page 42)

those "informal" activities of guessing and extracting mathematical concepts from the visible world around us, it neglects what may be the most interesting part for the general student, the most instructive for the future user of mathematics, and the most inspiring for the future mathematician. (Polya, 1966, pp. 124–125)

In Polya's view, mathematics consists of information and know-how. Regardless of how well schools impart mathematical information, if they do not teach students how to use that information, it will be forgotten. "To know mathematics is to be able to do mathematics" (Polya, 1969/1984, p. 574). "What is know-how in mathematics? The ability to solve problems" (Polya, 1981, p. xi).

To Polya, problem solving was a practical art, "like swimming, or skiing, or playing the piano" (1981, p. ix). One learns such arts by imitation and practice. Polya assumed neither that simply solving problems by itself with no guidance leads to improved performance nor that the study of mathematics by its very nature raises one's general level of intelligence. Instead, he recognized that techniques of problem solving need to be illustrated by the teacher, discussed with the students, and practiced in an insightful, nonmechanical way. Further, he observed that although routine problems can be used to fulfill certain pedagogical functions of teaching students to follow a specific procedure or use a definition correctly, only through the judicious use of nonroutine problems can students develop their problem-solving ability.

In Polya's formulation, the teacher is the key. Only a sensitive teacher can set the right kind of problems for a given class and provide the appropriate amount of guidance. Because teaching, too, is an art, no one can program or otherwise mechanize the teaching of problem solving; it remains a human activity that requires experience, taste, and judgment.

There are those today who on the surface affiliate themselves with the work of Polya, but who reduce the rule-of-thumb heuristics to procedural skills, almost taking an algorithmic view of heuristics (i.e., specific heuristics fit in specific situations). A heuristic becomes a skill, a technique, even, paradoxically, an algorithm. In a sense, problem solving as art gets reduced to problem solving as skill when attempts are made to implement Polya's ideas by focusing on his steps and putting them into textbooks. Although distortion may not be inevitable when educators try to capture within textbooks and teachers' guides what is essentially an artistic endeavor, the task is clearly a difficult one.

Of the three themes, we see problem solving as art as the most defensible, the most fair, and the most promising. But at the same time it is the most problematic theme because it is the most difficult to operationalize in textbooks and classrooms. The problem for mathematics educators who believe that problem solving is an art form is how to develop this artistic ability in students.

Because of the caricature most people hold of John Dewey, we are reluctant to bring his work into the discussion. But we believe that Dewey's ideas about problem solving complement those of Polya. Dewey does not provide all the answers; in fact, he demonstrates that the situation is even more complex than one might think. But he does give valuable direction and another way to think about problem solving.

(Continued)

(Stanic and Kilpatrick excerpt continued)

Although Dewey is clearly the major 20th century American philosopher of education and although he is blamed often and by various people for all that is wrong with American education, his influence on the school curriculum in general, and the mathematics curriculum in particular, has been minimal. A host of educators and psychologists ranging from Moore to Thorndike have praised Dewey's ideas; however, except for the lab school at the University of Chicago at the turn of the century, there is no example of his ideas being implemented as they were intended. What has been called progressive education did have an influence on the school mathematics curriculum, but the critique of progressive education Dewey (1938/1963) provided in *Experience and Education* shows how far from his basic ideas most other reformers were. Nonetheless, Dewey remains a major figure in American education because so many people have claimed a link with his work, including a few people who have actually taken the time to read Dewey's own writing rather than second-hand distortions.

Dewey did not often use the term *problem solving,* but it is clear that problems and problem solving were crucial in Dewey's view of education and schooling. What we refer to as problem solving Dewey usually called *reflective thinking.* Rather than being one way in which human beings deal with the world, problem solving was for Dewey the essence of human thought: Being able to think reflectively makes us human. Dewey distinguished among several types of thinking, but when he wrote *How We Think* in 1910 and revised it in 1933, to think meant to think reflectively.

Better than anyone else, Dewey combined the ideas of problem solving as means and problem solving as an end worthy of special attention. Dewey used much of *How We Think* to discuss how thought can be trained, so developing people's problem-solving ability was an important end for Dewey. But it was not an end separate from the progressive organization of subject matter that is a direct result of reflective thinking. That is, the same experiences that lead to the development of reflective thinking also lead to learning important subject matter. As simple and obvious as this may sound, our history of failures to accomplish the twin goals of helping students to develop problem-solving ability and organize the subject matter of mathematics is convincing evidence of how complex the task is.

Perhaps the greatest single misconception about John Dewey is that he was concerned with the child and not with subject matter. The problem, said Dewey (1902/1964), "is just to get rid of the prejudicial notion that there is some gap in kind (as distinct from degree) between the child's experience and the various forms of subject-matter that make up the course of study" (p. 344). Dewey argued that the child's experience "contains within itself elements—facts and truths—of just the same sort as those entering into the formulated study ... and [even more important] the attitudes, the motives, and the interests which have operated in developing and organizing the subject matter to the place which it now occupies" (p. 344).

For Dewey, experience was central, problems arise naturally within experience, teaching and learning consist of the reconstruction of experience which leads to the progressive organization of subject matter, and the reconstruction of experience requires reflective thinking (or problem solving).

Like Polya, Dewey placed a great deal of emphasis on the teacher. Dewey did not reject the idea of teachers transmitting information to students. In fact, he said

(Continued on page 44)

that "no educational question is of greater importance than how to get the most logical good out of learning through transmission from others" (Dewey, 1910, p. 197). Dewey said that the problem was how to convert such information into an intellectual asset. "How shall we treat the subject-matter supplied by textbook and teacher so that it shall rank as material for reflective inquiry, not as ready-made intellectual pabulum to be accepted and swallowed just as supplied by the store?" (pp. 197–198). Dewey answered his own question by saying that the transmitted information should not be something student could easily discover through direct inquiry; that the information "should be supplied by way of stimulus, not with dogmatic finality and rigidity"; and that the information "should be relevant to a question that is vital in the student's own experience" (pp. 198–199). According to Dewey,

> Instruction in subject-matter that does not fit into any problem already stirring in the student's own experience, or that is not presented in such a way as to arouse a problem, is worse than useless for intellectual purposes. In that it fails to enter into any process of reflection, it is useless; in that it remains in the mind as so much lumber and debris, it is a barrier, an obstruction in the way of effective thinking when a problem arises. (p. 199).

Teachers, then, can justifiably transmit information, according to Dewey, but only if the information is linked to the child's experience and problems that arise within experience. In a sense, subject matter is even more important for the teacher than for the student. The teacher needs to use her or his knowledge of subject matter in order to help the child reconstruct experience so that subject matter becomes progressively more organized for the child.

In "The Child and the Curriculum," Dewey (1902/1964) compared logically-organized subject matter to a map. The map, said Dewey, is a "formulated statement of experience" (p. 350). As students reconstruct their experience, they make a map of subject matter. They can also use maps constructed by others as guides to future journeys, but no map can "substitute for a personal experience" (p. 350). A map "does not take the place of an actual journey" (p. 350). Like Polya, Dewey was concerned with transforming logically organized subject matter into psychologically meaningful experience for students.

The process of thinking reflectively, of solving problems that arise within experience, was for Dewey, an art form. Dewey (1910) said that "no cast iron rules [for reflective thinking] can be laid down" (p. 78). He believed students should be "skilled in methods of attack and solution" (p. 78), but he expressed concern about an "overconscious formulation of methods of procedure" (p. 112). So, according to Dewey, skill is involved in reflective thinking, or problem solving, but reflective thinking itself is not a skill. In fact, Dewey expressed concern about too great an emphasis on skill acquisition. "Practical skill, modes of effective technique, can be intelligently, nonmechanically *used,*" he said, "only when intelligence has played a part in their *acquisition*" (p. 52).

Furthermore, Dewey (1910) believed not only that students should be "skilled in methods of attack and solution" but also that they should be "sensitive to problems" (p. 78). That is, proper *attitudes* were very important to Dewey:

> Because of the importance of attitudes, ability to train thought is not achieved merely by knowledge of the best forms of thought.

(Continued)

(Stanic and Kilpatrick excerpt continued)

> Possession of this information is no guarantee for ability to think well. Moreover, there are no set exercises in correct thinking whose repeated performance will cause one to be a good thinker. The information and the exercises are both of value. But no individual realizes their value except as he is personally animated by certain dominant attitudes in his own character. (Dewey, 1933, p. 29)

What is necessary, said Dewey (1933), is the union of attitude and skilled method. Dewey believed that the three most important attitudes to be cultivated are open-mindedness, whole-heartedness, and responsibility. Developing such attitudes was so important to Dewey that he said if he were forced to make a choice between students having these attitudes and students having knowledge about principles of reasoning and some degree of technical skill in reasoning, he would choose the attitudes. "Fortunately," he said, "no such choice has to be made, because there is no opposition between personal attitudes and logical processes .... What is needed is to weave them into unity" (p. 34).

Dewey's connection to Polya seems clear. Polya (1981) suggested that "instead of hurrying through all the details of a much too extended program, the teacher should concentrate on a few really significant problems and treat them leisurely and thoroughly" (Vol 2, p. 123). Dewey (1933) said that "fewer subjects and fewer facts and more responsibility for thinking the material of those subjects and facts through to realize what they involve would give better results" (p. 33)

Polya's and Dewey's belief that mathematics and problem solving are for everyone ties them to our professional forebears in mathematics education and the basic faith they had in human intelligence. Smith and Young could not or would not see in Dewey the opportunity to recast their view of the benefits of the liberal arts in light of a changing society. In a sense, we need to use the work of Dewey and Polya to recapture and revise the tradition embodied in the work of Smith and Young.

CONCLUSION

One consequence of recapturing this tradition is to take seriously the notion that problem solving really is for everyone. We need to look more at what children can actually do and to insist on broad evidence of what counts as ability to solve problems. In other words, we must study more carefully the role of context in problem solving. Some recent research shows that children who have trouble solving mathematical problems in school can solve comparable problems in out-of-school situations that are more meaningful to them. Taking seriously the notion that problem solving is for everyone means studying children in a variety of situations and providing examples to teachers of what children can do when an attempt is made to link subject matter to experience.

Again, neither Dewey nor Polya has all the answers, but they do help us with the basic issues of what problem solving is, why we should teach it, and how it is related to the progressive organization of subject matter. And their work provides for us a vehicle through which we might "critically examine our heritage as a field of study" by carrying on "a dialogue ... with our professional forebears" (Kliebard, 1968, p. 83).

An Emerging Theme: Teaching Mathematics through Problem Solving

Today, as we enter the twenty-first century, we are confronted with yet another shift in focus in the use of problem solving in the curriculum: *teaching mathematics through problem solving*, the theme of this volume. In a chapter appearing in the 1989 Yearbook of the National Council of Teachers of Mathematics, Tom Schroeder and Frank Lester (1989) insisted that, since the role of problem solving is to develop students' understanding of mathematics, teaching via problem solving is the most appropriate approach. They argued that proponents of this approach consider problem solving not as a topic, a standard, or a content strand but rather as a pedagogical stance. This approach has come to be referred to today as *teaching through problem solving*. The influence of Pólya's (1981) and Dewey's (1933) views on problem solving as an art are evident in this view of the role of problem solving in the curriculum.

This new view also closely parallels Stanic and Kilpatrick's theme of problem solving as a vehicle. In fact, problems that serve as vehicles for introducing or developing mathematical concepts began to appear in mathematics curriculum materials in the 1990s. Proponents of teaching mathematics through problem solving base their pedagogy on the notion that students who confront problematic situations use their existing knowledge to solve those problems, and in the process of solving the problems, they construct new knowledge and new understanding. Recent research in psychology and cognitive science has described learning as the individual's process of making sense of ideas on the basis of the individual's existing understandings (Greeno 2003; Sfard 2003). Theories describing how people learn, or construct knowledge, serve as the foundation for teaching mathematics through problem solving. To illustrate how teaching mathematics through problem solving has been put into practice, three examples, one each from the elementary, middle, and secondary school levels, are discussed in the following sections.

An Elementary School Example

One elementary school textbook series first published in the late 1990s presents the following situation. A second-grade class has read and discussed the Chinese folktale *Two of Everything* by Lily Toy Hong (1993), in which a poor old farmer finds a magic pot that doubles anything that is put into it. This context is then used to pose the following problem:

Our Class and the Magic Pot

What do you think would happen if our entire class fell into the magic pot? First write about how you would solve the problem. Then write about what would be one good thing and one hard thing about having a double class. (Economopoulos and Russell 1998, p. 46)

Although this problem may not seem very interesting or difficult at first glance, its placement in the curriculum provides an opportunity for children to explore a new mathematical idea before they have received any formal instruction in how to double numbers, especially numbers greater than 10—such as the number of students in the class. The children likely have never seen a teacher solve this problem or any problem like it before. In teaching through problem solving, the teacher trusts that the children will draw on their existing knowledge in a creative way and fosters their thinking about the problem she posed. After the children spend some time, often in small groups, exploring the problem situation, the teacher asks various children to share their solutions and their thinking about the problem. In addition to giving the children practice in problem solving, this activity helps them build their ability to use mathematical language. In this scenario, the entire classroom community holds a mathematical conversation about the solution to the problem.

Children use the mathematics they already know to solve the problem, and from their solutions, a new mathematical concept—the concept of doubling—emerges and may even be formalized. In particular, this problem brings to the children's attention the important mathematical notions of number patterns and relationships, and the teacher may introduce notation that shows the doubling relationship. In this way, the problem-solving experience creates the backdrop against which new ideas begin to take shape in the community of the classroom and in the minds of the children.

A Middle School Example

A middle school textbook contains problems that generate opportunities for students to engage in activities to enhance their emerging mathematical thinking processes, in this example, algebraic thinking (see fig. 3.1). Although this problem might be solved in a straightforward way in a traditional algebra class, it lends itself to investigation at the middle school level before students have had formal instruction in solving systems of equations.

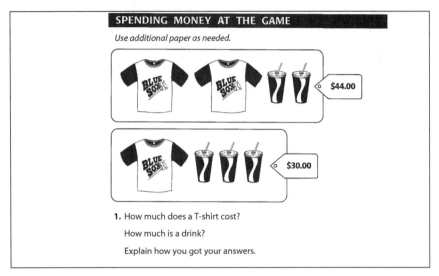

Fig. 3.1. Developing algebraic thinking in the middle grades (National Center for Research in Mathematical Sciences Education and Freudenthal Institute 1998, p.98)

Again, the placement of this problem in the curriculum affords students the opportunity to explore, in this example, the comparison of quantities. Several students' solutions to this problem incorporate the algebraic procedures they will learn more formally in their later study of algebra. For example, as student 1 describes his solution strategy, we can map the solution into formal algebra, identifying each of the student's steps as a formal algebraic manipulation. (The students' discussions of their solution efforts shown below are taken from a research study conducted by the author in collaboration with Jennifer Strabala.)

> *Student 1:*
>
> What I did to figure it out is I took the top picture, and I took 1 t-shirt and 1 drink away. It was $22. So the bottom t-shirt and 1 drink cost $22, but you still had two drinks left that cost $8 total so 1 drink cost $4 and 1 t-shirt cost $18.
>
> Formalized algebraic steps:
> $2S + 2D = 44$; so $S + D = 22$.
> $S + 3D = 30$, which can be written as $(S + D) + 2D = 30$.
> Through substitution, $22 + 2D = 30$.
> By solving for D, $2D = 8$; so $D = 4$.
> By solving for S, $S + 4 = 22$; so $S = 18$.

Yet another student approached the problem with a very different intuitive sense of what substitutions may be used.

Student 2:

To do this problem, I first crossed out the items common to both pictures. All that was left was a shirt in the $44.00 box and a drink in the $30.00 box. This told me that the shirt cost $14.00 more than the drink (y). I used this info and the original $30 box to make this problem:

$$3y + (y + 14) = 30$$

I modeled the problem like this:

$$yyy \ y \ 14 \wedge 14 \ 16$$

I crossed out the 14 from both sides and got this:

$$yyyy \wedge 16.$$

If $4y = 16$, then $y = 4$. [And] $4 + 14 = 18$. Therefore, a drink costs $4 and a shirt costs $18.

Student 2's use of the fulcrum to represent the equality in the situation is of interest to the teacher, who is using this problem both to draw out what the student knows and to build a more conventional notation to represent the relationship among drinks and shirts and total cost.

A High School Example

The use of problems to introduce new mathematics topics can be found in secondary school mathematics materials as well. For example, in the problem shown in figure 3.2, the students' use of their existing knowledge to approach new problems provides the backdrop for potentially rich mathematical explorations.

Borasi and Fonzi (in press) suggest the following problem as a means of engaging students in exploring concepts related to the area of certain geometric figures. The picture shown in figure 3.2 is given to the class, and the students are asked to propose a formula for the area of all such shapes. The students begin to explore the area of these shapes and draw on their existing knowledge of area. Their solutions reveal their depth of understanding of the area of familiar shapes as well as of the process of finding patterns and drawing generalizations. The problem also requires that students spend a significant amount of time developing and refining the definition for this class of shapes, referred to as "diamonds."

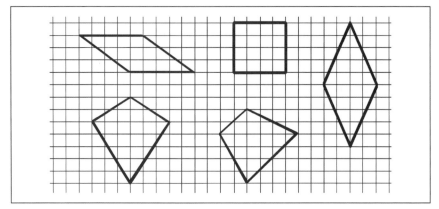

Fig. 3.2. Exploring area in secondary school mathematics (Borasi and Fonzi, in press)

This activity can generate for students several important experiences that simulate the work of mathematicians. First, the classroom community builds definitions and negotiates the limitations of different ways of defining a class of shapes. Second, the community finds the area of the shapes, looking for patterns and generalizing the process of determining area in an attempt to come up with a formula. Third, students propose a formula for the area of the shapes, justifying their thinking and reasoning to defend their proposal. Finally, students evaluate others' proposals, seeking to understand different explanations and challenging ideas that do not make sense to them. This process affords the teacher and students the opportunity to discuss various processes involved in doing mathematics, namely, developing definitions and formulas.

Conclusion

This chapter illustrates that problem solving has been an important component of the school mathematics curriculum for quite a long time—150 years or more—but that its role has changed over time. In some school mathematics textbooks today, problem solving now serves, to borrow from Stanic and Kilpatrick (1988), as a *vehicle* for developing deep understanding of mathematical ideas and processes. Proponents of this approach believe that engaging in productive problem solving leads to increased understanding. This approach, which involves confronting students with truly problematic situations to grapple with, is dramatically different from the approach promoted more than 150 years ago by Joseph Ray (1848) —an approach involving "gradual and easy steps." Whether the future will bring still other ways of thinking about the role of problem solving in mathematics instruction will be interesting to see!

Section 2

In the Classroom

CHAPTER 4

Signposts for Teaching Mathematics through Problem Solving

James Hiebert

A LL STUDENTS need a deep, rich understanding of the mathematics they study in school. It is not enough for students to know how to calculate the area of a rectangle, how to add fractions, or how to find percents, or even to memorize procedures for all these things and execute them with blinding speed. It is not enough, because knowing how to execute procedures does not ensure that students understand what they are doing. And unless students understand what they are doing, these procedures will not be very useful. Understanding is the key to remembering what is learned and being able to use it flexibly.

If, as the authors in this book emphasize, understanding mathematics is of utmost importance, why is the book about problem solving? In simplest terms, problem solving leads to understanding (Davis 1992). Students develop, extend, and enrich their understandings by solving problems. Some readers might find this approach odd and inefficient. Problem solving takes time. And if the problems really are problems, some students might not even solve them completely. Why not just teach students the concepts you want them to understand? The answer to this question is not simple. If it were simple, this book would not have been written. Understanding is best supported through a delicate balance among engaging students in solving challenging problems, examining increasingly better solution methods, and providing information for students at just the right time (Brownell and Sims 1946; Dewey 1933; Hiebert et al. 1997). Because the traditional teaching approach often has tipped the balance toward telling students too quickly how to solve problems, educators must correct the balance by thinking again about how to allow students to do more of the mathematical work. Students' understanding depends on it.

Signposts for Classrooms That Promote Students' Understandings

On the basis of observations of experts and the convergence of research evidence, one can identify several signposts to guide classroom teachers in the direction of giving students opportunities to develop deep mathematical understandings. Just as signposts along the road can highlight for travelers important information for reaching their destination, so signposts for the classroom can highlight for teachers essential features for helping students achieve the intended learning goals. If the learning goals are deep mathematical understandings, then the signposts all point to problem solving as the core activity. They stake out a new kind of balance among allowing students to struggle with challenging problems, helping them examine increasingly better solution methods, and providing appropriate information at the right times. The following paragraphs discuss three signposts; other chapters in this book point out additional signposts.

Signpost 1: Allow Mathematics to Be Problematic for Students

The idea that mathematics should be problematic for students is the most radical of the signposts. It is radical because it is very different from how most of us have thought about mathematics and students. Teachers have been encouraged to make mathematics *less* problematic for students. Parents assume that teachers should make mathematics less of a struggle; a good teacher helps students learn in a smooth, effortless way.

Allowing mathematics to be problematic for students requires a very different mindset about what mathematics is, how students learn mathematics with understanding, and what role the teacher can play. Allowing mathematics to be problematic for students means posing problems that are just within students' reach, allowing them to struggle to find solutions, and then examining the methods they have used. Allowing mathematics to be problematic requires believing that all students need to struggle with challenging problems to learn mathematics and understand it deeply. Allowing mathematics to be problematic does *not* mean making mathematics unnecessarily difficult, but it does mean allowing students to wrestle with what is mathematically challenging.

For many mathematics teachers, this way of thinking is new. They have learned that they are supposed to step in and remove the struggle, and the challenge, for students. The extent to which U.S. teachers hold this belief is revealed in a study of classroom mathematics teaching as part of the Third International Mathematics and Science Study (TIMSS). Margaret Smith (2000b) looked at a subsample of eighth-grade lessons from Germany, Japan, and the United States and examined the kinds of problems teachers presented to students and the way in which they helped students solve the problems. She found, in her sample, that about one-third of the problems presented in U.S. classrooms offered students the opportunity to explore relationships and develop deeper understandings. This percent was not dramatically different from the ones found in other countries. However, after presenting the problems, U.S. teachers almost always stepped in to show students how to solve them; the mathematics they left for students to think about and do was rather trivial. Teachers in the other two countries allowed students more opportunities to wrestle with the challenging aspects of the problems.

As will be pointed out in other chapters (see, e.g., those by Van de Walle and by Russell et al.), allowing mathematics to be problematic (or "problem-based," to use the term as Van de Walle prefers) for students does not require importing numerous special problems for students. Rather, it requires allowing the problems that are taught every day to be *problems*. For example, suppose third graders have just learned to solve problems like $324 - 156 = ?$ and then encounter $402 - 258 = ?$ Ordinarily, this problem is treated as a new one requiring new procedures, and teachers step in and show students how to solve problems with zeros in the subtrahend. Allowing mathematics to be problematic means allowing even these simple arithmetic problems to be real problems for students (Carpenter 1985; Hiebert et al. 1997).

This first signpost clearly changes everything. It affects the way in which all mathematics is treated, even the routine computation contained in the preceding examples. It points classroom practice in a new direction. It means that solving problems is the heart of doing mathematics, not a supplement to one's ongoing program. Allowing students to learn by solving problems leads to the next signpost: focusing classroom activity on the methods used to solve problems.

Signpost 2: Focus on the Methods Used to Solve Problems

John Dewey (1933) pointed out that the best way to gain deeper understandings of a subject is to search for better methods to solve problems. From a student's point of view, this quest requires the opportunity to share one's own method, to hear others present alternative methods, and then to examine the advantages and disadvantages of these different methods.

Suppose that a third-grade class is solving the problem posed previously: 402 − 258 = ? If the class has not solved a problem with a zero in the subtrahend before, they will likely produce several different solution methods. If they have base-ten materials, some students might break up one of the hundreds into 10 tens, then break up one of the tens into 10 ones, and then subtract 258, leaving 144. Other students might use a (flawed) written procedure and "borrow" 1 from the 4 (hundred); then change the 2 (ones) to 12, leaving the 0 unchanged; and then subtract to get 154. Still other students might add up from 258 to 402, counting the amount they had to add on and getting 144. Other methods will probably be suggested as well.

Learning opportunities for these students begin as they search for a method to solve the problem. Learning opportunities continue as they formulate a way to explain their methods to their classmates and justify their validity. Learning opportunities intensify as students listen to the methods of others and examine them, considering their relative advantages and deciding whether the alternatives provide better choices that they can adopt for subsequent problems.

The process of analyzing the adequacy of methods and searching for better ones drives the intellectual, and social, life of the class. Students should be permitted to choose their own method to solve problems but should commit themselves to searching for better ones. Discussions in class should revolve around sharing, analyzing, and improving methods. The focus always should be on the merits of the method, not the status of the presenter. Whether presented by the teacher or a student, correct methods should win popularity because of their mathematical advantages—they are efficient, or easy to understand, or easy to adjust to solve new problems, and so on.

Why place so much emphasis on examining and improving the methods used to solve problems? The payoffs are substantial. A first benefit is that examining methods encourages students to construct mathematical relationships, and constructing relationships is at the heart of understanding (Brownell 1947). Returning to the three-digit subtraction problem, examining the different methods that are likely to be presented provides a perfect opportunity to look again at how numbers can be decomposed and recomposed using hundreds, tens, and ones, and how subtraction can be conceptualized as taking away, finding a difference, or adding on. The problem presents many relationships to construct, relationships that extend students' understanding well beyond this particular problem.

A second benefit of focusing on methods is that students can learn from analyzing a range of methods, from flawed to primitive to sophisticated. By learning why some methods do not work, students can gain special insights that deepen their understanding and prevent them from making similar mistakes in the future. For example, examining the incorrect written procedure mentioned previously of "borrowing" 1 from the hundreds and making it 10 ones (changing 2 ones to 12 ones) presents another opportunity to think about how numbers can be decomposed and recomposed. Subtracting 5 from 0 to get 5 presents a chance to discuss the meaning of 0 as well as the "take away" meaning for subtraction. In short, focusing on methods creates an environment in which mistakes become sites for learning. This aspect is important because when mathematics is allowed to be problematic for students, making mistakes becomes a natural part of learning.

Because students learn from analyzing correct and incorrect methods, the class benefits from hearing a variety of methods. Variety might be more likely when the class is made up of a diverse population of students than when it is homogeneously grouped. Students with different backgrounds and different achievement levels are likely to think of the problem in different ways and produce different methods of solution. The interesting implication is that individual differences in a classroom become a resource that can enhance instruction rather than a difficulty that hinders good instruction.

A third benefit of focusing on methods is that the spotlight shifts from people to ideas. By focusing on methods and the ideas they contain, teachers can show students that all methods and ideas are sites for learning. Every student's contribution can help the class think about ways to improve the correct methods and avoid incorrect ones. When students see that the goal is to help the class, as a group, search for better methods and construct new mathematical relationships, the attention shifts from evaluating their response as correct or not toward examining what others can learn from the response. This focus is important because it provides a way for teachers to build a classroom culture in which all students feel welcome and appreciated. If mathematics is allowed to be problematic for students and they are encouraged to explain and justify their methods and examine the methods of others, students might become self-conscious and withdraw from the discussions (Lampert, Rittenhouse, and Crumbaugh 1996). Teachers should create an environment in which students enjoy participating as respected members of the group.

Signpost 3: Tell the Right Things at the Right Times

A third signpost that can guide classrooms toward providing opportunities for students to develop deep understandings is best phrased as a question: What mathematical information should teachers present, and when should they present it? For teachers using a traditional approach, this signpost is curious. They wonder, Doesn't good teaching mean presenting mathematical information clearly? Why even ask such questions as "What should be presented?" or "When should it be presented?" Shouldn't all mathematical information be presented as it comes along in the curriculum?

The fact that telling the right thing at the right time even becomes an issue shows how radical the first signpost is. Allowing the mathematics to be problematic for students changes everything. In this environment, teachers must think carefully about what information should be shared and when it should be shared. Presenting too much information too soon removes the problematic nature of problems. Presenting too little information can leave students floundering.

John Dewey faced the same situation in the 1920s. He had recommended that students be allowed to problematize their school subjects. Some educators interpreted this statement to mean that students should not be told anything. Dewey (1933) tried to correct this misinterpretation by saying that although teachers should not present "ready-made intellectual pabulum to be accepted and swallowed" and later regurgitated (p. 257), in many cases teachers can and should provide information for students.

Here are a few rules of thumb for telling students the right things at the right time. First, teachers should show students the words and written symbols that commonly are used to represent quantities, operations, and relationships (e.g., written notation for fractions, decimals, and percents; formats for writing equations; words such as *quotient* and *equivalent*). These are social conventions, and students cannot be expected to discover them. When should teachers present them? The best time is when students need them—when the ideas have been developed and students need a way to record the ideas and communicate with others about them. Rather than burden students with memorizing these conventions, the teacher should present them as beneficial aids.

A second rule of thumb is that teachers can present alternative methods of solutions that have not been suggested by students. Over time, teachers can develop a good sense for which solution methods for particular problems help students understand the main ideas and relationships that are contained in a problem. If students do not come up with these methods, teachers should feel free to present them.

Suppose that third graders are finding the area of a rectangle, say, 4 inches by 6 inches. After working on the problem for a few minutes, some students suggest using their square-inch pieces to cover the rectangle and counting the squares by ones; other students suggest counting the squares by fours; and one student suggests multiplying 4×6 (the class recently had been solving simple multiplication problems). After discussing these methods, the teacher suggests a slightly different one: counting the squares by sixes. This additional method allows the teacher to then lead a discussion comparing counting by fours and counting by sixes, which, in turn, introduces the concept of commutativity, including how 4×6 and 6×4 capture the act of counting and the ways in which they are the same and different.

Teachers should feel free to reveal alternative methods during the discussion of problems that students have already solved. The trick is for the teacher to present the method as one that students should examine, just as they examine other methods, rather than a method that is automatically preferred just because the teacher presented it. The teacher should ensure that students use a method because they understand why it is correct and because they find it useful.

A third rule of thumb for presenting information is that teachers should highlight the mathematical ideas embedded in students' methods. Students can invent and present methods for solving problems without being aware of all the ideas on which the methods depend. Consider again the third graders finding the area of a 4-by-6 rectangle. Many ideas and relationships are embedded in the various solution methods, and the teacher can make these ideas explicit. By restating and clarifying students' methods and pointing to the important ideas in them, teachers not only show respect for students' thinking but help guide students' attention to the important mathematics, thereby guiding the mathematical direction of the class.

How Different Is This Approach from Traditional Practice?

The kind of classroom practice described in this chapter, and in this entire volume, represents a fundamental change from business as usual. It will not be achieved by making superficial changes. It will be achieved only by rethinking our beliefs about two issues that lie at the core of mathematics teaching: the learning goals we set for students and how students can best achieve these goals.

This chapter is built on the premise that the traditional learning goals for students must be expanded and reshaped to include a deep understanding of mathematics (National Research Council 2001). Understanding has long been advertised as a goal for students. Many teachers obviously would like their students to understand the mathematics they study, but when asked to specify the goal for a particular lesson, most U. S. teachers in the TIMSS Video Study talked about skill proficiency; few mentioned understanding (Hiebert and Stigler 2000).

Valuing deep understanding of mathematics as an important goal for students is the first step. The second step is to help students achieve this goal. One way to support students' efforts to understand is to allow mathematics to be problematic for them. Why has this point received major emphasis in this chapter? It is based on a theory about how students construct understanding that is very different from the beliefs that many people hold about how students learn. In particular, the theory places great importance on the role of *struggle* in developing understanding. As mentioned previously, many teachers believe that their job is to remove struggles from students' learning experiences. But struggling, in a healthy sense and on the right kinds of problems for an appropriate amount of time, prepares students to make sense of relevant information, to piece together ideas in new ways, and to see the benefits of better methods of solution.

An important aspect of this theory is that deep understanding develops over time. Although quick insights can occur— sometimes while working on a single problem—significant and lasting understanding of mathematics develops gradually and accumulates over time as students solve increasingly challenging problems.

The changes called for in this book are fundamental. Teachers who take the recommendations seriously will face many obstacles as they revise their instruction to help students develop understanding through solving problems (Ball 1993; Lampert 2001; Schifter and Fosnot 1993). But the changes need not occur overnight and all at once. Change of this importance often happens in small steps, small steps that build on one another. Small successes can yield dramatic improvement if they are saved and shared and accumulate over time. Steady, gradual improvement often is more lasting than overnight reform.

Some encouraging signs are appearing. Many teachers are embracing new learning goals for students, creating for themselves new images of practice, and displaying rich models of what is possible in classrooms. If the mathematics education community can create a system in which teachers can record, accumulate, and share these images and models with others, classroom practice throughout the country might gradually become more aligned with the visions portrayed in this book.

Strategies for Separating

Malia Scott,
first- and second-grade teacher

In chapter 4, Hiebert discusses several "signposts to guide classroom teachers in the direction of giving students opportunities to develop deep mathematical understandings" [p. 54]. One of these "signposts" is a focus on methods: " . . . examining methods encourages students to construct mathematical relationships, . . . relationships that extend students' understanding well beyond [the] particular problem" [pp. 56-57]. In this grades 1–2 classroom, in which students have been consistently encouraged to develop and refine their own methods for addition and subtraction, students are examining methods for solving two-digit subtraction problems. Even though these students are young, many of them are ready to think about unfamiliar methods, and in the course of this analysis, they learn more about the mathematical relationships involved. Malia Scott writes about ways in which students are building on one another's ideas to develop sound methods for solving subtraction problems, but she also realizes that other students who are less active in trying new methods are nevertheless attending to the discussions of methods that are a regular part of the classroom work.

—Susan Jo Russell

This week, my group of second graders and several of the first graders worked on two-digit story problems involving separating. The students were asked to record two strategies for solving each problem. They then came together as a group and shared and discussed these strategies. As students offered new strategies, they recorded them on a "separating strategies" chart. I was interested to see the diversity of their thinking, their degree of comfort in listening to new problem-solving methods and refining their own strategies, and their willingness to solve subsequent problems in new ways.

I was pleased to find that all the students in the group had at least one good problem-solving strategy that they understood and were able to use consistently. However, the challenge of finding two ways of solving each problem really seemed to stretch their thinking. Earlier in the year, the group energy during discussion seemed to center on waiting to share rather than listening. In our more recent discussions, the students have been far more involved, actually listening closely to one another, asking questions, making comments, and adding their own ideas. During the days we spent on this work, I noticed a number of students trying to make sense of a new strategy.

One example of such an attempt occurred when Henry introduced the use of negative numbers in one of his strategies. For a problem involving subtracting 17 from 35, he came up with the following:

$$30 - 10 = 20$$
$$5 - 7 = -2$$
$$20 - 2 = 18$$

Marina was perplexed and told him that he "shouldn't have a minus after the equals." Henry explained, "You don't really have to stop counting when you get down to zero; the numbers just keep going into negative. It's like you owe somebody that much." I saw some doubtful looks, and Danielle maintained that Henry just could not take a bigger number away from a smaller number. However, despite their hesitation the previous day, several students were intrigued and tried to use Henry's strategy with their next problem.

After several days of continued discussion about negative numbers, at least half of my students had tried this strategy. Although the concept of negatives was difficult to grasp, the students were not deterred, and they listened carefully as they tried to make sense of the strategy in their own way. One of these students was Evan. Evan had been introduced to the conventional algorithm at home. For a first grader, his mathematics thinking was very advanced, but he did not have the wealth of strategies and flexibility in thinking possessed by many of my second graders. Evan preferred the traditional U.S. algorithms when solving problems, but I wondered about the depth of his understanding of the underlying concepts. Evan tried to use the algorithm with the new separating problems but was stumped by the first step in solving 48 – 29. He turned to pictures next, and then he tried Henry's strategy with negative numbers, which he was able to make sense of and use consistently. Finally, Evan returned to his algorithm of subtracting the ones first, and he used his new strategy to modify his previous one. He explained his thinking as follows for 48 – 29: 8 – 9 = –1 and 40 – 20 = 20, so 20 – 1 = 19. I believe that the process helped him understand the underlying structure of tens and ones more completely.

Another example of a student's attempt to make sense of another student's strategy involved Francesca and Marina. Marina began by looking carefully at the number she was subtracting and then breaking her problem down. She solved 35 – 17 as follows:

I knew that 17 = 10 + 7, so I made the 35 into a 10 + 20 + 5. The 10s cancel each other out, and then I took 20 – 7 and I had 13 left. I knew I had to add 5 back on to the 13, because the 5 belonged to the 35, and I wasn't taking away that number. So 5 + 13 = 18!

Francesca understood Marina's verbal explanation, and she modified and refined what she had done. Francesca, too, looked first at the number she was subtracting, giving special attention to the number in the ones place. For the problem 48 – 29, she explained, "I knew that I couldn't take 9 away from the 8, so I made the 8 into an 18, and that left 30." Her work is shown below.

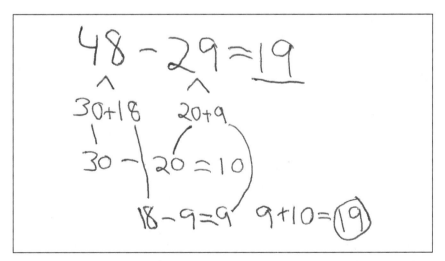

It amazes me that Francesca's strategy closely parallels the traditional regrouping algorithm, yet rather than memorize a recipe for an answer, she has developed her own problem-solving strategy, which demonstrates a sophisticated understanding of place value.

Several students are still most comfortable with strategies that rely on counting, but during discussion they are quite involved, and they comment on other strategies based on the structure and relationships between the numbers. Although they are not ready to "own" these strategies yet, they are obviously trying to make sense of them on their own terms. The daily discussions allow them consistent exposure to these new ideas and help me assess their understanding. Their contributions to the discussion demonstrate more complex thinking than their very concrete strategies on paper.

Finally, a comment from Emma validated the importance I had placed on group discussion for these problems. She announced to the group today, "I love to talk about my thinking. When I share with the class, I can usually figure out any mistakes I made, and I think my ideas get much clearer!"

CHAPTER 5

Designing and Selecting Problem-Based Tasks

John A. Van de Walle

I N PREVIOUS chapters, Lambdin and Hiebert effectively made the case for using problems as a major vehicle for engaging students so that their learning will be optimized and enjoyable. Solving problems focuses students' attention on making sense of the very mathematics we want them to learn. This chapter focuses on those tasks or problems that are at the heart of this problem-based approach. How do we choose them? What do they look like? How can we make them accessible to every child so that all children can learn?

Characteristics of Effective Tasks

A *problem* can be defined as any task or even an activity for which the students have no prescribed rules or memorized procedures that they can use to solve it (Hiebert et al. 1997; NCTM 2000). The terms *problem, task,* and *problem-based task* may carry different meanings in some contexts, but here they will be used interchangeably. An important point to emphasize is that a problem-based task need not be complex or elaborate.

Consider this task: "Which is more, 2/3 or 2/5?" Without a prescribed method of attack, this seemingly simple task can engage students in the meanings of numerator and denominator and help develop 1/2 as a useful fraction benchmark. For example, 2/3 and 2/5 each have two parts, but fifths are smaller; or 2/3 is more than 1/2, and 2/5 is less than 1/2. Each argument solves the problem. Students devising and evaluating these solutions are building important ideas about fractions. Comparing 6/8 and 4/5 involves different relationships. For example, 4/5 is 1/5 away from a whole, whereas 6/8 is 2/8 away from a whole. But 2/8 is the same as 1/4, and since fourths are larger than fifths, 6/8 is farther away, or smaller. Another might see these fractions as 12/16 and 12/15 and argue from that vantage point. A series of these tasks over several days can strengthen several aspects of fractional number sense.

To the basic definition of *task* or *problem* should be added three characteristics if the task is to promote student learning.

Task Characteristic 1: What Is Problematic Must Be the Mathematics

The oft-cited recommendation that students should be given "real world" problems or that students' personal interests should be included in student problems is worthwhile to consider, but an even more important consideration is that the task should focus students' attention on the mathematical ideas embedded in it. Making sense of a mathematical idea is often all that is needed to attract students' attention. The fraction-comparison task discussed previously has no context, yet the task can be quite engaging.

Context can often be used to introduce a problem or pose a setting for a task: "Carla is shopping and has only $2.25. She wants to know if she has enough money to buy an item that costs $.79 and one that costs $1.49. How can she solve this problem in her head?" The mathematics here involves the sum of 79 and 49. This calculation could be done in several ways (e.g., 80 + 50 – 2, or 110 + 18). When the sum of 128 is placed back in context, the mathematics also makes sense in context—Carla needs $2.28, so she does not have enough money. In the end, what students work on must be the mathematics.

Task Characteristic 2: Tasks Must Be Accessible to Students

Hiebert (this volume, p. 54) says that teachers should pose "problems that are just within students' reach"—challenging yet not inaccessible. Tasks that are too easy offer little opportunity for growth. Tasks too far out of reach can frustrate students and "turn them off." To know what is just within students' reach requires that you, as a teacher, develop good hypotheses about what concepts and skills your students will bring to the task you pose on the day you pose it (Simon 1995). Even the best curriculum materials or resource books can only suggest tasks that may be effective for a particular grade level. But only you know how well your students have developed ideas and what they are most likely to be ready for tomorrow.

Every class has a range of student abilities. Good tasks should be accessible to all your students. A task out of reach of students whose learning rates are slower will not contribute to their growth. Worse, it may cause feelings of inadequacy when the students are unable to contribute to discussions. These students will eventually retreat from participation. Similarly, tasks that pose no challenge will also provide little opportunity for growth and can cause disinterest.

Task Characteristic 3: Tasks Must Require Justifications and Explanations for Answers or Methods

Students need to understand that answers alone are not sufficient. A significant part of understanding mathematics comes from an analysis of the thinking that went into a solution. Every task should include clear expectations for how students will share their ideas and solutions. The format may be words, pictures, and numbers all used in a journal entry or a presentation prepared by a group on a large sheet of newsprint. For class discussions, it may be a simple admonition that students should be prepared to explain their answers, their methods, and why they think they are correct. When teachers establish this expectation explicitly and consistently, students come to learn that analysis is a central part of their mathematics work.

Writing or drawing pictures to explain one's reasoning has two important effects. First, the reflective act of analysis often causes students to rethink a solution, to more clearly understand their own ideas, and to share ideas with their partner or group members. Second, by putting their thoughts on paper, students are "rehearsing" for the discussion that will follow. Every student will be ready to participate, so the same confident or verbal students will not necessarily dominate the discussion.

All three of these aspects of effective problems are found in the following simple task: "Find some "clever" or efficient ways of figuring out what 6×8 is so that if you forget you will have an easy way to remember it. Explain each of the ways you find." Without any context, this task is engaging for even the best students in a third- or fourth-grade class and is accessible to all students. The mathematical content involves much more than a way to recall that 6×8 is 48. Consider just a few of the paths to get there: 5×8 and one more 8; three 8s are 24, then double that; four 6s are 24, then double that; ten 6s are 60, then take off 12. These ideas and others contribute to many interconnected ideas about multiplication and numerical relationships. The strategies can be applied to other facts. They provide an array of options for students who are having difficulties. A focus on processes or paths to a solution tells students that many ways exist to get answers and that each student's method will be considered, even if it is unique.

Selecting Tasks for the Classroom

If it were possible to design a "perfect" collection of tasks that would serve all classrooms at a grade level, this chapter would have no reason to be written, because someone would have already compiled such a collection. The children in any class differ in myriad ways even from the class across the hall and from child to child within the class. It is you, the teacher, who plays the crucial role in determining what tasks your students will experience from day to day.

Before Selecting a Task

Effective task selection requires reflection on two main factors in every lesson: (1) the mathematics involved and (2) the ideas brought to that mathematics by students.

Begin with the mathematics

Good task selection begins with the mathematics that you want your students to learn. Try to think in terms of conceptual ideas rather than rules or skills. Although measurable objectives are important (e.g., "The student will be able to ..."), focusing on such behavioral statements fosters a tendency to orient instruction toward a show-and-tell approach and away from conceptual development.

By way of example, consider the all-important topic of place value in the second grade. Typical objectives might require that students "identify the ones, tens, and hundreds digits in a three-digit number," "select the larger of two numbers up to 999," or "write the number that comes before and after a given number." Students are able to learn the names of place values, a rule for deciding on the larger number, or the sequence of number names and how to write them. These rules or procedures work because of the way the place-value system has been designed. However, learning the methods for getting correct answers does not necessarily help students understand the ideas behind the methods. The skills that we want our students to acquire are nearly always a direct outcome of a focus on the ideas that support them. Second-grade children who explore patterns on the hundreds chart, estimate quantities in jars of objects and then count and group them in bunches of ten, and play such games as "race to 100" (building 100 using tens and ones by rolling a die and collecting the indicated number of ones) are developing the ideas that will allow them to readily perform the skills that are on most second-grade objective lists for place value.

Allowing children to solve two-digit computation problems using their own methods can also enhance these same concepts for place value. For example, among the approaches students may use to add 36 and 48, some of the most likely ones are the following:

- Count by ones (1, 2, 3, . . . , 36, 37, 38, . . . , 82, 83, 84).

- Count on from 36 (36, 37, 28, . . . , 82, 83, 84).

- Add the tens (30 and 40 is 70), then add ones (6 and 8 is 14), then add 70 and 14 to get 84.

- Take 2 from the 36 and put it with 48 to get 50, then add 50 and 34 to get 84.

The discussion around these methods will contribute to all students' understanding of the base-ten system as well as help develop flexible computational methods.

Consider the ideas that students bring to tasks

The next step before selecting a task is to think about your students. You have been teaching them every day and listening to their ideas. You are the person most qualified to form hypotheses about what your students know and where they are with respect to acquiring the concepts the class is working on. Think about all your students rather than the majority or the broad "middle" of the class. As we discuss subsequently, an important consideration is to select tasks that are accessible by, and also beneficial to, all your students, not just some or even most. Hypotheses about students should continue to focus on their understanding rather than on what skills or procedures they either have or do not have.

Examples of Effective Tasks

Although many excellent tasks are clever, or elaborate, or complex, most good tasks are quite simple. The following sampling of tasks spans a range of grades and represents different areas of the curriculum. The purpose here is only to give you a better idea of what is meant by a problem-based task.

Sample task 1. Think about the number 5 broken into two different amounts. Draw a picture to show ways that 5 things can be in two parts. Make up a story to go with your picture.

This kindergarten or early-first-grade task is one of many variations to use when students are beginning to understand number in terms of parts and wholes. A similar task may ask students to find ways to break a bar of connecting cubes in two parts and find how many ways it can be done.

Sample task 2. Provide students with a collection of coins (real ones, pictures, or a list), and ask them to find the total in two different ways, for example, 8 nickels, 9 dimes, 2 pennies, and 7 quarters.

Here second or third graders obviously address skills with money, but, perhaps more importantly, they have a great opportunity to develop ideas related to tens and hundreds and to coordinate a variety of units. The class discussion around this task will almost certainly involve a variety of ways to make multiples of ten and see how 10 tens make 100.

Sample task 3. Find a way to measure our Halloween pumpkin, and then write a letter to our pen pals that will help them know just how large it is.

The task does not specify what type of measurement to make of the pumpkin. It might be girth, height, weight, or even volume. How the task is approached will vary considerably with the knowledge that children bring to the task. At first or second grade, informal units of length measure are likely. Older students may find creative ways to measure the weight or volume, and standard units are more appropriate. The problematic nature of the task also varies with the students. Younger students will wrestle with basic concepts of measure and how to communicate the data they find. Older students will have to find or devise appropriate measuring tools, select units, and communicate their findings clearly.

Sample task 4. A fifth grader was trying to put numbers in order from smallest to largest. This is what he did:

$$3.4 \quad 3.38 \quad 3.45 \quad 3.4026$$

What would you tell him?

One way to pose a task is to present a typical student error or an unfamiliar correct solution and have students confront it. For this task, students should have been exposed to, and have access to, a variety of decimal models, such as base-ten pieces, a 10-by-10 grid or perhaps a 100-by-100 grid, and number lines. However, the students should be the ones who decide how to represent the ideas and determine how to explain the ordering of the numbers.

Sample task 5. On your geoboard, what is the largest triangle you can make? Explain why you think it is the largest. Do other triangles exist that are the same size?

Sample task 6. Provide a shoebox and enough one-inch cubes to line up along the longest edge of the box. How many cubes will fit in the box? Once you have an answer and can explain your thinking, test the result by actually filling the box with cubes. Will your method work for other boxes?

These two measurement tasks are examples of situations in which students take their understanding of measure and work toward devising formulas. The triangle task may not result in a formula, but important groundwork for that formula will likely emerge. The box task can, depending on grade level and prior experiences, result in a meaningful formula for the volume of rectangular boxes.

Many excellent tasks are found in simple traditional story problems. For young children, solving the problems aids in the development of number concepts as well as understanding operations. The problems are likely to be solved using counters or drawings. From second grade on, a story problem can present computational problems with whole numbers, fractions, or decimals. A growing body of data suggests that children can construct reasonably adequate methods for adding, subtracting, multiplying, and dividing multidigit numbers without explicit instruction. Students' methods develop slowly over time as they share ideas and evaluate procedures invented by others.

The tasks described thus far might be given to individual students in a class or to groups working on the solutions, followed by a class discussion. Not every problem-based task has to fit this model. Many simple games require students to develop strategies that can develop number sense, estimation skills, or spatial reasoning. Some, but by no means all, computer activities have a built-in problem-based mode. (See the chapters by Battista [pp. 229–38] and by Crown [pp. 217–28] in this volume.)

Designing and Selecting Tasks for All Students

A problem-based approach for all students begins with an understanding that every child is a thinker having developing or emerging ideas. As students wrestle with problems, their ideas are going to be engaged, tested, revised, refined, and connected with other ideas they already possess. However, each of your students will do these things in her or his own way. This statement does not mean that all students will develop the same ideas or develop them at the same pace. But all children can think and all children can and must be given opportunities to learn. Interestingly, a problem-based approach to instruction may be the best way to make mathematics accessible to all students in a diverse classroom. For this outcome to occur in your classroom, you must keep in mind some important ideas:

- Focus on conceptual foundations.
- Plan and allow for multiple entry points.
- Reconsider what is meant by "practice."
- Listen carefully to your students.
- Create readily modified tasks.

Focus on Conceptual Foundations

A focus on conceptual foundations is an important idea for reaching all students in your classroom. It allows each child in the class to develop ideas at his or her own rate as the same concept is revisited many times in the course of weeks or even months. Those children whose rate of learning is slower may at first use more rudimentary or less sophisticated methods. For example, they may use counters and count all to solve addition problems rather than use mastered facts or number relationships. In the same class, students who are quicker to learn may develop useful methods early on and share these methods with others. Some of their strategies may never be learned by all students.

Put simply, a conceptual focus dramatically increases the number and variety of opportunities students have to engage in and develop good, long-lasting ideas. When the focus is on skills or procedures, the tendency is to lean away from a problem-based approach and rely more on show-and-tell, thereby decreasing opportunities for the students to develop ideas that make sense to them.

Plan and Allow for Multiple Entry Points

When considering a problem for your class, think about the most unsophisticated way that the problem can be solved or even approached. Will this way be accessible to all your students? Will it help them grow? What are some clever ways to solve the problem? Are any extensions or related challenges possible? Will these ways challenge your better students? If you can think of only one way to solve the problem, perhaps the task is not appropriate. Relax the criteria and see if it opens up options for more students.

Even the least sophisticated solution offers some opportunity for growth.

To illustrate the importance of using tasks that can be solved in several ways, consider the following task:

> Select a bag of counters, and tell how many are in the bag. Find an easy way to tell how many. Explain how you counted. Find a way to count that is easier than counting by ones.

Had the directions been "Make groups of tens and ones to find out how many counters are in the bag," the focus would be on the prescribed method of doing the task—following directions. In the original task, some students will count by twos or fives. The notion of using tens will come from those who have connected this idea with counting that may have occurred using a hundreds chart or other prior activities involving grouping by tens.

Here is another example:

> Use 8 two-sided counters to find addition combinations for 8.

For this task, some children will simply spill the counters repeatedly and write what they see. Some children will count every chip as they work, whereas others will begin to recall combinations and count only one of the parts. Some will notice that 3 and 5 is the same as 5 and 3, whereas others may argue this result. A few will try to order their results to see whether they can tell when they have found all the combinations. Some children may wonder whether all the combinations occur with the same frequency or whether a double combination always exists for any collection of counters.

Reconsider What "Practice" Means

Only rarely are important ideas fully developed in a single lesson. If we begin to think of practice as returning regularly to the same basic ideas but through new problem-based experiences, we begin to open up opportunities for all children in our classrooms. Let us examine the topic of equivalent fractions.

We want children to understand that the same quantity can be represented by different fractions. Eventually students should be able to use a symbolic method of changing a fraction into an equivalent form—perhaps with a given denominator. One possible task is this:

Use fraction pieces to find names for this region.
Find as many names as possible.

This same concept should also be approached with counters (e.g., "Find fraction names for 16 of 24 chips making up a whole"), with paper folding, with symbolic tasks, and with variations on each of these. Each of these tasks provides "practice" with the emerging idea of equivalence. Within a class of diverse learners, some will continue to struggle with the basic ideas at a very concrete level. Others will begin to notice numeric patterns as they write lists of equivalent fractions and go beyond what can be modeled with concrete materials.

Several points can be made here. First, you must be patient with students who learn more slowly. Accept them where they are today while encouraging and challenging them to develop more sophisticated ideas. If children are using tedious, inefficient methods to solve a particular type of problem, be sure that they are working to the best of their ability.

Second, even the best students need multiple opportunities to acquire difficult concepts or develop difficult skills. If a conceptual activity is followed too closely with a procedural skill or rule, all too often the rule becomes the focus and the poorly developed underpinnings are lost. For the inefficient learner, the danger of premature introduction of rules or procedures is even greater.

Third, students who grasp ideas quickly will most likely learn more about an idea than students for whom learning is difficult. With multiple opportunities to practice an idea, they can extend it beyond what most students need or develop a variety of avenues to the same end.

Listen Carefully to Your Students

Previously I noted that for a task to be just within the reach of your students, you should develop a good hypothesis about the ideas that students will bring to the subject. What ideas seem to be emerging as they work on related tasks? You need to explore this hypothesis with every child. A global "feel" for the class as a whole is insufficient.

To this end, it is important to listen carefully to every child. In a problem-oriented classroom, a significant portion of each lesson is devoted to discussion involving how problems were solved and why the results make sense—a significant listening opportunity. Another time to listen is when students are at work on a task. Sit with a child or a group, ask what they are doing, and have them explain their reasoning. You can also "listen" to what students write. Written work can suggest a probing question to pursue at the next opportunity.

The chapter by Yackel in this volume (pp. 107–21) is entirely devoted to this extremely important skill of listening to children. Given the diversity of learners in every classroom, listening carefully is paramount if tasks are to be designed or selected that meet the needs of all learners.

Create Readily Modified Tasks

Many tasks are easily modified by simply changing the numbers involved or by altering the question slightly. This approach is easily used with simple story problems.

> Tania was collecting seashells. Today she added {8, 20, 27} shells to her collection. Now she has a total of {12, 43, 51} shells. How many did she begin with?

Students select the first, second, or third set of numbers, depending on their individual comfort level with the size of the numbers. The operation reasoning remains constant, but each computation (12 – 8, 43 – 20, 51 – 27) offers a different level of challenge.

As another example, suppose you supply students with a collection of parallelograms cut out of tagboard. The collection includes squares and rectangles. Here are three tasks that can be offered in the same class, all of which are aimed at developing ideas about parallelograms but each at a different level of sophistication:

- Pick one *parallelogram*, and draw three different shapes that are like it in some way. Tell how your shapes are like the one you selected.

- Draw the diagonals, and see what you can find out about the diagonals of parallelograms.

- Make a list of properties that every parallelogram in this collection has.

In explorations such as these, often the children with learning difficulties or who typically require more time contribute ideas that no one else thinks of.

Commonly Asked Questions about Selecting Tasks

In the chapter by Russell and others, four teachers describe how they worked to engage their students in a problem-based approach to learning. These and other stories from teachers throughout this book illustrate clearly that allowing the mathematics to be problematic for students—allowing them to reason, explain, conjecture, and evaluate and defend ideas—is effective. It also is rewarding and challenging! Undoubtedly you have some concerns about this approach. Here are a few questions, commonly heard from teachers, that relate specifically to the issues of selecting good tasks.

Where can I find all the tasks I will need?

Examine the examples of tasks throughout this book; they are all quite simple. Avoid frantically searching for a clever problem for tomorrow's lesson. Instead, begin with the mathematics you want to teach. Many traditional textbook lessons can be changed to problem-based tasks with very little effort. Think about how you or your textbook would typically explain the main idea in a lesson or unit to your class, then create a parallel situation in which students are the sense makers instead of you. For example, instead of showing students how to change mixed numbers to improper fractions, ask them to find a single fraction name for 3 2/3.

A second suggestion is to make a habit of reading and collecting ideas for your own professional growth. Excellent resources are available in NCTM journals and publications, in resource books from other publishers, and from conferences and in-service activities that you attend. Teacher's editions often suggest activities that can become problem-based tasks. Soon you will develop a repertoire of ideas and approaches that you can call your own. The ideas you have reflected on, and have been exposed to, over time will guide or influence your design of the best tasks for your students. Hours spent flipping through resource books can often leave you with a task that is not appropriate for the particular needs of your students.

What about having students make up problems?

Wonderful occasions arise when, in the course of discussing a classroom problem, students will ask questions or make conjectures that are deeply connected with the ideas you are exploring. These questions or conjectures are often better than any task you could pose, because the students have ownership of the problem—they have a personal need to know. Be on the lookout for these opportunities. Encourage questions and conjectures. A question posed today can be the driving force of tomorrow's lesson. (See the chapter by English in this volume, pp. 187–98.)

A not-uncommon suggestion is that students should make up problems for themselves or for their classmates. Although this idea has some merit, student-designed tasks will almost certainly be about things they already know. You must be responsible for the tasks that move your agenda forward.

What happens if a task "bombs" or no one solves it?

Occasionally you will pose a task that is a bit out of reach for your students. After giving appropriate time and hints, it becomes clear that they are not going to get it. What should you do? First, be sure you are listening to your students. Ask yourself why are they not solving the problem. By identifying what they need to learn before solving the problem, you are identifying the mathematics for tomorrow's task. Temporarily set the difficult problem aside. Let students know that they will return to it later—then be sure that they do so.

Do tasks have to involve manipulatives or be "real world" oriented?

Although hands-on methods and realistic contexts are often important, do not let these considerations drive your choice of problems. Begin with the mathematics! Keep tasks simple! Many good tasks involve only pencil and paper or even mental strategies. Be wary of having students push materials around according to your rules and directions rather than their ideas. At times you may want to specify that a particular manipulative be used—for example, using counters for fractions instead of pie pieces or folded paper. A more common approach in a problem-solving environment is to allow students to select whatever method or materials they believe they need to solve a problem. Students should use manipulatives that make sense to them. They should use manipulatives when they need them.

As for context, wrap tasks in interesting data, story problems, and realistic settings whenever it is reasonable to do. Context helps connect mathematics with the world of students. Real contexts also help develop the habit of checking results against realistic expectations—"Does this make sense?" But remember, you should be concerned primarily with engaging students with important mathematics. Making sense of mathematics is inherently fun and interesting. You need not rely on context to engage students.

First Steps

Building your instruction around problem-based tasks can be a daunting proposition, especially at the beginning. Obviously the selection of tasks is only one component. To say that task design or selection is simple would be misleading, but it is far from impossible. Begin simply. Think about your lesson plans for next week. Pick the lesson you see as the most important—the one in which you will have to explain the most or the one dealing with the most important concepts. Make this your target lesson. Turn the explanations you would normally make into a task for your students to wrestle with.

If you are reading this book, you are certainly engaging in your own professional growth. Do not stop here. Continue to read good publications to enhance your sense of how to create problems for your students. It is challenging. It is possible. It is very rewarding.

Reassembling the Hundred Chart

Malia Scott, first- and second-grade teacher

One way to think of a "problem" is as "any task . . . for which the students have no prescribed rules or memorized procedures" (Van de Walle, this volume, chapter 5, p. 67). In other words, a task becomes problematic for students when they have to work through the mathematics that they are in the process of learning so that they can carry out the task. In this classroom episode, two students are working on their understanding of the structure of the base-ten number system and how this structure is notated. By placing numbers on a large hundred chart, they use the knowledge they have about how numbers are ordered and develop further understanding about how each decade is constructed and how patterns repeat from decade to decade. The teacher has designed a task that embodies the three characteristics that Van de Walle describes as crucial for effective problem-solving tasks. First, the task must be accessible to the students. In this case, the hundred-chart problem has enough structure to allow students entry yet is problematic enough that they must try out, consider, and revise their approaches. Second, the task focuses students' attention on important mathematics—the structure of the hundred chart highlights important patterns of the base-ten number system. And third, because they are working together and must agree on the placement of the numbers, they explain and justify their methods in the course of their work.

—Susan Jo Russell

81

For a second-grade mathematics class, I removed all the cards from our wall hundred chart and had students take turns working in pairs to reassemble the numbers. My class is very familiar with the activity in which several numbers on the hundred chart are removed. Students must use the patterns and organization of the chart to help them identify the missing numbers. This occasion, however, was their first opportunity to play with all the numbers missing.

One pair consisted of Roberto and Leo, both of whom were still struggling to develop a solid sense of our number system. Leo was beginning to recognize numbers in terms of tens and ones, but he struggled with the concept of place value.

Although this task was daunting for them at first, Leo and Roberto worked together beautifully. I was the lucky observer of a rich, captivating discourse, full of excellent observations and great strategies. Fortunately, I also had plenty of coverage in my room on that day, and I was able to sit with the two of them for the entire period and watch this activity play itself out (a rarity!).

They spread the cards out, face up in front of them, and began looking for a starting point. Leo first counted the spaces from the beginning by ones before he placed the 12 in its correct spot. Roberto shifted through the pile looking for the 1 and the 100. They both filled in several of the lower numbers before Leo found the 50. He was instantly animated as he realized, "Oh this belongs in the tens row!" He counted down the far column by tens and located the spot for 50. Leo had found a solid strategy, and he began searching for other "tens numbers."

Roberto meanwhile was filling in numbers quickly and randomly, usually finding the right area of the chart but often missing the correct slot. I decided to let him continue to see whether he too would find a more concrete strategy.

Gradually, Roberto began identifying rows as the "sixties row" or the "nineties row." This created some heated discussion as he tried to remove the numbers in Leo's carefully constructed tens column. Roberto looked at the end of his "fifties row," saw a 60, and replaced it with a 50 because, he believed, it did not fit his rule:

									40
	52	53		55					50
									60

Leo was quite confident of his tens column, and he explained why Roberto's change could not work.

Leo: See, you start here, and it's the tens row, so you count by tens [Leo ran his finger down the far-right column, and Roberto joined in as he counted]: 10, 20, 30, 40, 50, 60.

Roberto: What? What's going on here? But this is the fifties row, so this should be 50. [He pointed to the 60 spot.]

Leo: But you have to move down when you get to the end of the rows. This is 50, and then you go down to the next row and it's 51, 52, 53, 54.

Roberto looked skeptical. I could see that Leo's explanation seemed reasonable to Roberto, but he had not fully made sense of it.

The same issue came up again when he found 30s in the "twenties row."

Roberto: Whoa! What's going on here? This can't be. We are forgetting all the twenties. It goes 10s, 20s, then 30s. [He took all the cards out of the "twenties row" and picked up the 21] And this should go here [points to the 21 spot] 'cause there was a 20 at the end of this row up here, like you said! You move down and start again.

Leo: And look, it's a pattern, just like the first row! It's 1, 2, 3, 4, 5, 6, 7, 8, 9, 10. [He dragged his finger across the top row] All of our rows have the tens pattern, and here it'll go 21, like twenty and a one; 22, twenty and two; 23; 24; 25; 26; 27; 28; 29; and then it can't be twenty-ten, so it's 30!

Roberto: Yup. The second parts [of the numbers] should be the same in all our rows.

I was thrilled to hear these two making sense of the tens and the ones pattern in our number system in their own way. Certainly these observations and discussions were not new to our class, but previous to this activity, Roberto and Leo had remained largely on the periphery of these conversations about the hundred chart. Through their exploration they were able to establish meaning for themselves, and I could hear the excitement in their voices. They were listening closely to each other, and it was evident that they were using each other's strategies to further their own thinking. I was also surprised at how clearly and confidently these two boys verbalized their strategies and thinking. They had typically struggled to explain their ideas to others and had often been unsure of their strategies.

The two continued to work closely together, discussing the numbers and their placement. Leo began double-checking his placements based on the vertical pattern they had found.

Leo: Let's see, does 55 go here? Yup, that's the five row: 5, 15, 25, 35, 45, 55.

I was interested to note that he never used this strategy initially to locate a spot for a number, but he consistently used it to double-check his work. Leo realized that every row contains ten numbers. He was also confident that the numbers in his "tens row" followed the same pattern he used when he counted by tens. Did he realize that he was adding 10 each time he moved up or down any column on the board? I did not think so, but I wish I had questioned him more.

Roberto and Leo were able to successfully complete the chart, and they were proud of their work. When I asked them to go back and double-check to make sure they had gotten all the numbers right, Leo decided to count up from 1 to 100. Roberto moved quickly back up the board (he loved his new strategy!):

Roberto [running his finger across each row as he spoke]: Here's the nineties row, the eighties row, the seventies row, the sixties row, the fifties row, the forties row, the thirties row, the twenties row, the elevens row, and the ones row.

As I reflect on this lesson, I am reminded of the importance of giving students the opportunity to explore and develop their own strategies and construct meaning in their own way. Leo and Roberto were given the opportunity to revisit and explore a familiar problem in a very hands-on manner, which worked to their strengths. I could see the satisfaction and excitement on their faces as I hung the completed hundred chart. "I just love math!" I overheard Roberto telling Leo as they walked away.

On the other side of the coin, I am also faced with the perpetual "how"—how do I continue to provide students like Roberto and Leo with opportunities to explore concepts that the rest of their classmates have long since mastered?

CHAPTER 6

How to Focus the Mathematics Curriculum on Solving Problems

Susan Jo Russell
Rebeka Eston
Jan Rook
Malia Scott
Liz Sweeney

W HAT does it mean to have a mathematics curriculum that focuses on problem solving? At one time, many of us thought that a "problem solving" focus required unusual, unfamiliar, contextualized problems that looked entirely different from conventional classroom problems. These problems were often entertaining and interesting and sometimes dealt with important mathematics—but both students and teachers viewed them as completely separate from the rest of the mathematics curriculum. This chapter presents a problem-solving approach in a different sense—the use of problems to focus on the coherent development of important mathematical ideas that are core to the curriculum. As the examples in this chapter reveal, problems that engage students in reasoning about, representing, explaining, and reevaluating their ideas can be surprisingly straightforward. The choice of particular problems is not what defines a problem-solving curriculum. Rather, it is created through a coherent focus on mathematical ideas.

In this chapter, we recount episodes from four classrooms in which teachers made decisions about how to engage students with significant mathematical ideas. These stories illustrate how the interaction of students, teacher, and curriculum content can create a learning environment in which students' thinking about fundamental mathematical ideas is the focus of classroom activity and discourse.

The teachers in these episodes were participants in a small study group focused on the partnership of teacher and curriculum materials. The study group met for one year to discuss how to teach effectively using curriculum materials as a core but without considering the materials to be a script or a recipe. What characterizes a classroom in which a teacher is actively engaged in using and modifying such materials? What issues and decisions do teachers face? As part of their work, teachers wrote regularly about classroom episodes that illustrated such issues and decisions.

The four sections of this chapter illustrate four interrelated facets of using or modifying the curriculum to focus on solving problems:

- focusing on fundamental mathematical ideas,
- modifying problems to respond to students' evolving understanding,
- meeting a range of student needs, and
- developing representations and metaphors.

Episode 1, "Why Do You Always Call a Half a Half When Sometimes It's a Whole?" Focusing on Fundamental Mathematical Ideas

Teaching mathematics involves identifying important mathematical ideas for a particular grade or age, recognizing the ways in which these complex ideas develop over time, and listening and probing for students' developing understanding of these ideas. No matter how well a curriculum is structured to highlight significant mathematical ideas, the teacher's task is to decide, for a particular class, when and how to focus the students' attention on an idea that is central to their learning. Sometimes these ideas emerge in ways the teacher anticipated as she or he planned the lesson. At other times, ideas arise unexpectedly from students' thinking, and the teacher has to decide whether to pursue them. Lucy, a fourth-grade teacher, recounts the following story about how a student in her class raised an important issue about fractions:

My fourth-grade class was about two weeks into a curriculum unit on fractions. We had been working fairly successfully, I thought, breaking squares into halves, fourths, eighths, thirds, sixths, and other fractional parts in a variety of ways. The students seemed to recognize how shapes that looked different could be equivalent fractions, and they were developing an understanding of common equivalents, such as 1/2 = 2/4, 3/6 = 1/2, and 3/4 = 6/8. I thought things were going well when, during a class discussion, Jessie, looking very perplexed, asked a question that had been bothering her for several days: "Why do you always call a half a half when sometimes it's a whole?" Other students protested, "Because it's not a whole, it's a half," "What are you talking about? You know what a half is—when you cut something into two pieces, you get a half, and there's another half." But Jessie was persistent: "No! When I cut something into two pieces and I take my piece, it's a whole. Like those brownie problems—when I cut my brownie into two pieces and I take my piece, I get a whole piece."

I sat back for a while and listened to the students interact around Jessie's question. Some tried to use a pizza example as the basis of their argument: when you buy a pizza, it's usually cut into 8 pieces; when you take a piece, you are taking 1/8 of the pizza. But Jessie remained unconvinced. This example seemed to be the same as the brownie example she had proposed: "When I take my piece, I'm taking a whole piece." After letting the discussion go on for a while, I asked if others in the class thought about one-half the same way Jessie did. I thought she might be the only one, but then a hand went up and then another and another. Soon, some of the students were saying that they understood what Jessie was saying and were equally confused about it.

We can imagine situations in which Jessie's question would be brushed aside. After all, most of the students (and all the initially vocal students) seem to understand what is going on—that half of a brownie is still half of the brownie, even when it becomes someone's whole portion. Before moving the class on to the planned work, the teacher could easily answer Jessie's question with a simple clarifying statement—for example, "Well, yes, Jessie, if you think of the piece of brownie you get as a whole piece, then it is a whole, but it is still half of the original brownie." Would this statement be enough to satisfy Jessie and clear up her confusion? Also, the possibility exists that Jessie might never have asked her question. The fact that she brought up her question and persisted in her argument in the face of immediate disagreement from other students suggests that some things of importance are going on in this classroom—*(a)* that students know that their ideas are valued and *(b)* that mathematics is about thinking through ideas, challenging ideas that are being discussed, and developing logical arguments to support an idea or call it into question.

Jessie may or may not be confused, but she has brought up a central idea about fractions—that a fraction is a fraction in relation to a particular unit whole. A quantity is named differently when it is considered in relation to a different unit. Lucy chooses to wait and listen before making a decision about how to intervene. She recognizes several important elements in this situation. First, Jessie is wondering about a central mathematical idea. Second, once they hear Jessie's argument, several other students have the same question. Lucy may also be considering another common aspect of learning about a complex idea such as fractions: students' apparent understanding of some aspects of a topic may conceal a lack of understanding of fundamental ideas. The relation of a fraction to a unit whole may seem obvious when the unit has been clearly identified, for example, when students are cutting up squares that represent brownies. But do students have the flexibility to keep track of the mathematical relationships between piece and whole as different units are considered? If I have two slices of the three pizzas we ordered for our meal, with each pizza cut into eight slices, am I eating two *whole* slices, a *quarter* of a pizza, or a *twelfth* of the whole meal?

Here is a moment at which a teacher must make a decision about how to problematize the curriculum. Although a good curriculum can alert teachers to the fundamental mathematical issues that might arise, it cannot possibly anticipate everything that will happen in class—or when it will happen. The teacher must listen to students' talk and observe their actions, analyzing these discussions and behaviors in relation to the mathematical agenda for the class and making decisions about when to stop and focus on an essesntial mathematical idea. Lucy, who had been involved in a series of teacher development projects, had been thinking hard about mathematics with other colleagues for several years. She comments on the importance of the teacher's interaction with the curriculum:

I wonder how I would have handled Jessie's question three or four years ago. I don't think that I would have understood the significance of what she was asking. I might have just dismissed the idea as a minor confusion—something that she would get over as we moved along. I might not have even heard the question. To Jessie's credit, she did not let the issue rest. She forced us to rethink what we had done over the past weeks, to go back a bit, to retrace our steps, to think of those fractional pieces again and how they relate to the whole.

Although the written curriculum keeps marching along, mathematical ideas do not develop in straight lines or all at once but, rather, in fits and starts, circles and backtracks. A crucial aspect of problematizing the curriculum is taking advantage of moments in students' thinking that focus—or refocus—the class's attention on fundamental mathematical ideas.

Episode 2, "The Counting Jar": Modifying Problems to Respond to Students' Evolving Understanding

A focus on the basic mathematical ideas underlying students' learning leads to the need to modify core activities to fit students' evolving understanding of a set of ideas. In the following episode, a kindergarten teacher recounts how she used an activity from the written curriculum materials, then gradually modified it over the course of the year so that it would continue to be problematic for her students. The activity is called "The Counting Jar," a classroom routine for kindergarten in *Investigations in Number, Data, and Space* (Scott Foresman, 1998), that is done periodically throughout the year. It involves three steps: first, students count the number of objects in the jar, which vary in size and amount from one time the activity is used to the next. Then students represent the number of objects in some way on paper, and finally, they create an equivalent set of objects. When Gloria first read the description of this activity in the curriculum, she noticed that it was similar to another familiar class activity in which students estimate the number of something in a jar, then count. At first she thought that this activity would be pretty much the same, but as she tried it out, she found that it was more appropriate for her students:

By reading carefully the description of the counting jar in the curriculum guide, I became aware of a shift in my thinking. I once thought that I was providing a challenge for the children by asking them to estimate the quantity in a jar. Their estimation would, I thought, provide a context for practicing counting. I now realize that often either my young children would be frustrated by the estimation or it would seem silly to them—the actual counting seemed meaningless. We would often count the contents of the jar together. I look back now and realize that more times than not, I was doing all the counting, with the children chiming along in unison. I used to say that I was modeling ways to count for the children and thought that was enough. Now, with the counting jar, my students are independently counting all the time. As they count, I become more and more aware of their comfort level and proficiency with the process. In this three-step routine, students can utilize the help of others in the first two steps; they can count with a partner to determine the quantity of the original set, and they can look at another child's paper to see how he or she represented the total, but they have a very hard time avoiding doing the last step—creating an equivalent set of objects—on their own. I feel much more secure that all children are doing the work, and, in fact, I can observe which parts they seek assistance for and which they can do independently.

However, as the year went on, Gloria found that when she brought out the counting jar, some students began complaining, "Do we have to do this again?" She began thinking about how students' ideas about counting were evolving and how she might modify the counting-jar activity: "I wanted to think of a way to alter the counting jar just a little to see if I could provide a challenge for these students without losing the focus of counting and making it too difficult for others." She began by increasing the number of objects in the jar. When there were 31 items, rather than 17 or 20, she found that many students miscounted, providing the opportunity for discussing counting strategies, double-checking, and ways to ensure accuracy. In the spring, she introduced another variation:

My newest adjustment to the counting-jar activity is to strategically place subsets of objects in the jar. Last week I put 17 plastic bunnies in the jar—5 were yellow, 5 were red, 5 were blue, and 2 were green. It can take several days for each child to complete the three steps involved in the counting-jar routine. By the fourth day I noticed that everyone had finished. This [completion] usually is my signal to bring the counting jar and recording chart to a class meeting so that we can discuss any new insights and confirm the exact total. The meeting began, and as usual, we acknowledged the representations and confirmed the total. Everyone agreed that it was 17. We looked at how to write the number, because most, if not all, of my students now write the number as opposed to drawing a picture or making tally marks. Reversals are common, and so I use this occasion as a good opportunity to briefly discuss handwriting and strategies for recalling how to write a number.

This meeting had gone smoothly and had not taken very long, so I decided to take on the idea of the subsets even though no one had noticed this aspect on their own. To start, I asked, "Is there anything else that you notice about these bunnies?" After a brief silence, Joseph said, "They are plastic." I nodded and waited a few more seconds. Carly raised her hand next, "They are different colors." I asked, "What do you notice about the colors?" The following conversation ensued:

Martina: They are blue and green and yellow and red.
Kim: There is the same number of red and blue ones.
Teacher: What do you mean?
Kim: There are 5 red and 5 blue ones.
John: Yeah, and 5 yellow ones.
Anika: There aren't five green ones. There are only 2.
Teacher: Did anyone notice this before? [There was a long pause. I assumed the silence meant that no one had.] Now that we have noticed how many bunnies are in each color group, can that help us find another way to tell how many bunnies there are altogether? [Again a long pause ensued. Finally Pake spoke.]
Pake: I know that 5 and 5 makes 10.
Kim: I can count 5, 10, 15, 20.
John: No, 17! 5, 10, 15, 16, 17.
Teacher: Does everyone follow what John and Kim and Pake just said?

I looked around. Some children were nodding their heads yes, but most were not. We recounted the bunnies together, grouping them by colors although still counting by ones so that everyone could follow. By now we had been sitting for a long time, so I decided to leave the discussion there. I was delighted that some of the children could make use of the subsets and could find a new way to arrive at a total. I also realized that this activity was all done in the support of the whole-group meeting. I look forward with great anticipation to see what will happen the next time I put a similar set of objects in the counting jar.

Gloria was able to use her written curriculum as a starting point, then carefully observe how students interacted with the task and modify the task to meet her students' growing understanding about number. To do so, she had to take into account both what she knew about her students and how the mathematical ideas they were working on can develop. Counting by ones leads to thinking of numbers as being composed of larger units as those ones are combined into groups. Eventually these ideas lead to understanding how our number system is constructed of ones, tens, hundreds, and so forth. For now, some students are beginning to count the objects by using larger chunks—in this instance, fives—and one or two students are starting to coordinate two different units—counting by fives and by ones ("5, 10, 15, 16, 17") to construct a number.

In reflecting on her decisions, Gloria recognizes both what she learned from the written curriculum and her own role in revising it: "I have learned a great deal by watching my students work with the counting jar and now feel much more secure about making subtle changes. I know that the changes I make are mathematically sound and directly linked with the goals I have set for my students."

Episode 3, "The Same Gone and the Same Left": Meeting a Range of Student Needs

A crucial aspect of the teacher's work in problematizing the curriculum for students is taking into account the range of student needs that exist in every classroom. Students who are struggling, students who are doing fairly well but are not going beyond what is expected, students who easily solve most problems, students who can tackle problems beyond what most of their peers are ready for—all these students need problems that engage them in working on significant mathematics. In Gloria's episode, several students were ready to think about coordinating different units, and Gloria's modification of the counting-jar activity allowed those students to work on this idea. In the following episode, Margery, a fifth-grade teacher, works with three girls who are struggling in mathematics.

Margery's class has just completed the first two sections of their fractions unit. As she thinks about how the class is doing as a whole, she identifies three students who seem to be having great difficulty with basic ideas about comparing fractions. Two of the students are bilingual. The third one says she hates mathematics;

Margery describes her as a student who "tries hard not to get involved in any mathematics conversation and attempts to disguise the 'not knowing' with angry indifference." During a time when the rest of the class is writing, Margery meets with the three girls. She begins with a question she frequently asks, encouraging students to take responsibility for their own learning: "What are some ideas about fractions that you don't completely understand?" No response is forthcoming from the three girls, who look, respectively, sad, scared, and angry. "Clearly," Margery notes, "these are familiar feelings for them in this difficult mathematics terrain. So many overlays of emotions are evident once one equates 'not knowing' with failure." So Margery asks, "What do you understand?" After a long pause, some conversation begins. Here is Margery's account of the rest of her meeting with the girls.

> *Maria:* It's about parts.
> *Pauline:* Parts can be big, or they can be small.
> *Maria:* All the parts in each one have to be exactly the same as each other.
> *Cara:* I don't know anything. Well, the thing has to be the same size.
>
> The pauses are long here, and I'm trying to figure out what's the right place to enter, whether these three students share some common ground.
>
> *Cara:* [with some impatience] It could be about candy bars.
> *Pauline:* We could break them into pieces.
> *Teacher:* Can we think of a context, a story about candy bars and pieces?
> *Cara:* Yeah, we had candy bars and we wanted to eat them, and we didn't want you to catch us, so we broke them into pieces to sneak them.
>
> I decide to go with this idea. It reminds me of another problem that has proved to be powerful for comparing fractions in my class, a scenario involving loaves of bread sliced into different numbers of slices. We draw four rectangles to represent candy bars, one for each of us. We note that they are all the same size. No one is really hooked.
>
> I then pose the following problem: Cara wants to eat her candy, and since she sits near me, she has to break it into small pieces so I will not notice, so she divides her rectangle into sixteenths. Pauline hardly ever breaks the rules and decides she is too nervous to con-

tinue after she breaks her candy bar into halves. Maria divides hers into quarters. I decide that I want a candy bar, too. I divide mine into thirty-seconds, smaller than Cara's pieces.

We decide that Cara eats seven pieces, Pauline eats one, and Maria eats three. I decide that I am just as rebellious as Cara, and I eat fourteen. They comment on my diet. On a large piece of chart paper, we make a drawing and put Xs on the pieces consumed. The girls actually show some animation now. We name the fractional part that each has eaten and label the drawing, which looks like this:

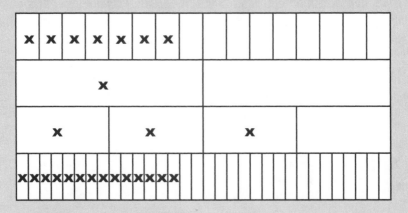

The mood is more relaxed. I am confident that some fraction ideas, not just language, are becoming clearer. As we look at the drawing, I ask, "So, who ate the most?" All three look at me as if I am very silly, as if my question is so obvious as to be ridiculous. I ask again, "So really, who ate the most?"

> *Cara:* You did, of course! [The other girls nod in agreement.]
>
> *Teacher:* How do you know that?
>
> *Maria:* You ate the most pieces.
>
> *Cara:* You ate way more than anybody else. Pauline only had one piece, and Maria only had three.
>
> *Teacher:* What does the drawing help you know about who ate the candy?

I am thinking that this is a pretty good question because I know they will "see" the answer in the representation. But Pauline answers, "What we said—Cara ate seven, I had one, Maria had three, and you had fourteen. You ate the most." What is it about the number of pieces and the relationship of that number to the whole that is not clear to them? What is it about the numerator that captures them and causes them to ignore the strong visual model? Is nothing about this problem familiar to them? Do we abandon this activity, or do I find a way to push it further? I try, "If I disagreed with you, how could you prove that you are right?" Nothing. Moments like this are so challenging.

I am thinking that, even with the drawing, they are not yet visualizing the parts eaten, the parts remaining, and how these parts relate to the whole, so I suggest that we actually each cut out our candy bars, then cut them into two parts—what we ate and what was left. We each put down the part we ate, and I ask again, "Who ate the most?" Three light bulbs come on, three students see something, and from the energy of it, I would guess it was for the first time. They observe that Maria ate almost the whole candy bar: "3/4, 75 percent," they say. And they note that Pauline ate "1/2, 50 percent." Clearly they have picked up something more than vocabulary during these last couple of weeks. They notice that sneaky Cara and the off-the-diet teacher ate the same amount. They appear on the edge of understanding something:

Cara: How come the numbers are different if the amounts are the same?

Pauline: I think it's like 3/6 and 4/8 and 5/10 are all 1/2. Different names for the same-size piece. [Pauline projects confidence as she says this—it sounds like a lot more than just words.]

Cara: But she ate more pieces than me.

Maria: Yeah, but she ate the same amount. You both have the same gone and the same left.

One of the difficulties in problematizing the curriculum for students who lack confidence and understanding in mathematics is that the teacher must consider both emotional and cognitive aspects of the students' learning. The teacher must not only find or create the right problem but also bring students to a place where they are willing to enter the problem. In designing a problem that both provides the teacher with some insights into what the girls understand and gives them a way to clarify and move forward in their own mathematical understanding, Margery uses multiple sources of information. First she draws on her knowledge of the fundamental mathematical ideas in comparing fractions (as in Lucy's class, the importance of the relationship of the fraction to the unit whole). Second, she uses her knowledge of problems and representations that have been effective in helping students compare fractions. For example, she mentions the loaf-of-bread problem that she has used to help students visualize how to compare fractional parts. Third, she must work with what she learns from her real-time interaction with the students as she struggles to find points of entry and understanding.

Teaching students with a range of experiences, needs, competence, and confidence is not the exceptional situation; it is the situation that every elementary school classroom teacher faces. Although problems for students like these may, in comparison with what their peers are working on, seem simple, the tasks must be problematic for these students to engage them in working through mathematical ideas.

Episode 4, "The Elevator Way": Developing Representations and Metaphors

As we saw in Margery's episode, representations of mathematical situations are important anchors for problematizing. Without the drawing of "candy bars," the three fifth graders would have had no way to compare the fractional parts. Looking only at the numbers, they focused on the numerators and compared the quantities as if the numerators alone indicated relative size. By representing the relationship of whole and parts and actually cutting out the parts they needed to compare, they were able to see the quantity represented by each fraction and to relate the numbers to the quantities (for example, seeing how two different fractions can indicate the same amount).

Representations and metaphors provide an anchor for students as they investigate problems and a basis for interaction with one another about their problem-solving process. Part of the teacher's role in problematizing the curriculum is to choose, develop, and help students develop representations and metaphors, then analyze whether and how these representations support students in their mathematical problem solving.

Curriculum materials and mathematics manipulatives offer many kinds of representations, some of which have been used for decades in mathematics education—for example, geometric solids, rectangular arrays, fraction pieces, and connecting cubes. But representations are not magic bullets. In Margery's episode, representing the fractional relationships with a picture did not automatically illuminate the mathematical ideas for the students. Margery had to work to engage the students with the representation in a way that helped them compare fractional parts. In the next episode, Sarah is listening to the ideas of her first- and second-grade students about subtraction. They have commonly used a number line and connecting cubes—two different ways to model subtraction. However, class discussion reveals that students have different ideas about how to use these materials to model subtraction. One student comes up with a metaphor using a familiar situation that helps the students visualize the relationships on a number line.

For the past few years, I have been interested to note how my students come to make sense of the number line. It requires a certain amount of sophistication in their thinking, and although I encourage my students to use and make sense of a variety of different strategies, the number line presents a challenge that few of them seem to be able to resist trying out. The number line actually measures distance or spaces between numbers rather than concrete sets or objects, a concept that has seemed difficult for my students to fully understand at this age.

In my combined first–second grade this year, we have not discussed how to use the number line as frequently or in as much depth as in the past. Most of my second graders seem to have a fairly solid understanding of the concepts behind the number line, but my first graders are still struggling. I have also had the uncomfortable feeling that, because I haven't given them much opportunity and time to discuss and explore their understanding of this strategy together, most of the first graders have gleaned "rules" for using the strategy, primarily from me.

Recently, as part of our daily routine, "Making Today's Number," many of my first graders and several of my second graders gathered to share "ways to make 12," the day's date. Many of the students had explained their answers and strategies for solving the problem. Latasha offered her solution, 18 − 6 = 12, and explained that she used the number line to figure it out: "I counted back from 18, 17—that's 1, 16 —that's 2, 15—3, 14—4, 13—5 and 12, that's 6. So 18 minus 6 makes 12." I accepted her articulate explanation and did not probe any further to see how clearly she actually understood what she was doing with the number line.

Will got up to share his answer and his strategy: "I came up with 18 minus 7 equals 12. I used the number line, and I counted down." He demonstrated on the number line, pointing as he counted from 1 to 7, starting with the 18 and landing on 12:

		7	6	5	4	3	2	1		
10	11	12	13	14	15	16	17	18	19	20

Keith commented, "I don't think that works, 'cause I know 8 minus 7 equals 1, and that would make 11." I assumed that Keith was thinking about subtracting 7 from the 8 in 18. Will looked confused at this point, so I intervened, "It looks like you and Latasha used the same strategy, and you both even started with 18, but you subtracted different numbers. Could this work? Let's try to figure it out."

Latasha explained her strategy again and then added, "Just like you told us, you never start on the number, you start counting down on the next number." I cringed. It sounded like my own voice regurgitated. How much of this did Latasha actually understand? I asked, "Why do you need to do that? Why not just start on 18?" Latasha replied, "Because you can't start on that number. You're supposed to start on the next one down." She shrugged.

I asked Will to explain his thinking a little bit more. He said, "Well, I wanted to take away from 18, cause I knew I had to get to 12 and that would be a takeaway. So I counted back." He demonstrated his strategy again. I asked, "Can anyone else help us out here? Both these strategies seem to make some sense, and also seem similar, but Latasha and Will thought about the problem differently. What should we be thinking about when we use the number line?"

Several students offered analogies using cubes, and I was wondering how thinking about counting cubes would help with the number-line model, in which the spaces between the numbers are counted, not a set of objects. I tried a different question, "Latasha started by counting down to 17 first instead of starting on 18. Does this work?" Many of my first graders looked confused at this point, but my second graders came to the rescue:

Toshi: Well, it's like you're already on 18, so you can't count 18 again. You have to count down.
Teacher: Can anybody explain what Toshi just said?
Flavia: You already counted 18. You are already there. So you can't count it again. So if you are taking away, you have to take away by going to the next number.
Thomas: I think I understand! Say I was at the Prudential Center. [Thomas loves buildings and landmarks.] If I was on the 18th floor and I wanted to go down on the elevator, if I wanted to go to the 12th floor, if I got on, I am at the 18th floor, so the next floor I go to is the 17th floor.

It took me a moment to realize how well this analogy worked. The class suddenly perked up, vitalized by concrete terms and images that they could visualize and understand. A buzz of conversation was heard as they discussed Thomas's idea. Will, whose incorrect answer had catalyzed this conversation, said, "Yeah, I get it. If you got on at the 18th floor and you go to 18, you don't go anywhere." Keith acted Thomas's idea out with his hands as he explained, "You have to go to the next floor. The 17th floor is 1, 16th is 2, 15th—3, 14th—4, 13th—5, 12th—6! That's 6 floors down!

This episode brought up several issues for me as a teacher. I would like to continue to develop my ability to question students—pushing them toward higher-level thinking and clarifying their understanding of concepts but without leading them to a prescribed solution. Latasha's explanation of her problem was, in reality, a recitation of a memorized rule I had given her, not a demonstration of her understanding of a difficult concept. Latasha had given me the answer I wanted to hear, and I mistakenly moved on without probing any deeper.

However, I was very pleased with Thomas's ability to synthesize information and clarify a difficult concept and strategy with a very simple, concrete example. I was also happy to find a larger number of first graders using the number line successfully in our next few sessions. They described this strategy as "the elevator way" of solving a problem. I am reminded of the importance of providing students with the opportunity and meaningful context to think about problem solving naturally through their own discussion. I feel as though I am constantly struggling to find a middle ground—to provide students with the opportunity to share their thinking and explore a variety of strategies without losing many of my students. They have difficulty listening to one another for long, but the sharing component is a vitally important step in the development of their thinking. This time I chose to push the discussion, and ultimately, many of the students became engaged and gained a stronger understanding of a difficult concept.

Sarah, like Lucy in the first episode, could simply have corrected Will's wrong answer. By asking her students to consider the two solutions to the problem, she problematized the situation even for students who had initially solved the problem correctly. Sarah recognized that "correct" use of a representation can indicate that students have learned a procedure only but have not constructed for themselves how the representation models mathematical relationships. Sarah challenged her students to think through why and how the number line can be used to represent subtraction. Their discussion resulted in the development of a new metaphor for understanding the "counting backward" method of solving subtraction problems—which, in turn, offered all the students a new way to think about this class of problems. Encountering, using, contrasting, and analyzing a variety of representations is one way of deepening the work that students are doing as they focus on core mathematical ideas.

Conclusion

No set of curriculum materials, no matter how carefully researched and tested, can anticipate all the ways in which ideas develop in a particular classroom's mathematical community. In the four classroom episodes recounted here, the teachers all use curriculum materials to guide their work, but none of them expect the curriculum to do their teaching for them. They are actively engaged in learning from both the written curriculum and their students. In none of these cases did the teacher simply move on in the face of a confusing or difficult moment or try to settle an important mathematical question quickly. Their focus is not on how to "cover" the sequence of activities suggested by the curriculum but on how to engage students in thinking about significant mathematical ideas through judicious use of the written curriculum. They take seriously what the curriculum materials have to offer, but they are vigilant and analytic as students of their students' thinking. They think hard about when to open the book for guidance—and when to close it so they can pay attention to what their students have to say.

How Many 4s in 100?
Where Do We Go from Here?

Nancy Buell, fourth-grade teacher

In this episode, Nancy Buell faces two issues that all teachers face every day: (1) how to engage all students in the class in working on significant mathematical ideas, and (2) how to engage all students in class discussion about their ideas. These two intertwined challenges are inevitable as teachers consider the diverse needs and strengths represented in the classroom. In some situations, a single problem can engage all students at their own levels. At other times, a teacher must modify a problem slightly—perhaps by changing the numbers in the problem—to make it more accessible or more challenging. But sometimes the design of problems requires more differentiation to engage very different students in the same set of mathematical ideas. This kind of modification requires that teachers clearly identify the mathematics content students need to work on and assess the understanding that different students have about that content. In their study of factors of the multiples of 100, some students in this class have a sense of what a factor is and how it relates to a multiple. However, a significant number of students in the class do not have a well-developed understanding of the relationship between a factor and a multiple. As Nancy works with them, she realizes that they need to visualize and analyze how a factor relates to a multiple before they can profitably develop and test conjectures about the multiples of 100. The evolution of work over several days in her classroom illustrates her modification and differentiation of problems in response to students' evolving understanding and the range of students' needs (see Russell et al. in chapter 6 for further discussion of this theme).

—Susan Jo Russell

THIS week we worked from our curriculum materials to review the factors of 100 as well as the factors of some other numbers. In the discussion that followed, some students made observations and predictions about how knowing the factors of 100 would help them find factors of 400. Nell hypothesized that all the factors of 100 would be factors of 400. Pete speculated that 400 would have 4 times as many factors as 100 for a total of 36 factors; other students thought that it would not have that many. Nell and Gayle were fairly sure it would have no more than twice as many. So, of course, I set my plans aside, and the students worked to find all the factors of 400. They worked alone or in twos or threes. That day, I let them choose whomever they wanted to work with. Mostly they chose to work with students at their own level of understanding.

I noticed that about half the class found a lot of factors right away and soon were fairly sure they had identified them all. I met with the half that had finished, and we talked briefly about the strategies they had used to find the factors. Their strategies included the following:

- testing all of the factors of 100 to see whether they were factors of 400;

- testing multiples of 4, since 400 is 4 times 100;

- dividing by a known factor to find its factor pair; and

- looking at the factor pairs of 100 and multiplying one number of the pair by 4.

No one suggested trying every number in order or trying numbers at random. Most of the discussion in this group centered on predictions about factors of other multiples of 100. In general, they thought that the larger the multiple of 100, the more factors it would have. They were happy to go off and explore other multiples of 100 to test this conjecture.

I then met with the other half of the class. Most of this group had identified only a few of the factors of 400 at this point. We began sharing strategies, but the discussion was very different from my discussion with the first group. These students did not seem to have a plan for choosing the numbers they tested other than the factors of 100, an idea that had come up in our whole-group discussion before students began exploring on their own. This group tested numbers by skip counting. If they landed exactly on 400, they knew that the number by which they were skip counting was a factor. I sensed that their understanding of factors was limited to numbers that worked in this activity. Only one student connected the idea with making rectangles using connecting cubes.

We all started this investigation together three days ago, and now we are in very different places! I am glad that I met with the two groups separately, because if we had had a whole-class discussion, it would have been dominated by the observations and predictions of the stronger group. I might well have missed the fact that a substantial number of students are still unsure of what a factor is and how it relates to multiplication and division.

Over the next two days, one group explored factors of other multiples of 100. I had asked the group to find the factors of other hundreds numbers, to look for patterns, and to think about how they knew whether they had found all the factors. I got together with them a couple of times to share their progress. They spontaneously pointed out patterns, made conjectures, and wondered aloud. They were interested in hearing and thinking about others' ideas. The discussion was lively, and the ideas just kept coming. Students said they were surprised that 400 had fewer factors than 300. They had thought, after finding factors for 100, 200, and 300, that the number of factors would keep increasing as the hundreds multiple increased. Someone mentioned that 100 and 400 had an odd number of factors, whereas 200 and 300 had an even number of factors. I asked why that outcome occurred and what they would predict about larger multiples of 100. They were off on a new exploration.

Meanwhile, I had posed a different problem to the second group, designed to focus their attention on how the factors of 100 were related to the multiples of 100. I asked them to find how many 4s are in 100, in 200, in 300, and so forth. Then they had to tell how they knew how many 4s are in 300 and also describe any patterns they noticed. They continued exploring how many 5s, 10s, 20s, or 25s are in the multiples of 100 up to 1000. Most of the students chose to work relatively independently, seldom checking in with one another. Very quickly, most of them abandoned other strategies and began dividing on the calculator to find the answers.

Although students were finding the correct answers, I was still dissatisfied. I believed that they had arrived at a method to get the right answer but that they had not necessarily acquired much understanding of why that answer was correct. They were not visualizing and analyzing how the multiplication relationship between 4 and 100 gave them information about the multiplication relationship between 4 and 200 or 300. I then posed a problem they had not done before, one that did not involve a factor of 100: I asked them what tools they might use to find how many 15s are in 300. They suggested using a calculator, a 300 chart (similar to a 100 chart but with thirty rows, with ten numbers in each row), money, and connecting cubes. I then asked the students to use the 300 chart, money, and cubes to model the relationship between the factor 15 and its multiple 300 to find the number of 15s in 300.

First the students worked as a whole group to skip count on the 300 chart by 15s. We marked an X on each count. When they got to 300, I asked where the answer was. They said it was the number of Xs we had made. Someone pointed out that you could count down the Xs in the fives column and multiply by 2 to figure out how many Xs appeared altogether, because for each X in the fives column, a corresponding X appeared in the tens column.

Working with money to find the number of 15s was not obvious, since we do not have a 15-cent coin, but Angela made piles of one dime and one nickel to build up to one dollar. She ended with one dime left over. Then she made identical arrangements for the other two dollars. She counted the piles and got eighteen 15s. She said that the three leftover dimes were 30 cents, or two more 15s, for a total of 20 fifteens.

The students seemed engaged, with everyone looking and listening. Most of them offered comments along the way—in contrast with the way most of them operate in whole-class discussions. The pace of the discussion was slower, and the students had time to figure things out. We were able to stay focused on the question of how to use the tools and how each number was represented.

Before I asked anyone to show how he or she might use the cubes, I asked the students to think about it. Then I had them verbally share their ideas with a partner. I wanted to make sure that no one was going to let someone else do the thinking, since we would have only enough time for one person to share a strategy. Gary said that he could do it by making groups of 30 cubes. Laurel tried to correct him, but I suggested that we should see what he meant. Carefully counting to make sure he had 10 cubes on each stick, Gary made groups of 3 sticks plus 1 extra stick to make 100. He did the same for two more hundreds. Then he made the extras into another group of 30. He then counted the groups of 30 by twos to find the number of 15s. I was amazed that Gary— who is my weakest student in mathematics and who still has to count the sticks to be sure that each contains ten cubes—could come up with such a strategy. At this point the students were already late for art class. As Nina said, "When math is fun, it's easy to forget about time." Of course, that comment made my day!

I think that both groups of students benefit from working separately at times on problems designed for them. In whole-class discussion, we sometimes get off on ideas that intrigue some students while others have not finished grappling with foundational ideas and strategies. With both groups working on problems that engaged them in thinking—at their level of understanding—about the relationships of factors and multiples, both groups were able to proceed at a comfortable pace, present their ideas with confidence, and get excited about exploring mathematical ideas.

CHAPTER 7

Listening to Children: Informing Us and Guiding Our Instruction

Erna Yackel

THE FOLLOWING incident took place in a fourth-grade class that was working on developing fraction concepts by using fair-sharing problems in a small-group collaborative setting. At the conclusion of the small-group work, the class discussed their solutions to a problem that asked them to show how to share three pizzas equally among eight people. One pair of students said that they would cut each pizza into eight equal slices and give each person one slice from each; their solution is shown in figure 7.1a. Another group suggested cutting each of the first two pizzas into four equal slices and giving each person one slice, then cutting the third pizza into 8 equal slices and giving each person one slice; their answer is shown in figure 7.1b.

The following discussion took place:

Teacher: [Addressing the entire class] Are you telling me that 1/4 is the same as 2/8 (pointing to the written symbol 1/4 in fig. 7.1b and then to 1/8 + 1/8 in fig. 7.1a)?

Michael: They are *if* [emphasis added] you cut it [the 1/4] in half.

Imagine that you are the teacher in this fourth-grade classroom. What have you just heard? What is the significance of Michael's remark? Is it significant mathematically, or is it a trivial comment about how to make the two diagrams look the same? I

The author would like to thank Frank Lester and John van de Walle for comments on an earlier version of this chapter.

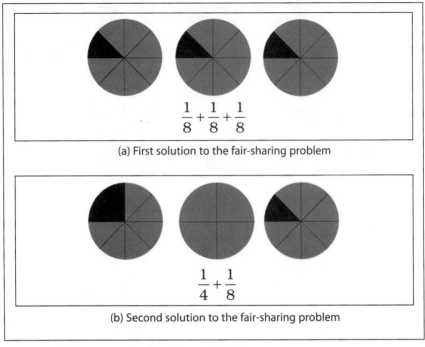

(a) First solution to the fair-sharing problem

(b) Second solution to the fair-sharing problem

Fig. 7.1. Solutions to the fair-sharing problem

invite you, the reader, to stop and think about possible interpretations of Michael's comment and about how you might direct the discussion from here. What might you say in response to Michael's comment? Are any "big" mathematical ideas involved that might be pursued? If so, what are they? Would you attempt to follow up on them? How? If you did, how would you attempt to involve the entire class in thinking about these ideas? We return to this example later in the chapter to discuss these questions.

The purpose of this chapter is to focus on listening to children. Listening includes attending to what children do as well as to what they say. In general, listening to children in the mathematics classroom involves attempting to figure out how they interpret and solve mathematical problems. A common practice in elementary school is to call on various children to share their solution methods after individual or small-group problem solving. The stated purposes of this approach often include to establish that a problem can be solved in more than one way, to demonstrate that we value the children's thinking, to give children the benefit of hearing other solution methods, and to provide children the opportunity and responsibility of explaining their problem-solving attempts. However, this practice can easily devolve into a routine that does not go beyond "collecting" students' solutions. In this chapter, I want to challenge us to think about ways to use listening to children in the mathematics classroom to advance the discussion, that is, to move children forward in their thinking and enhance the learning of all children in the classroom.

What We Can Learn about Children's Conceptual Understanding by Listening

A primary purpose of listening to children is to gain an understanding of their mathematical conceptions. Consider the solutions to the problem shown in figure 7.2, given by second-grade students early in the school year.

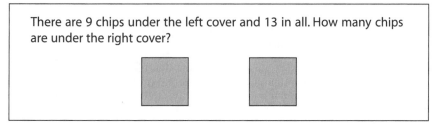

There are 9 chips under the left cover and 13 in all. How many chips are under the right cover?

Fig. 7.2. The "how many chips?" problem

Chantrell solved the problem by saying "10, 11, 12, 13" to herself, putting up one finger with each number word. She looked at her fingers and, without counting them, said "4." Jameel said, "It'd be 4. I figured it out like, I said, 10, 11, 12, 13, and when I got to 13 I stopped. It's 4 because 1, 2, 3, 4, that's the same as 10, 11, 12, 13." Rasheed's answer was also 4. He said, "8 + 4 was 12, and if I had 9 plus 4, it would be 13." Other children in the same class needed manipulatives other than their fingers to solve this problem. For example, some children counted out 9 cubes and then used trial and error to figure out how many additional cubes they needed to have a total of 13.

By paying careful attention to what the children said, we notice that their solutions are at various levels of sophistication. Chantrell used a double-counting approach. Although she said the words "10, 11, 12, 13," she knew that these number words did not represent the answer to the problem. She needed to know *how many* number words she had spoken, that is, to keep track of her counting acts. She did so by putting up one finger every time she spoke a number word. Significantly, she knew how many fingers she had up by simply recognizing the finger pattern for 4. From this single solution we are able to learn quite a bit about Chantrell's concept of number. First, she understood the need to double count. Second, she had a way to keep track of the double counting. Third, she understood that the answer to the question was not the last word spoken but the number of fingers she used in tracking her double counting. Fourth, she had a finger pattern for 4 that she recognized.

Jameel, like Chantrell, used double counting. However, he did not use his fingers to keep track of how many times he counted. Further, in saying, "1, 2, 3, 4, that's the same as 10, 11, 12, 13," Jameel showed that he was explicitly aware of his double-counting activity. He was able to reflect on this activity and was aware of its character. Thus, although both Chantrell and Jameel used a double-counting solution, by listening to what they said and noting their activity, we know that Jameel's understanding of number is more sophisticated than Chantrell's.

Rasheed's solution was of a completely different character and indicates yet another level of sophistication. He did not rely on counting but used a fact that he already knew as the basis for reasoning about the answer. He used what is called a "thinking strategy."

The task presented above is a typical problem task in second-grade mathematics instruction that is problem based. The children were engaged in problem solving precisely because they were developing their own methods based on what made sense to them. Contrast this approach with the situation in which the teacher presents an example and works it out with the class prior to their individual solution activity. In this situation, we would be reluctant to say that the students had engaged in problem solving. Instead, they typically would interpret the situation as one in which they were to use the same method demonstrated by the teacher, even if they or other students had contributed to the development of the sample solution.

Using Information Gained from Listening to Children to Plan for Instruction

If we ask children to engage in problem solving, we should be interested in what they figure out. As the previous example shows, listening to what children have to say gives us a window into their thinking. As such, it is an invaluable tool for informing us and guiding instruction. The crucial question is, How can we, as teachers, make effective use of such information in planning instruction? Having such information might seem more perplexing than enlightening; for example, the solutions given by the children in the previous illustration were very diverse. In the following paragraphs, I suggest how a teacher might use the information provided by these children's solutions.

In this example, the range of conceptual possibilities in the class includes using counting-on solutions at various levels of sophistication, using thinking strategies, and, for some children, using manipulative materials with trial-and-error approaches. Since Rasheed was the only student in the class who used a thinking-strategy solution, we might decide to select instructional activities that provide opportunities to develop thinking strategies at the same time as they foster mental imagery for those students who are using manipulative materials in a trial-and-error fashion. For example, the teacher might decide to use the following double-ten-frame activity.

In this activity, the teacher displays a quantity of chips in a double-ten-frame, using a different color in each of the two frames. The task is to figure out the total number of chips shown. Children are explicitly encouraged to figure out the answer *without counting*. The display is shown for just a few seconds and then hidden from view. After children have had a few minutes to think about what they have seen, the image is displayed again briefly, then again hidden. The teacher repeats this cycle several times, then the pupils share the number of chips they think are present and how they figured it out.

For this activity to foster thinking strategies, a useful approach is to pose a carefully selected sequence of tasks. For example, consider the sequence of four tasks shown in figure 7.3.

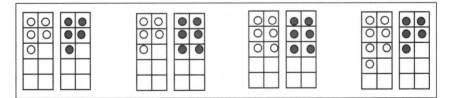

Fig. 7.3. The double-ten-frame instructional task sequence

This sequence of tasks gives opportunities for fostering thinking strategies in several ways. The problems are, from left to right, 5 + 5, 5 + 6, 6 + 6, and 7 + 5. Thus, a solver could use task 1 and the thinking strategy of adding one more to solve task 2. Likewise, a solver could add one more to task 2 to solve task 3. Finally, a solver could solve task 4 either by noticing that two more have been added to the first frame in task 1, thus the answer is two more, or by relating task 4 to task 3. In this last situation, the student might notice that one more chip is in the first frame and one fewer is in the second frame, or that one chip from the second frame has been "moved" to the first frame; so the answers are the same. Further, and most important, the chips have been arranged to preserve the visual image from one task to the next as much as possible, increasing the likelihood that children will notice the changes. For example, a child who might not think of relating 5 + 6 to 5 + 5 when the tasks are posed orally or symbolically might notice that just one more chip is present in the visual material. In this sense, the visual material contributes to children's ability to develop a basis for using thinking strategies. In addition, visual material allows children to make sense of another's thinking-strategy solution because they can "see" what the other child is talking about, especially if the teacher points to the visual material when the thinking-strategy solution is given.

We have no guarantee that the children in this class will use thinking strategies to solve these tasks; however, we can make conjectures about how they might proceed. We as teachers are in precisely this position when planning for instruction. Information gained from listening to children is useful for making conjectures about how they might solve subsequent tasks. For example, we know that Chantrell capitalizes on finger patterns when counting on; thus, she might notice the visual patterns and how they change from one task to the next and use that information in solving the tasks. In that instance, we would expect her to notice that 6 is one more than 5 and use 5 + 5 = 10 to help her figure out 5 + 6. In fact, the first task, 5 + 5, was selected deliberately because most children in second grade know that this sum is 10. Many students who generally use counting strategies will not need to count to solve this task. In this way, students' attention is called to a known fact at the beginning of the task sequence.

We conjecture that Jameel might also use a thinking strategy rather than a counting solution. His remark, "1, 2, 3, 4, that's the same as 10, 11, 12, 13," indicates that he explicitly links two number sequences in double counting. In the example given previously, Jameel did not use a known result as a starting point. Because 5 + 5 is the first task in the sequence, Jameel will likely, from his approach to double counting, be able to capitalize on the fact that 6 is one more than 5. He might think, for example, that "1, 2, 3, 4, 5, 6 is just one more than 1, 2, 3, 4, 5, so 5 + 6 must be just one more than 5 + 5."

As for other students, Rasheed has already demonstrated that he can use thinking-strategy solutions and has some number facts at his disposal. And those students who needed to use manipulatives have visual materials available when the ten-frames are in view. They can count the chips, given sufficient "peeks." However, one purpose of hiding the visual material is to encourage children to develop mental imagery and to use those images to solve the tasks. In this way, the similarity of the chips from one task to the next prompts children to think about "one more" or "one fewer" even if simply as a means of mental economy.

This example shows how we can plan instruction on the basis of specific information gained by listening to our students' responses to a problem-solving task. The approach described involves anticipating students' solutions on the basis of prior knowledge of their solution methods in other situations. This approach is similar to the Japanese lesson plan, in which the primary emphasis is on the students' activity (Stigler, Fernandez, and Yoshida 1996). When creating their lesson plans, Japanese teachers anticipate a variety of student solutions and plan the guidance or advice they will offer for each solution. The discussion that occurred in the double-ten-frame task sequence shows that such sequences can provide a productive learning experience for children at a variety of conceptual levels. The child who needs to count all items has an opportunity to do so through repeated showing of the visual material. A child such as Rasheed, who already uses thinking strategies, has the opportunity to become more proficient, to come to "just know" more number facts, and to develop expertise in explaining his thinking to others.

Learning to Listen

Listening to students involves two aspects for teachers to consider. First, we must hear what students say. Second, we need to have a way to make sense of what they say and do. In the preceding sections of this chapter, I assumed that the teacher in question both heard and made sense of the children's remarks and activity. In this section, I discuss how we, as teachers, can come to make sense of what children say and do.

In a discussion of listening in the classroom, John Mason (1994) comments on an incident in which a student's comment was not heard. Mason says,

> What strikes me initially is the *not-hearing* [emphasis added]. I felt a resonance between this incident and

many others I have participated in. I recognize so clearly
being caught up in the flow of what I am thinking that it
is only later when I listen to a tape that I realise that I
have not 'heard' what a student or colleague was saying
to me. (p. 185)

Mason goes on to say that typically we have some expectations
about what students or colleagues will say, but often we are
unaware of our expectations. Only when the response differs from
what we expect do we become aware of the discrepancy. That
point of awareness offers a moment of choice when we can make
a deliberate response rather than follow along a previously anticipated path. It can be a moment of learning for us as teachers.

Consider the following example that took place in a second-
grade classroom early in the school year. The teacher wanted his
students to use thinking strategies to solve problems. He planned
an instructional activity in which he presented tasks in pairs, with
the intention that students use the results of the first task to solve
the second task. For example, after a child answered that 3 plus
3 equals 6, the teacher said, "Now that we know that 3 plus 3
equals 6, then 3 plus 4 would equal what?" For the first three
pairs of number sentences, the children called on by the teacher
responded as he anticipated, solving the second number sentence
in the pair by adding one to the result of the previous number sentence. However, when the teacher called on Jorge to explain the
result of 5 plus 6 "if we know that 5 plus 5 equals 10," Jorge did
not respond as the teacher had expected. Instead, Jorge said,
"'cause I counted 5 on this hand, and then I counted 6. . . . I
counted 5 and counted 6 more; that makes 11." The next child
called on also gave a counting solution, counting on 5 more from
6 to end up with 11. In an attempt to cope with this unanticipated situation and achieve his instructional goal, the teacher made
a deliberate move and specifically called for something different.
He asked the class, "Do you have anything different? . . . What do
you have [that is] different?" Travonda responded by saying that
she first added 3 to 5 to get 8 and then added another 3 to get 11.

As a result of this seemingly insignificant incident, this
teacher realized that students solve problems in ways that make
sense to them, not necessarily in ways that he has in mind. While
Jorge used a more primitive method than the teacher anticipated,
he was both surprised and impressed by Travonda's response.
The teacher understood, at least implicitly, that the type of mathematical thinking involved in Travonda's solution is potentially
productive and should be encouraged. This realization had signif-

icant implications for his instructional decision making. Subsequent to this incident, whenever he posed a problem to students, he asked them how they solved it and called for them to give solutions that were different from those already given. However, after this incident he no longer planned lessons geared toward eliciting specific types of solutions. In particular, he continued to pose many tasks sequenced to make thinking-strategy solutions possible, but he ceased prompting students to relate the tasks as he had in the example of the number-sentence pairs. He now understood that to expect all children to use a predetermined method to solve certain types of problems is an inappropriate goal for a lesson.

This example illustrates Mason's claim that moments of discrepancy between our expectations, as teachers, and what the pupils say and do can be specific points of awareness and offer opportunities for us to choose deliberately how to respond. Such moments occur in the midst of classroom lessons and confirm what others have noted, namely, that the primary site of our learning is in our own classrooms, as we attempt to resolve dilemmas and pedagogical problems that arise for us in the act of teaching (Cobb, Yackel, and Wood 1988).

We can also easily imagine situations in which we fail to notice something of potential significance. Mason points to the need to develop what he calls the "discipline of noticing." He suggests imagining asking a question in the classroom and being surprised by the response. Then imagine choosing to tell the students what you are thinking about and taking time to listen to what they say. According to Mason, this tactic is one way that we can sensitize ourselves to notice opportunities to alter what we are attending to, that is, to make ourselves more aware. As a result, things that were previously outside of our awareness can then become significant.

We are also sensitized to noticing when someone else prompts us to think about students' activity in a way that we have not previously considered. As an example, consider the following incident that occurred in one of my own mathematics methods classes for elementary teachers. These preservice teachers were given a set of balance problems (see fig. 7.4 for examples) and cubes, packaged in sticks of ten cubes each, and asked to figure out how pupils might solve the tasks using the cubes.

Most of the preservice teachers reported that to solve the first task, they counted 15 cubes, then 8 cubes, and then counted the number that they had altogether. When asked, "How did you count the cubes?" most of the teachers were surprised by the

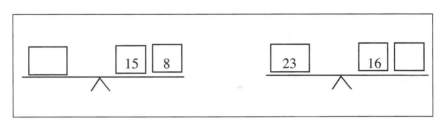

Fig. 7.4. Sample balance tasks

question. Only after more detailed questions had been asked—such as "Did you take a ten-stick (without counting it) and then count 11, 12, 13, 14, 15 to get the 15, or did you count 1, 2, 3, all the way to 10, and then continue on with 11, 12, 13, 14, 15? How did you get the 8? Did you count 1, 2, 3, 4, 5, 6, 7, 8, or did you break two cubes off a ten-stick?"—did the preservice teachers become aware of distinctions between ways of counting the cubes. The subsequent discussion in the class focused on the relationship between children's conceptions of number and how they use cubes. For example, a child who creates 15 by placing a ten-stick with five individual cubes shows evidence of beginning to develop a tens structure for number, whereas a child who creates 15 by breaking the sticks of 10 apart to create a pile of 15 individual cubes shows no evidence of having a tens structure.

Although this example might seem to be more related to children's potential physical activity than to their verbal remarks, this type of "noticing" is precisely what Mason refers to when he says that we need to learn to "listen." The preservice teachers involved in this exercise found that it sensitized them so that later, when they were in elementary school classrooms teaching lessons to children, they noticed how the children used the cubes.

The Value of Understanding Children's Mathematics

As the preceding discussion shows, we need to be knowledgeable about children's mathematical conceptions and how they develop if we are to hear and make sense of what children say and do, that is, become knowledgeable about children's mathematics (Steffe and Kieren 1994). Understanding children's mathematics involves more than understanding the relevant mathematical concepts from an adult point of view. It involves knowing about how children develop the concepts, about various levels of sophistication, and, most important, knowing about the conceptual foundations for big ideas in mathematics, such as place-value numeration, multiplicative units, and fractional numbers. For example, the conceptual foundation for place-value numeration is co-ordinating units of different rank, that is, units of ones, tens, and hundreds (Steffe, Cobb, and von Glasersfeld 1988). Consequently, instruction that focuses on coordinating units is foundational to children's understanding of adding and subtracting multidigit numerals with regrouping. Teachers who know about coordination of units can more readily make sense of the solutions children give, including the errors children make, when adding and subtracting with regrouping.

Experience shows that the important considerations for teach-ers are the practical implications for the classroom, not the inti-mate details of the underlying research (Cobb, Yackel, and Wood 1988). How do teachers gain such information? A primary means is through participating in professional seminars and conferences and reading professional literature, such as the teacher journals published by the National Council of Teachers of Mathematics.

The Role of Children's Errors in Shaping Instruction and Enhancing Learning in the Classroom

One challenge of listening to children's explanations of their mathematical thinking is to figure out how to deal with errors. Several mathematics educators provide insights into how to han-dle such situations. In a provocative article titled "Children's Right to Be Wrong," the author argues that children's errors are a nat-ural and necessary part of their conceptual development (Labinowicz 1987). By figuring out why something is erroneous, a child makes progress in understanding. Von Glasersfeld (1988) says the same thing in a slightly different way:

> It is absolutely essential that you [the teacher] take as the primary principle the notion that what the child says or what the student does in response to some stimulus that you have presented makes sense to the student. Therefore, when the student produces something that from the teacher's point of view is an error, that's the most interesting thing because it's not an error to the student. From the student's point of view that is the rea-sonable answer to give, and it is the teacher's task to dis-cover in what way the student made sense of this. Because it is only when you have discovered that, or at least some hypothesis that covers the evidence you've

had that you can conjecture something that will lead the student out of this way of thinking into another one. And I very deliberately say another one, because you are never sure which way the student is going to go. Obviously experienced teachers have either intuitively, or by analyzing their experience, found ways that work very often, but even those ways are never absolutely foolproof.

As both of these educators suggest, dealing with errors directly can bring about significant learning. A common misunderstanding of the current emphasis in mathematics education on children's self-generated methods is that we should accept all answers and all methods equally, regardless of whether they are correct. However, that approach ignores one of the most important opportunities for learning and can leave children confused about what is mathematically acceptable. In fact, it can lead to the serious misunderstanding that any answer is valid. The responsibility of attempting to figure out how the child is thinking, as well as of conjecturing some means of assisting the child in altering his or her thinking, rests squarely on the teacher's shoulders. Fortunately, in classrooms in which social norms foster children's listening to, questioning, and challenging one another's thinking, other children in the class often provide crucial support by offering their own interpretations of a child's erroneous thinking and their own suggestions on how to alter the approach (see Stephan and Whitenack [chapter 9, this volume]).

The following example illustrates the potential of errors in enhancing learning and also shows how one teacher used a student's error to guide her instructional decision making. Students in a fifth-grade class were working in small groups to solve a number of fair-sharing fractions tasks, including the problem presented at the beginning of this chapter. One small group of four boys had divided each of the pizzas into eight equal pieces and had shaded in one piece in each to indicate what each person would get. Their diagram was the same as the one shown in figure 7.1a. However, they could not agree on what to give as an answer. Two of them argued that the answer should be 3/24, whereas the other two argued that the answer should be 3/8. When the teacher approached the group, they explained their disagreement. Roberto said, "See, there are 24 pieces in all. Count them. Eight here, 8 more makes 16, and 8 more makes 24. Each person gets 3 of these 24 pieces so the answer is 3/24." Manuel said, "But each of these pieces is 1/8, and each person gets three of them. So each person gets 3/8." From listening to what they said, the teacher knew how each of the boys made sense of the situation. She had to decide how to proceed. Using von Glasersfeld's language, we would say that she was in the position of having to make a conjecture about what approaches might be effective.

In this example, the teacher had encountered this situation before because Roberto's solution is a common one for this problem. From her previous experience with such solutions, she knew that the underlying issue was the unit of the fractions involved. For Roberto, the unit was the entire quantity of pizza, all three pizzas. All three pizzas yield 24 pieces, and each person gets 3 of the 24 pieces, or 3/24 of the pizzas. For Manuel, the unit was one pizza. Each person gets 3 pieces each of 1/8 of a pizza, or 3/8 of a pizza. The teacher was also aware that the question of what is the unit in such fractions problems as this one is a difficult conceptual issue. Therefore, she initiated a discussion with the group about their interpretations of the problem and how they each made sense of their answers. In the process, the issue of what the unit is for the fraction given as the answer became an explicit topic of conversation. When the class convened to discuss their problem-solving efforts, the teacher specifically called on Roberto and Manuel to share their thinking so that the entire class could benefit from the discussion. Again the issue of what the unit is for the fraction became an explicit topic of discussion.

When the class session was over, the teacher was aware that the students would need to revisit this issue. Therefore, she planned to continue having the class work on the same type of problems for the next several days. Listening to the disagreement in Roberto and Manuel's group informed the teacher and guided her instructional decision making, both in the immediate class session and for subsequent sessions. In this example, a disagreement between two students was treated as—and hence, became—a significant opportunity for learning.

Conclusion

To conclude, we return to the example presented at the beginning of this chapter. In that example, when the teacher asked, "Are you telling me that 1/4 is the same at 2/8?" Michael replied, "They are if you cut it [the 1/4] in half." I asked you to consider what significance Michael's remark might have and to think about what action, if any, you would take in response. I also asked you to consider any "big" mathematical ideas that might be pursued.

One interpretation is that Michael was attempting to describe how the two diagrams might be made to look alike—so that you could "see" that each person gets three pieces of the same size in each instance. Another interpretation is that Michael was pointing to an important "big" idea, namely, equivalence of fractions, although he may not have been explicitly aware of it himself. Recall that this incident took place in a fourth-grade classroom. These students had no formal knowledge of fraction equivalence and no arithmetic techniques for determining equivalence. Consequently, in this situation, one might argue that the only means the students had to determine equivalence was that these methods were two different ways to share the pizzas equally, so the resultant amounts had to be the same amount to eat. Following this line of reasoning, 1/4 must be the same amount of pizza as 2/8. However, that was not Michael's argument. He said, "They are [the same] if you cut it [the 1/4] in half." His comment seems to imply that for him 1/4 and 2/8 are not the same. They are the same only if the 1/4 piece is cut in half.

If we think about how fractional numbers are introduced in elementary school, typically 1/4 is described as one of four equal parts and 2/8 is described as two of eight equal parts. According to this definition, 1/4 is not the same as 2/8; it is only equivalent to 2/8. From this perspective, Michael's remark was profound. He was articulating a major notion within fractional concepts. We do not say that two fractions are equal unless they are identical. Otherwise, we say that they are equivalent, meaning that they represent the same quantity (the same amount of pizza to eat). Further, to think about the equivalence of two fractions, one must reconceptualize one of the fractions to make it comparable to the other. In this instance, Michael reconceptualized the 1/4 by imagining cutting it in half. To complete the reconceptualization, one would have to cut all the 1/4 pieces in half to yield eight pieces of equal size in the pizza. Alternatively, one could reconceptualize 2/8 as 1/4 by thinking of each of two 1/8 pieces as forming a unit. In that view, four such units would make up each pizza, and each of those units of two 1/8 pieces would constitute 1/4 of a pizza.

I was present in the class when this incident took place, although I was not the teacher. I did not think of all these ideas on the spur of the moment. Instead, I thought of them later, as I contemplated what might be the significance of Michael's comment. His comment has helped me understand that as early as fourth grade, some children are aware of the conceptual complexities related to the way fractional numbers are defined and to notions of equivalence. It has helped me understand that instruction involving fractions in the intermediate grades must address these complexities head on. Approaches that rely on using arithmetical techniques to establish equivalence would not begin to address the conceptual issues that Michael is deliberating. The instructional implications of his remark are enormous because the very basis of dealing with equivalent fractions using arithmetical approaches is challenged.

The main theme of this chapter is that listening requires us as teachers to adopt a *pro*active rather than a *re*active stance. Labinowicz (1985) pointed out that we see what we understand rather than understand what we see. The same can be said for listening. We, as teachers, hear what we understand, not the other way around. Thus, we must learn to listen. We can do so by sensitizing ourselves to notice discrepancies between what children say and what we expect them to say. In the process, we become more aware of our expectations and can be prepared to listen for alternatives. Another way we can learn to listen is by informing ourselves about children's mathematics. In particular, we can use both our experiences with pupils and professional development opportunities to build our own understanding of how children develop mathematical concepts. The more we understand, the more we will be prepared to hear. And the more we hear, the more we can use what we hear to influence and guide our instruction.

Listening to One Another: "Ears Open, Mouths Closed"

Liz Sweeney, fifth-grade teacher

What does listening "look like"? What are our expectations for students' listening behaviors? If a student is quiet and looks attentive, is that demeanor a sufficient indicator of listening? Liz Sweeney is a fifth-grade teacher with many years' teaching experience in a large urban school system. Well into her teaching career, she became involved in professional development that led her to rethink her role and the students' role in the mathematics classroom. As her practice changed, whole-group discussions became more central to the process of learning mathematics, and this shift, in turn, raised questions for her about how students participate in those discussions—both when they are talking and when they are not. In chapter 7, Erna Yackel discusses how "listening requires ... a *pro*active rather than a *re*active stance" (p. 121). In this story, Ms. Sweeney reflects on what she is learning about students' listening and how she is working proactively with her students to make shared criteria and goals for listening explicit in her classroom. "Ears open, mouths closed" may sound like the beginning of a set of rules from a classroom in which students are seen and not heard, but it takes on a different meaning and intent as "deep listening" is practiced in this classroom.

—Susan Jo Russell

L ONG ago I realized the value of whole-class discussions. They have pushed students' and teachers' thinking to places where I, as the teacher, might never have gone. Changes in my mathematics class—from teacher-directed, quiet, right-and-wrong, individual rote work to loud, energized group investigations in which ideas get tossed around with the enthusiasm of a springtime ball game—have brought about complexities in my teaching that continue to challenge me.

Which change has been most crucial? A confusing endeavor for me, both in class and, repeatedly, in my personal and professional reflection, is active listening. I almost hesitate to write about it. "Listening" seems very elusive, yet what I have learned is that it is essential to the process of learning. As a teacher, I experience the struggle that is required to listen to the students to get some insight into their mathematics ideas. Without deep listening, how do we know what students are thinking? How do we know what questions to ask, what mathematics issues to raise, what the next mathematics "lesson" should be? Listening to students opens up new territory for teachers in our classroom practice.

In this story, though, I would like to focus on students' listening to the mathematics thinking of their classmates. Since I, as the teacher, was not doing all the talking any more, I could not enforce all the listening! At first I did not realize the dramatic significance of this shift. I was not sure of my expectations. I anticipated that the desired outcome would happen more easily, that students' careful listening would simply be a secondary—and effortless—effect of my teaching mathematics differently. This result was decidedly not what happened!

In this unfamiliar environment, some disconnection clearly existed between teaching and learning, between good curriculum and students' engagement, between my expectations and student outcomes. At first, I did not even know what questions to ask, but gradually I formulated these:

- What does it mean for students to listen to one another in this truly hard way?

- What does listening "look like"?

- How do we get students to use listening as a tool for learning mathematics?

- How do we, as teachers, create structures and, even larger, a culture where deep listening happens?

- How does the curriculum support students' listening to one another?

- How can the work itself be compelling enough to engage the students in active listening?

- How do we get students invested in someone else's ideas about mathematics?

- What makes the work richer and more rewarding to do with others than alone?

- What shifts in students' behavior are necessary for learners to develop these new skills?

Even as I review my questions, I am reminded that I did not arrive at them easily. As I think about how I have worked on this process in my own classroom over the past couple of years, I see clearly that it involves a lot of messy trial and error—very small steps, very deliberate moves, many classroom conversations, and much reflection. I will try to share the process honestly.

Building a structure did not come easily. Each September, I would talk with the students about the importance of listening. Later, if I commented that certain students were not listening, they would always respond that indeed they were. I knew that they were not, but I was baffled as to how listening could be measurable—just what did listening behavior look like? Together, our class created a chart of what we thought were observable listening behaviors:

In our classroom, LISTENING looks like this—

1. Eyes on the speaker,

2. Hands empty,

3. Mouth closed, and

4. Ears open.

We added each behavior to the list only after considerable discussion and agreement. We believed that "eyes on the speaker" focused the listener's attention and showed respect. "Hands empty" came from the theory that the brain could pay attention to only one message at a time, and the "thing" that might be in the hands—paper clip, elastic, whatever—frequently, and not unexpectedly, captured the brain's attention. We stipulated "mouth closed" because, clearly, to listen when talking is difficult to do. "Ears open" began to touch on the next level of listening: it is about really taking in what other people are saying, and, although it is not actually observable, it was a reminder of the importance of concentration on the speaker's message.

We also decided that people would be addressed by name. We practiced ways of entering into conversation: "I agreed with Marya when she said . . . ," "I was confused when Felicia said . . . ," or "I disagreed with Malcolm when he said . . . ." These respectful, although somewhat artificial, formulas provided a safe way for the students to question their peer or present an alternative view.

We established a "thinking time," a few minutes prior to working in a group, or even working independently, during which we "listened" to our own thoughts. We all agreed that we would be able to articulate at least one idea about the investigation and would go around the group sharing it before the actual work started. We refined this concept by agreeing that if one could not get comfortable with the problem, being able to articulate a question or explain the "sticking place" would be appropriate. After the mathematics class, we would have some "reflecting time"—more specifically related to the development of listening and not the actual mathematics—in which students would write about something they learned from another student's thinking.

Much more remains to be said here, and much more work remains to be done to establish the classroom culture in which this kind of listening can take place—a culture in which respect and safety, purposefulness, hard work, perseverance, and responsibility are paramount. And to support the development of students' listening to one another, the curriculum itself must be both compelling and appropriate. If the work authentically engages students and gives them a reason to persevere, to jointly muddle through the frustration, listening becomes an essential tool. In the enthusiasm of a team's rising to the challenge and doing the shared hard work of the mathematics, listening grows from its own need. Students listen because they need to listen to do the mathematics in which they are personally engaged. If the curriculum engages them and the culture supports it, students listen well because they are doing what they want to be doing—being successful mathematicians.

CHAPTER 8

Reflecting on Teaching Mathematics through Problem Solving

Frances R. Curcio and Alice F. Artzt

Stella: I'm trying to figure out a way to prepare a lesson that involves some important number concepts and make it enjoyable for the kids. I was thinking about giving out a hundreds chart—the children are familiar with it, since we've used it to find patterns. I could ask them to mark off the two-times table in one color and the three-times table in another color and then ask them what they notice. I would hope they notice that some numbers, such as 6, 12, and 18, are marked with two colors. Then I could give them a word problem that would relate to common multiples.

Claire: I like your idea of giving them a hundreds chart, but I would give them the word problem first. I think children have an easier time understanding numbers when they are related to a real-life problem.

Stella: Do you know a problem we could use?

Claire: Well, I once used a Ferris wheel problem with my sixth graders, but I think it would be too hard for your third graders. Kids love certain foods, so you could ask something like "Every other day the cafeteria workers serve chocolate milk for lunch. Every third day the cafeteria workers serve pizza for lunch. On which days can we expect to have chocolate milk and pizza for lunch?" What do you think?

Stella: I think that's a great problem, especially since I know the children love chocolate milk and pizza. I'll bet they'd have fun solving that problem, and in the process, they'll be generating the multiples of 2 and the multiples of 3, giving them practice with their times tables. All the children know the two-times table already, and they can skip count starting with 3. Besides the hundreds chart that's posted, there's a calendar they could use, and there are other tools around the

Vignette 1. A first-year teacher, Stella, discusses ideas for a lesson with a more experienced colleague, Claire.

Vignette 1 (Continued)

room, so they can explore their own way to solve it. My kids usually think of bet-ter ideas than I have, and it's best if they think for themselves.

Claire: What if the students all come up with different ways of looking at it? How will you bring their ideas together?

Stella: I could pick the group that seems to have it figured out and let them present their ideas. What do you think?

Claire: Or you could start the conversation by saying, "Anybody notice any patterns? Do you disagree? Do you agree? Why do you disagree? Why do you agree?" Just enough to get a sense that the kids are thinking about the pattern. What do you hope they will say?

Stella: I hope somebody will notice that the days for chocolate milk and pizza are divisible by both 2 and 3.

Claire: What if nobody notices that? How can you get them to see it themselves?

Stella: I might say, "Let's look at this together. I notice something about this. Look at it. What are you noticing there?"

AFTER reading vignette 1, one might guess that these teachers are engaged in planning a lesson on common multiples. We agree that this interpretation of the conversation would be accu-rate, but we would like to suggest another vantage point for analy-sis. Specifically, we could say that Stella and Claire are engaged in problem solving, the problem being *how to teach a lesson that will engage their students in problem solving to learn important mathematics.*

Although being a problem solver oneself is widely accepted as a necessary condition for being able to teach children mathemat-ics through problem solving (National Council of Teachers of Mathematics 1991), teachers need more than mathematical problem-solving ability to be able to teach children effectively. And although lists of problem-solving steps and heuristics are widely available, teachers face challenges as they attempt to engage their students in a way of doing mathematics that will lead to deep understanding.

If one accepts the vision of "teaching as problem solving," one would agree that teachers engage in problem solving as a regular part of their work (Carpenter 1988). Recent literature on teaching as problem solving (Artzt and Armour-Thomas 1998, 2002) has focused on teachers' underlying knowledge, beliefs, and instructional goals and how these aspects affect teachers' thinking before, during, and after teaching a lesson. These works reveal that the nature of teachers' instructional practice—that is, the *tasks* they design, the *learning environment* they create, and the *classroom discourse* they orchestrate—are directly affected by the nature of their underlying knowledge, beliefs, and goals.

Using this conception of teaching, teachers who wish to empower their students to become mathematical problem solvers must understand that problem solving occurs in phases: (*a*) *before*—preparation to solve the problem, (*b*) *during*—actual problem solving, and (*c*) *after*—verification of the solution (Artzt and Armour-Thomas 1992; Garofalo and Lester 1985; Pólya 1945; Silver 1987). Furthermore, teachers must set specific goals for their students when they engage in problem solving. In this chapter, we discuss "nested problem solving," that is, teaching mathematical problem solving within a teaching-as-problem-solving framework. Throughout this examination, we discuss how teachers' knowledge, beliefs, and goals and their problem-solving behaviors can be transferred to their students in ways that develop the students' understanding of important mathematics.

Nested Problem Solving

Although the context of the teacher's and the students' problems are quite different, the problem-solving phases they go through are similar. To begin, let us define the two problems we consider in this chapter. The teacher's problem is to help students acquire an understanding of common multiples. The students' problem is to solve the cafeteria problem (see p. 132). In the next three sections, we examine each phase of the problem-solving process from both the teacher's and the students' perspectives. By so doing, we hope to reveal the connections between the teacher's knowledge, beliefs, goals, and problem-solving behaviors and the opportunities she gives her students to engage in authentic problem solving to learn an important mathematical idea. Table 8.1 summarizes the parallel phases of problem solving for teachers and students.

Phase 1: Before Solving the Problem

The Teacher Plans the Lesson

The teachers involved in the conversation in vignette 1 refer to their *knowledge* about their students (e.g., "I think it would be too hard for your third graders. Kids love certain foods"; "I know the

Table 8.1. *Parallel Phases of Problem Solving from the Teacher's and the Students' Perspectives*

TEACHER'S PERSPECTIVE	Phase	STUDENTS' PERSPECTIVE
Review the curriculum, and refer to appropriate resources. Focus on important information about the content and about students' current knowledge, interests, and abilities. Consider possible ways to teach the lesson so that students are placed at the center of instruction. Prepare the plan.	**Before**	Read the problem carefully, focusing on understanding special vocabulary. Focus on important information, and try to ascertain what the problem is about. Consider possible ways to solve the problem. If possible, develop a plan.
Implement the lesson plan. Observe and question students to determine where they are in the solution process. Provide guidance as needed, and consider other instructional strategies.	**During**	Begin to solve the problem as planned. Assess the effectiveness of the problem-solving approach being used. Explore other possible ways to solve the problem, as needed.
Look back on the lesson to assess the effectiveness of instruction. Determine what to change if the lesson is to be taught again.	**After**	Look over all work, and make sure that it and the answer make sense. Consider other ways to approach a similar problem.

children love chocolate milk and pizza"; "All the children know the two-times table already, and they can skip count starting with 3"), their *beliefs* about how their students will learn best (e.g., "I think children have an easier time understanding numbers when they are related to a real-life problem"; "My kids usually think of better ideas than I have, and it's best if they think for themselves"), and their *goals* for their students' learning (e.g., "I'm trying to figure out a way to prepare a lesson that involves some important number concepts and make it enjoyable for the kids"). Note that the teachers' *knowledge, beliefs,* and *goals* are the underlying determinants of the nature and quality of their instructional practice.

Also present in vignette 1 are the kinds of questions that will be asked to determine students' understanding and how to proceed with the lesson (e.g., "You could start the conversation by saying, 'Anybody notice any patterns? Do you disagree? Do you agree? Why do you disagree? Why do you agree?' Just enough to get a sense that the kids are thinking about the pattern"). The discourse described here is designed to place the students at the center of instruction as well as to provide a vehicle for the teacher to *monitor* (i.e., analyze and gauge) the extent of the students' understanding. Claire tries to get Stella to anticipate how she will modify her instructional strategy if the students do not notice a pattern on their own (i.e., "What if nobody notices [a pattern]? How can you get them to see it themselves?"). Stella suggests an approach that would provide scaffolding for children without showing them a pattern (i.e., "I might say, 'Let's look at this together. I notice something about this. Look at it. What are you noticing there?'") These interactive cognitions of monitoring, guiding, and assessing are crucial to any problem-solving endeavor and to the quality of student-centered instructional practice. Yet teachers find these areas of instruction to be the most challenging.

The art of teaching rests with the teacher's ability to be aware of the different levels of students' understanding at any given moment during a lesson and then know how to act on this awareness. This ability includes formulating questions that will reveal the nature of students' understanding or lack of understanding. For example, such questions as "How does this remind you of a problem we solved before?" "How did you get your answer?" "Does your answer make sense?" "Why did you use that method?" are useful for eliciting students' explanations that reveal what and how they are thinking about the problem. On the basis of this information, teachers need to make on-the-spot decisions about how to proceed. For example, students' actions may reveal weaknesses in their current understandings that impede their progress. In such instances, teachers should adjust their questions to address these gaps.

After discussing ideas for the lesson with Claire, Stella developed a lesson plan (see the Appendix). In planning a lesson, she has taken into consideration the tasks that will facilitate students' involvement and understanding, the discourse that will engage all the children in thinking about the mathematical concepts, and the learning environment that will promote students' active engagement with the problem.

Specifically, the two teachers have designed a task, "the cafeteria problem" (stated on the next page), that they believe will be of interest to all the students and will lead them to discover common multiples. By suggesting that the students work together in pairs, thereby allowing them to explore the problem without her direction and to select the tools that will help them best represent the problem, Stella has inherently shown respect for her students' abilities and has thereby created a comfortable and supportive learning environment. Furthermore, the suggestions she has made about the type of questions she will ask them shows that she is ready to guide them in the direction of the goal for the lesson—learning about common multiples—without inhibiting students from expressing their own ideas.

The Cafeteria Problem: Starting tomorrow, every other day, the cafeteria workers will be serving chocolate milk for lunch. Every third day, the cafeteria workers will be serving pizza for lunch. On which days can we expect to have chocolate milk and pizza for lunch?

Students Analyze, Explore, and Plan How to Solve the Problem

After launching the lesson and polling the children to determine how many like chocolate milk and pizza, Stella asked Amos to read the problem, which was posted on the chalkboard. When asked whether they had any questions about the problem, several children were not sure what "tomorrow" meant in the context of this problem—they were not sure when to start "counting." Stella suggested that they decide with their partners how to proceed and that they select tools to use to explore the problem. What follows in vignette 2 is an excerpt of a discussion between two students, Jaime and Antoine.

As the children worked, Stella noticed that Antoine appeared to be somewhat confused. She saw that the way the two children chose to represent the problem using the calendar would probably not lead them to her goal for the lesson, finding common multiples, so she suggested that instead of using the calendar, which seemed to be creating unnecessary confusion for them, they should use the hundreds chart. When Antoine asked, "How can we use a hundreds chart? It doesn't have any dates on it," Stella suggested that they record the information from the problem on the chart just as they were doing on the calendar; then she moved on to another group.

This short classroom excerpt shows that the teacher's plan for her students to take charge of their problem solution got off to a productive start. Note how the teacher encouraged her students to examine the conditions of the problem and what the words meant.

Jaime: Tomorrow will be Tuesday, so let's look at the calendar and start from there.

Antoine: What should we do, count it as a chocolate milk day?

Jaime: No, let's say that starting tomorrow the problem starts and then on Wednesday, we can have chocolate milk.

Antoine: OK. So Wednesday, October 31st, will be chocolate milk. Then Friday, November 2nd, will be chocolate milk. Let's mark it on the calendar. [The two children walk to the calendar on the wall.]

Jaime: How far should we go? To January?

Antoine: No, let's just finish November. We marked October 31st and November 2nd. Now what do we do? Skip to Monday?

Jaime: Yeah, I guess. But, Monday doesn't count because we had chocolate milk on Friday.

Antoine: OK, so then November 6th, 8th, then we have Saturday.

Jaime: So let's jump to Monday, November 12th, and then Wednesday, November 14th.

Antoine: Let's do pizza now. I like pizza. So go back to Wednesday, October 31st.

Jaime: No, we gotta start with tomorrow—Tuesday—and start counting from there. So that'll be...

Antoine: OK, that'll be Thursday, November 1st, but there's no match with pizza.

Jaime: Keep going: Tuesday, November 6th, then Friday, November 9th.

Antoine: I'm getting mixed up.

Jaime: No, we got a match on November 9th.

Antoine: But we didn't get anything for October. We'd better make believe it's November and start there.

Jaime: It's OK, let's just keep going.

Vignette 2. Two students, Jaime and Antoine, work on the cafeteria problem.

However, rather than answer their questions directly, she encouraged them to work with their partners to develop a better understanding of the problem. As a result, the students independently explored the problem and slowly developed their plans for solving it (e.g., "Let's mark it on the calendar," "Let's finish chocolate milk first," "Let's just finish November"). The children in vignette 2 chose to use the calendar as a tool to solve the problem. Even though the calendar did not turn out to be an effective tool, the students' exploration of its use fostered their greater depth of understanding of the problem and its many facets. It provided a concrete vehicle for modeling the problem. In the next section, we show how the teacher analyzed and modified her implementation of the lesson plan as the children analyzed and modified their work.

Phase 2: During the Solution Process

The Teacher Implements the Lesson Plan as Students Implement Plans for Solving the Problem

Following her plan for the lesson (see the Appendix), the teacher allowed her students to solve the problem in pairs. Different tools (e.g., calendars, hundreds charts) were available for the students to use when solving the problem. As she circulated through the room, listening to what the children were saying, she was essentially assessing how well her plan was working for them. As she passed by Antoine and Jaime, she noticed that they were running into difficulty as they marked the calendar. Stella recalled that when she introduced the problem, they had asked what "every second day" meant. To solve the problem, the children had to answer such questions as "Which day do we start with?" "What do we do about counting when the weekend comes?" "What do we do when the month changes?" Stella realized that each time the children encountered one of these questions, they were essentially monitoring their own problem solving. In fact, when Antoine became worried that the dates in October were not being used, he modified his original plan and decided to start with November.

Stella could see that using the calendar was presenting some insurmountable difficulties—not only for Jaime and Antoine but for other children as well. Even if the students circled the correct dates for chocolate milk and for pizza, the presence of weekends and the changing month prevented the idea of common multiples from emerging. Rather than follow her plan to allow the students to continue using a calendar, Stella decided to steer the students in a different direction by suggesting that they use the hundreds chart. By monitoring students' work, the teacher discovered that she had to modify her plan because allowing the students to continue would derail the problem solution. Although allowing students to initiate and follow through on their ideas is important, teachers must assess what the students are doing and sometimes offer guidance that will help steer the process in a more productive direction.

Once the teacher redirected Jaime and Antoine's efforts, Antoine was not sure what to do next. Jaime suggested starting with 1 and counting by twos and then by threes. They identified the common multiples as the numbers marked with two colors.As Stella continued to walk around the room, she noticed that most of the children in the class chose to use the hundreds chart, and they marked off the multiples of 2 and the multiples of 3. She recorded which children were using the calendar and listened carefully to their conversations, planning to have them share their difficulties during the whole-class discussion.

> *Jaime:* So let's write down the numbers that are colored in red and blue. [He writes the numbers 6, 12, 18, 24, 30, 36, … on his paper. Antoine waves his hand to get the teacher's attention. Stella walks over.]
>
> *Antoine:* Look! We figured it out. These are the numbers.
>
> *Stella:* So what do these numbers mean to you? Think about that, and then you may want to share it with the rest of the class when we come back together as a group. [Antoine looks at the board where the problem is posted and reads it aloud to Jaime.]
>
> *Jaime:* But what are those days? How are we gonna know which days we have chocolate milk and pizza?

Vignette 3. Jaime and Antoine try to make sense of their solution.

Phase 3: After the Problem-Solving Effort

Students Look Back at Their Solution (Vignette 3)

The children have followed Stella's suggestion to use the hundreds chart and believe they have solved the problem. Although they have found the common multiples of 2 and 3, which was the teacher's original goal for the lesson, they have not answered the question posed in "the cafeteria problem"—that is, they have not identified which days they will be served chocolate milk and pizza. When the teacher approached the children, she tried to make them aware that they must look back at their work. By suggesting that they examine the original problem and make sure that their answer makes sense, she is emphasizing the essential role of reflection in problem solving.

The Teacher Reflects on the Lesson

Stella's interest in having her students look back on their solution can be related to her eagerness to look back on the lesson. It can also be related to the way she has her students revisit the stated cafeteria problem to see whether their answers make sense. Stella's original intent for the lesson was that the students learn about common multiples. Had it not been important to her to emphasize "looking back," she might have been tempted to accept

Stella: I just taught the common multiples lesson, and I'd like to talk about it.

Claire: Sure. What happened?

Stella: Well, remember my idea of making the calendar available as a tool? It turned out to be a problem because the date changes each month and weekends were interfering with the multiples of 2 and 3.

Claire: So what did you do?

Stella: I'm not sure that I should have done this, but I told the kids to use the hundreds chart instead.

Claire: So how did it work out?

Stella: At first I thought it worked great, since the kids came up with all the right multiples. But then, when I wanted them to look back on their work, they still had to go back to the calendar. This took us far away from the discussion of common multiples. I'm starting to wonder how I might change the cafeteria problem to make it work better.

Vignette 4. Stella describes her concerns about the lesson to Claire.

the students' list of common multiples as the solution and then centered the conversation on those numbers. Instead, she encouraged students to examine the context of the problem, which brought them back to the dates on the calendar, which took them away from the goal of her lesson. Of course, after the discussion about the days they would have chocolate milk and pizza, she did return to the numbers they found on the hundreds chart and the idea of common multiples, but the lesson carried over into the following day and took much longer than she had planned.

Stella's respect for the role of looking back was also clear in her comments to Claire after the lesson (vignette 4). She thought deeply about the difficulties that she had had in implementing the lesson. She reflected on how the calendar had created unnecessary confusion for the children and how it had not helped them arrive at the idea of common multiples. And even after she had gotten the students to use the hundreds chart, they had still needed to return to the calendar. Finally, she questioned how she might revise the cafeteria problem so that it would better support her instructional goals. By looking back, teachers are able to evaluate the effectiveness of their instructional approaches, and learners are able to evaluate the effectiveness of their solution strategies. In both situations, this evaluation can be the vehicle for continuing progress and deepening understanding.

Closing Comments

Our purpose in this chapter has been to explore the parallels between the process of teaching a mathematics lesson that leads to deep understanding and the process of solving a mathematics problem. Teaching is complex and often unpredictable; so, too, is problem solving. A "good" lesson requires planning and can take a multitude of forms. Likewise, making a plan to solve a mathematics problem is essential, and typically, not just one "right way" exists to solve a problem.

Improving one's teaching skills involves risk taking and the willingness to try new approaches. Similarly, improving one's problem-solving skills involves taking risks and trying new approaches. Monitoring and regulating one's teaching require "tuning in" to learners by listening to and observing them. Analogously, monitoring and regulating the solution to a problem require "tuning in" to the underlying features and mathematical relationships embedded in a problem. Teachers who reflect on a lesson are able to analyze, refine, and revise the plan for an appropriate follow-up lesson. Correspondingly, looking back on a solution to a problem allows learners to compare the outcome with the original goal, determining the suitability of the solution and thus expanding their problem-solving schemata.

The intermittent and sometimes concurrent incidence of problem-solving processes during instructional practice has made this exposition particularly intriguing for us. The interesting similarities that have emerged between teaching a lesson that leads to deep understanding and solving a mathematics problem suggest that through a problem-solving approach to teaching, one might, in fact, become a better teacher of mathematics.

Appendix

Topic: Number—Common Multiples

Grade: 3

Aim: What are common multiples, and how can we use them to solve problems?

Objectives: To explore a contextual mathematics problem using a variety of tools (e.g., the calendar, the hundreds chart, Unifix cubes, Cuisenaire rods)

To share problem-solving strategies

To discuss patterns of multiples using a hundreds chart

To define "common multiples"

To examine selected times tables to find common multiples

To compare prime and composite numbers when finding common multiples

To determine whether problem solutions make sense

To formulate and solve extension problems

Prior knowledge: Children have had experience finding patterns on the hundreds chart.

Children know how to read a calendar and use the calendar to determine dates of events.

Children have used Cuisenaire rods and Unifix cubes to solve problems.

Materials: Calendar (posted on the wall); hundreds chart (posted on wall and individual sheets) and colored pencils or markers; Cuisenaire rods; Unifix cubes

Launch: By a show of hands, how many children like chocolate milk?

By a show of hands, how many children like pizza?

By a show of hands, how many children like both chocolate milk and pizza? Well, those of us who love chocolate milk and pizza are going to have a real treat in the cafeteria on selected days—and it is our job to figure out which days we will have the treat. Here is the situation (post the problem on the chalkboard):

The Cafeteria Problem. Starting tomorrow, every other day, the cafeteria workers will be serving chocolate milk for lunch. Every third day, the cafeteria workers will be serving pizza for lunch. On which days can we expect to have chocolate milk and pizza for lunch?

Development:

Steps of the Lesson	Student Activities and Expected Reactions/Responses	Teacher's Responses to Student Reactions and Things to Remember
Let selected children read the problem, and ask them to restate it in their own words.	Some children may have trouble understanding "every other day" and "every third day." The problem is open ended in that they will not know how many common multiples to find.	Relate every other day with every second day.

(Continued)

Appendix—Continued

Steps of the Lesson	Student Activities and Expected Reactions/Responses	Teacher's Responses to Student Reactions and Things to Remember
With children working in pairs, allow them time to explore the problem using any tools they select.	Some students may elect to use the calendar. Some students may elect to use Unifix cubes or Cuisenaire rods to model the problem. Some children may choose to use a hundreds chart.	This tool may help them answer the problem, but unless the calendar begins with "1" tomorrow, the common multiples will not be revealed. These tools may be confusing for some children to keep track of the multiples; ask them to record or draw a diagram of what they are doing. This tool may be useful in revealing the common multiples of 2 and 3.
After about fifteen minutes, bring the class together to share their problem-solving strategies and solutions.	Children using the calendar may show their solution by skip counting. Children using Unifix cubes or Cuisenaire rods may show their solutions by grouping or aligning the cubes or rods. Children using the hundreds chart may show their solutions by skip counting and marking multiples and common multiples.	Record the days (not the dates) that chocolate milk and pizza are served. Record the multiples and common multiples over diagrams of the cubes or rods. Circle the common multiples on the hundreds chart, and compare the solutions obtained by using the different tools.

Steps of the Lesson	Student Activities and Expected Reactions/Responses	Teacher's Responses to Student Reactions and Things to Remember
Have selected children use two different colors to mark the multiples of 2 and 3 on the hundreds chart, identifying the numbers that are marked twice.	Some children may have trouble connecting the different representations of the problem (i.e., calendar and cubes or rods with hundreds chart). Try to have all children focus on the hundreds chart, having children who used the chart explain their strategies.	Ask, "Why are some numbers on the hundreds chart marked twice? What does this double marking mean?" Introduce the term *common multiple*. Ask, "How can common multiples help us solve our problem?"

**Assessment/
Summary:**   When we celebrate the one hundredth day of school, should we expect to have chocolate milk and pizza served? Why or why not?

What would happen if the cafeteria workers decided to change the days that pizza is offered to every sixth day, continuing to offer chocolate milk every other day? Should we expect the days for having chocolate milk and pizza to be the same as in our original problem or different? Why?

What is a "common multiple"? How do we find common multiples?

Assignment: Write and solve a problem that uses common multiples. Be prepared to share the problem with the class tomorrow.

Ordering Rectangles: Which Is Bigger?

Jan Dwyer, third-grade teacher

Fran Curcio and Alice Artzt point out in chapter 8 that "teachers engage in problem solving as a regular part of their work" (p. 127). In this story, Jan Dwyer describes her own teaching as a problem-solving activity. To find out what her third graders know about the length and area of rectangles, she engages them in a problem—ordering a set of rectangles—that provides an opportunity for both teaching and assessment. Before class, she thinks through what mathematical ideas she will focus on and what kinds of questions she will ask her students about their thinking. During class, she circulates and listens as students are working and then engages the whole class in discussion about their work. By noting what strategies each student brings to solving the problem, she develops an overview of the ideas students have about different measures of the rectangles, and then, building on the students' ideas, she chooses a focus for further problem solving. When the class is over, she has a much clearer idea of how her class as a whole is thinking about the length and area of rectangles, and she can begin to plan further experiences to meet the needs of the range of students in her class.

—Susan Jo Russell

I WANTED to find out what my class of bilingual third graders understood about length and area. Because many of them struggle with mathematics, I decided to use an activity from a second-grade curriculum that I thought would be appropriate for their independent working level. The activity—ordering a set of rectangles (fig. TS6.1) (see Akers et al. [1998] for the complete activity)—would allow entry points for the range of students in my class, and I thought that I would learn a great deal about my students' reasoning. Before class, I thought about the following:

- The mathematics that students will engage in:
  - ▲ Ideas about length and area—do they notice and use both of these measures?
  - ▲ Numerical and visual strategies to compare the size of shapes
  - ▲ Attention to the attributes of rectangles—width, length, and area
- The kinds of questions I will ask:
  - ▲ How did you decide that one rectangle is bigger than another?
  - ▲ How did you compare them?
  - ▲ How did you prove your idea to your team?
  - ▲ What does biggest mean to you?
  - ▲ What part of the rectangle are you looking at?
- Expectations about what I will learn from these questions:
  - ▲ What aspects of the rectangles do the students attend to?
  - ▲ What materials and strategies do they use for determining and proving their conclusions?

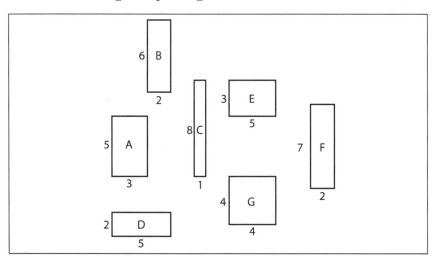

Fig. TS6.1. Rectangles used in the activity

Each student organized his or her own set of rectangles (fig. TS6.1); then, in small groups, the students discussed and compared what they had done. I noticed three basic kinds of ordering:

1. Four students chose C as the tallest rectangle, but beyond that, their reasoning was inconsistent. At times they compared height and then switched and compared width. They compared one rectangle with another next to it, but they did not seem to get the big view of how all the rectangles were related as a group.

2. Eight students ordered the rectangles by the longest side (fig. TS6.2). When two rectangles were the same height, they ordered them according to width. They explained, "C is the tallest. G and E are the same, but G is fatter, so it's bigger than E," "All the shapes are straight up and down, and they go down like stairs."

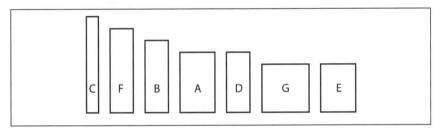

Fig. TS6.2. Ordering of rectangles for eight students

3. Six students agreed with the order of C, F, B, and A "because they are tall," but they ordered the three last rectangles differently so that they had no rectangles of the same height (fig. TS6.3)—"They look like stairs this way, too."

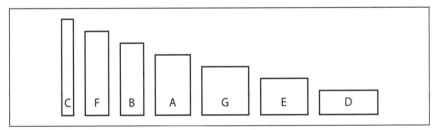

Fig. TS6.3. Ordering of rectangles for six other students

When the whole class came together, the children were very pleased that many of them agreed on the order of so many rectangles, and they were very interested in one another's explanations for the different ordering of the last three. Luis, looking at the ordering shown by the third group of students, said, "If you turn D and E this way, you have to turn all of them. Look, now C's the smallest." Luis rearranged the rectangles very quickly, sliding them into their new positions on the floor so that they were ordered according to the length of the shortest side (fig. TS6.4).

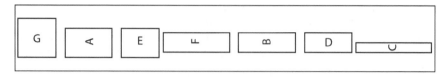

Fig. TS6.4. Luis's new ordering of the rectangles

Many children agreed that Luis's new order was fine, too. Others looked doubtful. I asked, "How can the biggest change? How can the biggest now be the smallest?" Luis responded, "See, when you look at them this way" [indicating the short side with his hand], "C gets smaller, so they still go down like stairs. They look like a train." Many murmurs of agreement were heard, "Biggest going this way."

At this point, someone said, "D and F are the same size." Gladys picked up B, F, and D and placed one rectangle on top of another. "I just thought of something," she said. "See, if I put D on top of F, I have some extra here and here. And I'm just thinking that this little piece is like that little piece if I moved it. No, I guess F is bigger than D, but I'm getting confused. . . ." A number of students seemed to agree with what Gladys was saying. I decided to see whether we could go further with Gladys's idea. When I had thought about the mathematics ideas in this lesson, I had hoped that students would notice that different measures can be considered in ordering the rectangles. So far, most students had focused on length. Now Gladys's comparison of D and F provided an opening to consider the space inside the rectangle. I asked, "So are some of you changing your minds about biggest? Does biggest mean tallest all the time?"

Carlos then said, "Fattest. If you put G and C together, then G has more space." Rufino placed rectangle C on top of G, folded down the extra length of C, and showed that C could cover only half of G. He said, "G's like 16 chocolates and C's like . . . um . . . 8 pieces." I asked, "If these were chocolate bars, which do you think would be the biggest?" Many children answered, "G," but others did not offer an opinion.

"Now that we've found several different ways to put the rectangles in order, Carlos and Gladys are bringing up a question about which rectangle has more space. Let's work on a new problem to help us think about this idea." I asked everyone to work on three questions and to find a way to prove their thinking: Which chocolate bar has the most chocolate? Which has the least chocolate? Are there any chocolate bars that have the same amount of chocolate?

While the children worked, I circulated around the room, watching and listening. Many students proved their decisions by covering the rectangles with one-inch tiles and then skip counting by rows to find the total. A few children began to identify the rectangles as "the 16" or "the 12," whereas some children identified them as arrays—"the 1 by 8," "the 4 by 4," "the 3 by 4." Some students folded, cut, and moved pieces to compare. Only two students did not find a satisfactory way to determine the largest and smallest chocolate bars. David cut different rectangles to make them the same size, but he did not use this method to decide which had been bigger before he started cutting them. Kateria insisted that the rectangle that had fifteen tiles was the same size as the rectangle that had sixteen tiles. David and Kateria were two of the four children who had not seen the rectangles as a whole collection that could be ordered; they had attended to different attributes for each comparison of neighboring rectangles during the ordering activity.

I learned a great deal about my students' thinking in this hour. I think that the activity was right for their independent working level, so I was able to get them to dig a bit deeper. They investigated different ways to order the rectangles by length and then, with the new context of candy, looked at the "space," or area, of the rectangles. Most students used the inch-square tiles as a unit to measure the area. I would like to continue with problems that will help them think about how to measure and compare familiar shapes. Rufino was particularly facile in comparing shapes, noticing right away that the area of C is half the area of G, for example. I would like to find ways to spur him on with this line of thinking. David and Kateria really concern me. I am not sure that they understand the meanings of "equal" and "the same." I wonder what they would do with a set of rectangles for which only one dimension varied.

We need more vocabulary development, as well. The children used hand gestures and language from their environment to describe or explain their decisions. At times, they seemed frustrated because they lacked words that would make their meaning clear. I plan to work with them on such words as *length, width,* and *area* and help them develop a vocabulary list that will be useful to them as they articulate their ideas.

CHAPTER 9

Establishing Classroom Social and Sociomathematical Norms for Problem Solving

Michelle Stephan
Joy Whitenack

PRINCIPLES and Standards for School Mathematics (NCTM 2000) states that problem solving means "engaging [students] in a task for which the solution method is not known in advance" (p. 52). In addition, students also engage in genuine problem-solving activities when they have opportunities to create personally meaningful solutions to messy problem situations. One of the hallmarks of genuine problem solving is that classroom discussions focus on students' methods for constructing solutions, not simply their answers to the problem.

To foster discussions that center on students' solution processes, the teacher and students must create and sustain a risk-free environment in which students' reasoning, not getting answers, is valued. Students are more likely to develop productive

The investigation reported in this paper was supported by the National Science Foundation under grant number REC 9814898 and by the Office of Educational Research and Improvement under grant number R305A60007. The opinions expressed do not necessarily reflect the views of either the Foundation or OERI. The members of the project team involved in this investigation included Paul Cobb, Beth Estes, Koeno Gravemeijer, Kay McClain, Beth Petty, Michelle Stephan, and Erna Yackel.

The authors wish to thank Lisa Gross for her suggestions and comments on an earlier version of this article.

problem-solving attitudes if they "play a role in establishing the classroom norms ... where everyone's ideas are respected and valued" (NCTM 2000, p. 185). Because the teacher and the students together establish these norms, both of their roles are important. More specifically, two types of classroom norms are crucial for establishing an environment in which problem solving is valued: *social norms* and *sociomathematical norms*. Social norms involve shared agreements about what discussing one's ideas means and how one goes about doing so. Sociomathematical norms involve agreements about what counts as different, sophisticated, efficient, and acceptable mathematical ideas (Yackel and Cobb 1996). As the teacher and students talk about what counts as knowing and doing mathematics, these discussions enable students to explain their reasoning, ask clarifying questions, and listen to other students' ideas. These norms are essential for engaging students in productive problem-solving situations.

In this chapter, we use examples from one first-grade classroom to illustrate how the teacher and the students create a genuine problem-solving environment as they establish classroom social and sociomathematical norms. We describe how Ms. Smith, a first-grade teacher, began to establish a problem-solving environment in her classroom, but we have seen similar problem-solving atmospheres at work across elementary-grades contexts. We believe that such a proactive role can be extended and tailored to other elementary grades.

In her classroom, Ms. Smith engaged students in two interrelated instructional sequences, arithmetical reasoning and linear measurement, that placed problem solving at the heart of the students' activity. (See Stephan et al. [2001] for a more elaborated discussion of this classroom.) As we look at excerpts from the classroom discussions, we consider the teacher's and students' important roles in helping establish the classroom norms. In particular, we highlight how Ms. Smith used questioning techniques about the students' work not only to help them explain the procedures they used but also to help them articulate the mathematical reasons behind those procedures. Our examples also illustrate that the students shared their ideas as they became increasingly aware of what being a participating member of the classroom community means.

Social Norms

Social norms refer to the expectations that the teacher and students have for one another regarding their ways of acting and communicating in the classroom. Yackel and Cobb (1996) suggest that social norms for genuine problem solving include expecting students to be able to do four things: (1) explain and justify their solutions, (2) attempt to make sense of explanations given by others, (3) agree and disagree, and (4) ask clarifying questions in situations in which they misunderstand or are confused. Helping students develop mathematical dispositions in which they share their ideas, discuss others' ideas, and so on, is always a challenge. A particular challenge for the teacher is deciding how to help students understand the extent of their responsibilities during whole-class discussions, particularly when they have not previously been expected to explain their thinking.

Teachers often develop their own strategies for helping students learn that explaining, listening, and asking questions of one another is valued in the classroom. For example, sometimes the teacher initiates these new norms by stating her or his expectations during problem-solving activities: "Your job is to listen to Perry and see whether he thinks about the problem the way you did," "You've got to understand Meagan's thinking," or "We're really interested in how you are thinking about this problem." At other times, the teacher spends a few minutes during, and at the end of, class highlighting instances in which students listened to and tried to understand one another's solutions. The students also play an important role during these discussions as they attempt to explain and justify their ideas, ask clarifying questions, and so on. As we show subsequently in our classroom example, students, too, initiate conversations about norms for engaging in whole-class discussions.

As would be expected, at the beginning of the school year, conversations between the teacher and students and among students are extremely important for establishing the norms in the classroom. As the school year progresses, the teacher and students must continue to nurture an environment in which the students can communicate their ideas. For example, although Ms. Smith and her students had previously established the social norm that students were to ask questions if they did not understand a classmate's ideas, as late as March, the teacher and students continued to talk about the students' responsibilities during whole-class discussions. The discussion below took place after the students had measured part of the classroom floor with a "footstrip," a piece of paper on which they had traced five of their footprints, by placing the footstrip end to end four times. In the middle of the discussion, one of the students, Melanie, observed that twenty of the students' feet were the same length as four footstrips. As the discussion continued, the teacher asked the other students whether they had a question for Melanie:

Teacher: Ohhh, so twenty is the number of feet, but it's only four footstrips, it's not twenty footstrips . . . it's just four. How many people agree with what Melanie says? [Some students raise their hands.] How many people have a question for her? [Only Alice raises her hand.] Alice?

Alice: Well, I have a question for the whole class. Umm, but not for the people who raised their hand. Well, if they didn't understand Melanie and what she said and agreed with what she said, then they would all have questions.

Perry: [Perry has raised his hand.] Ms. Smith said, "Raise your hand if you agree with what Melanie said." Some people raised their hand, and some people didn't. And the, umm, somebody said raise your hand if you don't agree, and they don't answer?

Teacher: Yeah, I was just wondering about that myself. That's why I was really wanting to see what people do, because I think it's ..., I'm really interested to know how you're thinking about this. So if you're not sure about what Melanie said, or you disagree with her, you need to say so.

In this excerpt, Alice noticed that the students who did not understand Melanie's explanation did not raise their hands to ask a clarifying question. For Alice, her classmates did not feel obliged to indicate whether they understood other students' thinking. As such, she and Perry explicitly challenged their classmates, pointing out that their responsibility was to indicate misunderstandings. After Alice initiated this shift in the discussion, the teacher had an opportunity to ask whether other students understood Melanie's thinking. At this point, the discussion shifted from a discussion about "talking about mathematics, to talking about talking about mathematics" (Cobb, Wood, and Yackel 1993). That is, the conversation shifted from discussing Melanie's solution to discussing how and when students could contribute to the discussion. Interestingly, the students seemed to take responsibility for sustaining the previously established ways of communicating in the classroom, illustrating that both teacher *and* students play roles in maintaining the norms for communicating mathematical ideas in elementary-grades classrooms.

Students should play an important role in developing and sustaining the classroom social norms. Thus, during whole-class discussions, student-student interactions should also be fostered. Unfortunately, too often, when student-teacher dialogue occurs, the teacher and the student engage in one-on-one discussions that often do not include other students. To encourage *all* students to contribute to discussions, the teacher should ask other students to explain their classmates' ideas. By using this strategy, the teacher urges students to use their own words and ideas to reconstruct what a classmate has shared. In doing so, students have an opportunity to think out loud and, in some instances, to rethink a classmate's ideas in light of his or her own ideas. As such, these instances are learning opportunities for the student who is sharing as well as for those students who are listening to the conversation.

In addition to asking students to verbalize other students' ideas, a teacher can encourage students to address their questions directly to their classmates. For instance, when a student, Aimee, was confused about a classmate's (Pat's) solution to a problem and posed a question to the teacher, Ms. Smith immediately said, "Aimee, can you talk to Pat about that?" Ms. Smith further encouraged this type of student-student interaction by saying, for example, "Do you understand?" "Ask him a question if you don't understand," and "Who's got a question for Meagan? Ask her." These types of interactions encourage students to ask their classmates to clarify their thinking. In time, student-student interactions during whole-class discussions become commonplace.

In summary, helping students explain their thinking, understand someone else's thinking, and ask clarifying questions is an ongoing process during problem-solving investigations. Teachers and students begin to establish these norms at the outset of the school year as situations arise during whole-class discussions. Throughout the school year, the teacher and students must continue to discuss their roles in whole-class discussions. We have discussed three specific strategies that teachers might employ to maintain healthy social norms in the classroom:

- encouraging students to explain their thinking;

- asking a student to explain another student's solution method; and

- directing students to pose their questions directly to classmates instead of to the teacher.

Furthermore, the teacher can use discussions precipitated by students to find out about their understanding of their responsibilities during whole-class discussions. Students should be encouraged to—

- share their ideas and their understandings about how to engage in problem-solving discussions,

- ask questions, and

- indicate their agreement or disagreement with others' ideas.

Sociomathematical Norms

Sociomathematical norms are social norms that are specific to mathematical activity. They involve the *criteria* for what counts as a mathematical argument, explanation, or representation. One social norm, for example, may be that students explain their solution methods, but the teacher and the students must decide together the acceptable forms for a mathematically valid justification for the solution. As is true for social norms, establishing sociomathematical norms is very important if genuine problem solving is to take place. One example of a sociomathematical norm is what counts as an acceptable mathematical explanation (Yackel and Cobb 1996). Another example is deciding on the role that pictures might play in supporting communication and reasoning, what we refer to as what counts as acceptable *mathematical notation*. In the sections that follow, we focus particularly on the processes that Ms. Smith and her students went through to establish these two sociomathematical norms.

What Counts as an Acceptable Mathematical Explanation

At the beginning of the school year, Ms. Smith began working with her class to establish what constitutes an acceptable mathematical explanation. When creating and sustaining a problem-solving environment, many teachers ask such questions as "How did you know that?" or "How did you get that answer?" Although these questions encourage students to explain their reasoning, students often explain only the calculations, that is, the steps they used, that led them to their answer. These students, who may be regarded as *procedure oriented*, give explanations that suggest they are focusing only on the procedure for getting an answer. In contrast, some students give explanations that are *conceptually oriented*, that is, they include in their explanation their *interpretation* of the problem situation that led to their calculation (cf. Thompson et al. [1994]).

When elementary-grades students are asked to explain their thinking, typically they provide procedurally oriented justifications. When the teacher tries to initiate a shift to conceptually oriented explanations, helping students make this shift can be quite challenging. We illustrate with an example that occurred at the beginning of the school year. In the following episode, the teacher had posed the problem "Lena has eleven hearts. Dick has two hearts. How many more hearts does Lena have than Dick?" We enter the discussion as Sandra explained what the problem was asking:

Teacher: What was it you wanted to know?

Sandra: What the answer was.

Teacher: What kind of answer were we trying to find? What was it we wanted to know about the hearts?

Sandra: Who has more.

Teacher: Is this what we want to find out? Can you read what the problem says and decide what we want to find out?

Sandra: Okay. It says, "How many more hearts does Lena have than Dick?"

Teacher: Good. Now who can tell me in your own words what we want to find out? [Meagan raises her hand.] Meagan!

Meagan: How many more hearts does Lena have than Dick?

Teacher: That's exactly what it says. How many more hearts does Lena have than Dick? That's what we want to know. Does everyone understand what Meagan said? Do you want to ask her a question? Can you ask her a question if you don't understand, because she's trying to explain it to you, right, Meagan?

Meagan: [Nods yes.]

Mitch: I don't understand, but I don't know what to ask.

Teacher: Maybe somebody else has a question. Sandra?

Sandra: I think she needs to explain it again.

As can be seen in this excerpt, Sandra indicates that she knows that she is supposed to look for an answer to the problem, but we know little else about her thinking. The teacher attempted to shift the discussion toward understanding the problem situation by asking, "What kind of answer were we trying to find? What was it we wanted to know about the hearts?" By asking these questions, she communicated to Sandra and the other students that finding the answer is certainly important, but understanding what the question is asking is equally important. Like Sandra, other students were not accustomed to giving conceptually oriented explanations. In fact, such students as Mitch did not know how to ask questions to help them understand a classmate's interpretation. Ms. Smith had to employ another strategy to help students describe how they thought about the problem.

What Counts as Acceptable Mathematical Notation

Because some students in the example did not know how to engage in conceptually oriented discussions, the teacher decided to draw pictures to help them explain their thinking. However, the students did not know how to use their pictures to communicate their ideas to others, so this issue, too, became an instructional challenge for the teacher. During subsequent discussions, the teacher and the students began to establish what counted as acceptable mathematical notation. To illustrate this process, let us return to the example, as the teacher and students continue to discuss the problem. We reenter the discussion after Meagan has explained her answer of 11.

Teacher: Will you explain it again for us, Meagan? And everybody's going to listen really carefully because we want to understand what you're saying.

Meagan: We're trying to find out how many more hearts does Lena have than Dick.

Teacher: Did everybody hear what she said? Put your hands up if you understand. Hands up if you're not sure what she's saying. Mitch, do you have a question now? [He doesn't answer.] Does anybody have a question for Meagan? Why did you say eleven, Meagan? Where's the eleven?

Mitch: Were trying to figure out how many more does Lena have than Dick.

Teacher: Can you draw us a picture maybe to show us? Can anybody draw us a picture? Who wants to go up and draw a picture? We need somebody. Who's gonna be the brave one?

Perry: [Perry comes up and draws a picture of a stick person. See fig. 9.1.] I'm drawing a picture of Mitch saying he doesn't understand.

To our surprise, Perry interpreted the teacher's request to draw a picture as an occasion to show that Mitch did not understand. The teacher, of course, had expected a picture that showed how Perry was thinking about the problem.

Because they did not have enough time to address this issue at the end of the lesson, the teacher chose to continue their dis-

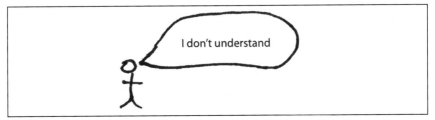

Fig. 9.1. Perry's drawing of a stick person that shows that Mitch does not understand

cussion the next day. During the next lesson, the teacher posed a similar problem for the students. After the students had solved the problem, the class reconvened to share their solution methods. To begin the discussion, the teacher asked a student to draw a picture to show how she had solved the problem "If there are 11 cats and 3 dogs, how many more cats are there than dogs?" Interestingly, the student drew a picture of a cat and a dog, not eleven cats and three dogs. Furthermore, she did not use her picture to explain her thinking.

To initiate a shift in how students might use their pictures to explain their thinking, the teacher drew the following picture on the board as another student explained that she had compared eleven cats with three dogs (see fig. 9.2).

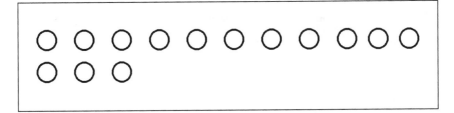

Fig. 9.2. The teacher's drawing of circles to represent eleven cats and three dogs

As a consequence of drawing the picture, the teacher and the students could refer to it during the ensuing discussion. Also, the teacher could ask questions related to the picture. For instance, the teacher could ask, "Can you pretend that each circle here is a cat [pointing to the top row] and that each circle here is a dog [pointing to the bottom row]? How many dogs are in the bottom row?" Thus, drawing the picture was an important instructional strategy. On the one hand, the students had opportunities to consider their and others' ideas as they looked at the picture. For instance, students who had difficulty keeping track of their counting had opportunities to understand the problem, to compare the two collections using the picture, and, more important, to understand how their thinking was different from their classmates' thinking. On the other hand, the teacher and the students began to establish how and when particular mathematical notation might be used to illustrate and support their mathematical ideas. Note that the teacher implicitly communicated that she valued this type of notation by first drawing the picture and then asking students questions about the picture. By engaging the students in these types of discussions, the teacher began to establish with her students what counted as acceptable mathematical notation.

Establishing and Reestablishing Sociomathematical Norms

The teacher's proactive role during discussions contributed, in part, to the types of explanations that the students began to give and the notation that they began to use as they explained their thinking. The students, too, played an important role as what counted as acceptable explanations and acceptable mathematical notation continued to evolve. To illustrate our points, we visit another discussion that occurred several days later. In our example, two students, Porter and Phil, gave different explanations of, and solutions to, the problem "There are 15 bugs in a box and 9 bugs in a jar. How many more bugs are in the box?" When Phil gave what the teacher considered to be a procedure-oriented explanation, she went to the board and drew tally marks to represent each collection (see fig. 9.3). After the class agreed that each of the tally marks stood for the number of bugs in the box and in the jar, Porter explained how he got fifteen for the answer.

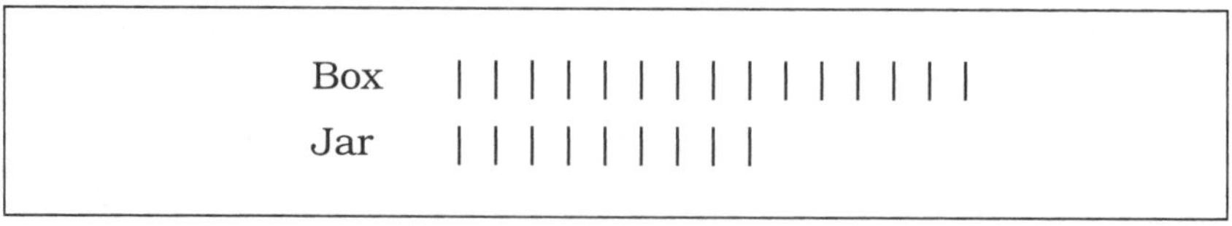

Box | | | | | | | | | | | | | | |

Jar | | | | | | | | |

Fig. 9.3. The teacher's drawing of tally marks to represent fifteen bugs in a box and nine bugs in a jar

Porter: I did it like, I knew it because it says says ... I knew that 15 was a bigger number than 9. So I knew that was the right one and that's how I answered it.

Phil: The way, it's like yours except if they both had nine [points to the first nine tally marks after the word *box*], but they didn't, and I added on six more [points to the six more tally marks in the box] would be fifteen. So there's fifteen in here and nine in here. But if they both had nine, there'd be nine in the box and nine in the jar. I added on six more so there's fifteen in the box. So the box has six more bugs than the jar.

As the discussion continued, Porter asked Phil a question about his thinking:

Porter: Phil, how did you know you wanted to put six more on?

Phil: This is the nine [points to the first nine tally marks in the box], and these are the six I put on [points to the six tally marks]. I was imagining that was the nine [points to the box] and that was nine [points to the jar], then I put six more in here [the box] and that would make fifteen in here and nine in here still [draws a line after the first nine; see fig. 9.4].

Fig. 9.4. Phil's drawing of a line to mark off the nine bugs

Students, such as Phil in this example, began to develop explanations that described how they interpreted the problem. Phil, for instance, used the teacher's diagram to explain how he could compare the two collections. If Phil had given a procedure-oriented explanation, he might have said, "I counted up from nine and stopped at fifteen. That gave me six more." He would have simply explained how he counted to solve the problem. Instead, Phil used the teacher's diagram to justify *why* he counted on six more from the nine bugs in the box (i.e., he pretended that each container had an equal number of bugs). Interestingly Phil's rich explanation was initiated by Porter's question. Porter wanted to know *how Phil knew* which procedures to use to solve the problem. By asking this question, Porter prompted Phil to explain the reasoning behind his procedures, that is, he asked Phil to provide a conceptually oriented explanation. As illustrated here, the students, rather than the teacher, began to initiate these types of discussions. This exchange happened several days after our first example; clearly, shifts in what counts as acceptable mathematical explanations can change in a matter of days.

As they determined what counted as an acceptable mathematical solution, the teacher and students continued to establish what counted as acceptable mathematical notation. During Phil and Porter's discussion, for instance, they referred to the pictures to explain and understand Phil's ideas. Although the teacher had drawn the picture of the collections, the students readily used this picture to talk about their ideas without prompting from the teacher. So again, the teacher and the students helped establish how and what kind of notation they might use to explain their ideas. The teacher had drawn the picture before the students began to explain their thinking, and the students referred to the pictures as they explained and justified their ideas. Hence, the teacher and the students continued to substantiate what counted as acceptable mathematical notation.

As students developed conceptually oriented explanations, they continued to establish how they might use pictures to explain and support their thinking. As such, these two sociomathematical norms seem to be related. Because students must be able to give reasons for the procedures they use to arrive at a solution, they can refer to pictures to explain why they solved a problem a certain way. The pictures can also help them consider certain interpretations. Seeing the two collections juxtaposed may enable students to realize why one might "match" and then read off the difference between the two collections. Hence, developing conceptually oriented explanations and establishing acceptable mathematical notation seem to be interrelated.

Some Reflections

Why are conceptually oriented explanations important for mathematical discussions? Conceptually oriented explanations give students opportunities to articulate, and give other students opportunities to understand, reasons for performing certain procedures. Students such as Porter had opportunities to think about the mathematical reasons behind Phil's procedures. If Phil had not been able to provide a conceptually oriented explanation, Porter might not have had a chance to understand Phil's thinking. Although our examples are taken from a first-grade classroom, we suggest that teachers and students at all elementary-grade levels can foster conceptually oriented explanations. Students who have been in classrooms in which conceptually oriented explanations are valued may continue to provide these types of explanations as they progress through the elementary grades. However, if students have not been in such classrooms, the teacher faces a special challenge. The older students are, the more accustomed they may have become to traditional school instruction. When a fourth-grade teacher, for example, first attempts to change her or his expectations for when and how students participate in discussions, she or he should expect resistance. Upper-elementary-grade students may not understand why the norms are being changed after they have been successful in previous classrooms with more traditional norms. Therefore, we suggest that upper-elementary-grade teachers explain to their students from the outset of the school year not only their new expectations for their students but also the reasons they value this kind of mathematical communication.

The longer students have participated in traditional instruction, the more time and effort the teacher may need to establish the type of problem-solving environment we advocate. Similar to our examples, upper–elementary-grade teachers must help students understand his or her expectations for their reasoning and explanations of their ideas. The teacher may have to illustrate students' ideas on the chalkboard and have the students refer to these representations as they explain their reasoning. As students become more comfortable with representing their ideas, the teacher's role may shift to that of highlighting the students' contributions. For instance, the teacher may ask the students to talk about why the pictures help them understand a classmate's thinking. With this question, she implicitly communicates that she values how they use their pictures to share their ideas. At other times, the teacher may explicitly communicate to the students that he or she likes how they show their thinking. During these types of discussions, the teacher and the students together establish norms for communicating and reasoning about mathematical ideas.

We conclude this section by offering one caveat. In the examples we described, the teacher always drew a picture and initiated discussion around it. However, students eventually began to draw pictures as a way to *solve problems* and to *communicate their reasoning to others.* Although tally marks, circles, and so on may help students communicate their ideas, the time may come when the teacher realizes that students default to using pictures to solve problems without considering other, more efficient methods. For this reason, the teacher must recognize these instances as junctures at which the class must reconstitute how to reason efficiently and elegantly. The teacher may need to initiate an explicit discussion in which she or he encourages students to draw pictures *only* if they are necessary. When possible, students should try to solve problems mentally or by using more efficient methods rather than by counting tally marks by ones. By reconsidering methods of solving problems and communicating their ideas, the teacher and students continue to establish sociomathematical norms for engaging in problem-solving activities.

Conclusion

Our discussion has pointed to the roles of the teacher and the students in building productive problem-solving environments in elementary-grade classrooms. As we have maintained throughout this chapter, the teacher and the students together create and sustain a community in which knowing and doing mathematics are continually supported as children engage in problem solving. In many classrooms, such as the one described in this study, the teacher and students create an environment in which the students are free to express their thinking. However, as we have indicated in this chapter, students generally share their *procedures* rather than their reasons for performing those procedures. Genuine problem solving is more than asking students, "How did you figure that out?" Although this question moves discussions beyond those heard in traditional classrooms, by asking these types of questions, the teacher may implicitly communicate to students that he or she values only the mathematical procedures they have performed. As we suggest in this chapter, the teacher and students can coestablish the social and sociomathematical norms that promote a problem-solving environment in which conceptually oriented explanations are valued. Environments in which such discussions take place make problem solving more accessible to all students.

Motivating Students to Engage in Problem Solving

Jennifer Strabala, sixth-grade teacher

In chapter 9 of this volume, Stephan and Whitenack point out that to "foster discussions that center on students' solution processes, the teacher and students must create and sustain a risk-free environment in which students' reasoning, not getting answers, is valued" (p. 149). Jenny Strabala's story illustrates how she realized that her job was to establish a classroom climate that motivates students to engage in real problem solving involving important mathematics. She describes an online pen-pal project with college students who were preparing to be teachers. Her "experiment" illustrates how even reluctant children can come to accept in the classroom social and sociomathematical norms that are much different from what they had experienced in the past. Through her project, over time, Jenny was able to establish a classroom norm in which students valued careful, detailed explanations of, and justifications for, their thinking. By requiring students to write explanations of their solutions to their college pen pals, Jenny found a way to get her students excited about problem solving, and, just as important, she got them to strive for clear mathematical writing and a deep understanding of mathematical ideas.

—Frank K. Lester Jr.

I N BEGINNING to plan for my sixth year of teaching sixth-grade mathematics, I was looking for ways to motivate my students to explore mathematical ideas in problem-solving settings. In these settings, I wanted to encourage my students to come up with their own ways of approaching and making sense of the mathematics, and I wanted those opportunities to be the means for discovering and learning the foundational mathematics topics in the sixth-grade curriculum. But I ran into some difficulties in getting this outcome to happen. Any given class seemed to contain very enthusiastic students who really enjoyed the freedom of being able to figure things out on their own; in the same class were students who had a much harder time with this type of learning. The ones who had the most difficulty were often the same ones who would ask me to tell them how to do it the "right" way. These students seemed to become easily frustrated, give up, sit back, and let other group members do all the tough thinking. I often heard complaints from students that "Johnny' doesn't do his part" or "I am doing all the work for my group, and the others aren't even trying." I had to find a way to motivate the ones who gave up too easily.

I discussed some of my frustrations with Professor Beatriz D'Ambrosio at Indiana University–Purdue University at Indianapolis (IUPUI). We decided to collaborate in an attempt to motivate some of these hard-to-reach students. We set up a partnership between two of my sixth-grade mathematics classes and Dr. D'Ambrosio's IUPUI class called "Math for Future Elementary Teachers." Through this partnership, each of my students was assigned an online pen pal—one of the college students—with whom they would discuss and write online letters about the group problem-solving activities we were doing in mathematics class. I hoped that this pen-pal experience would provide a meaningful, real-life mathematics learning experience while increasing individual accountability and participation. My students showed great enthusiasm; they seemed to take a lot of pride in the idea of having college partners. I heard such comments as "We are lucky" and "We must be smart."

The students were given their college partner's names; each college student was assigned one first-period student and one sixth-period student. I explained to my students that they would have to accept three very important responsibilities:

1. They would be given problem-solving tasks to work on in pairs or small groups. At the same time, their college student partners would work on the same problems. Partners would then write about their strategies for solving the problems and any difficulties that resulted from their efforts.

2. The college students would be allowed to ask them questions about their work.

3. They would write their own problems for their college partners to solve.

(For a more complete discussion of the college pen-pal project, see Tunc Pekkan [2002].)

Before giving them a problem to solve, I told the class that the next day they would each write an e-mail letter to their IUPUI partner about their strategy for solving the problem. We then tried a think-pair-share approach to the problem: I handed out the problem to each student and told them to spend five minutes on their own, silently trying to solve it *(think time)*; then they would have five minutes to discuss it with their seat partner *(pair time)*; and finally, they would have a chance to discuss solutions in groups of four and with the class *(share time)*. What follows are some of my observations and reflections on this approach to motivating students to engage in serious problem solving. The discussion makes reference to two problems, the "T-Shirt and Drink" problem and the "Birthday Money" problem:

T-Shirt and Drink Problem

> At the state fair, Felipe bought 2 T-shirts and two soft drinks for $44.00. Heather bought one T-shirt and 3 soft drinks and paid $30.00. How much does a T-shirt cost? How much is a soft drink? Explain how you got your answers. (National Center for Research in Mathematical Sciences Education and Freudenthal Institute 1998, p. 80)

Birthday Money Problem

> Carman received some money for her birthday on Friday. That night, she took her friend to dinner and spent half her money. Then she tipped the waiter $6. The next evening, she went to dinner alone, spent half of what she had left, and tipped the waiter $2. The next night, she went to dinner again, spent half of what she had left, and tipped the waiter $1. At this time she had $6 left. How much money did she get for her birthday? (Fesler 1995, p. 72)

From the beginning, I saw an increase in the students' motivation to solve the problems. And as the project progressed, many of the students became quite concerned about what they were going to write to their pen-pal partner—much more so than they had been when they had written for a more traditional class assignment. After pair time, I had several students share their solutions with the whole class, making sure that a variety of solutions were presented. As the students shared with the class, I noticed some students jotting down notes to help them remember the different strategies.

The first problem for which students were asked to write to their college pen pals was the T-Shirt and Drink problem. When I read the students' online messages about their solutions to this problem, I was pleased with how many of them made reference to another student's method of solving it. Kathy wrote, "We shared our ways of doing the problem, and I understood Mark's better than my own." I noticed that some students gave excellent, detailed descriptions of how they solved the problem; others gave almost no detail at all; and many others fell between these two categories.

For example, Jacob wrote the following:

> I just finished my T-shirt and drink problem. What did you get on it? I got $18.00 for a shirt and $4.00 for a drink. I got this by first dividing the 2 shirts and 2 drinks for $44 by 2, and got 1 drink and 1 shirt for $22. Then I thought of the one shirt and 3 drinks for $30 had 2 more drinks than the one that cost $22. Then I put that it cost $8.00 for 2 drinks because it cost $30 – $22 = $8. So I divided $8 by 2 and got $4 for one drink, then I subtracted $4 from $22 and got $18.

Jacob's writing is one of the more detailed first writing samples. He stated his answer and was very thorough about the process he used to arrive at his solution.

The following excerpt, from Libby's letter, is an example of one that gives some detail, but it definitely has room for improvement:

> I figured out that a drink costs $4.00. And a T-shirt costs $18.00. I figured this out using different combinations. My answer works because $18 \times 2 = 36$; $4 \times 2 = 8$, $36 + 8 = 44$. And $4 \times 3 = 12$; $12 + 18 = 30$.

Although she told how she knew that this answer worked, she did not discuss how she arrived at her solution. Aaron gave even less detail when he wrote, "My answer is $4.00 for a drink and $18.00 for the shirts. Is that what you got?"

After reading their first attempts at communicating with their partners, I could see that their explanations left plenty of room for improvement. I decided that we needed to discuss what I expected in their writing. I told them that their focus should be on their thinking and how they solved the problem, not on the answer. I went on to tell them, "Even if you can't find the answer, you still can write about your thinking and what you tried, how you know it didn't work, what you learned from these attempts, and so on...." I read some samples to the class to demonstrate detailed writing and not-so-detailed writing.

A couple of weeks after we had this talk clarifying my expectations for their writing, I read the following letter from David to his partner regarding the Birthday Money problem:

I couldn't find out the answer to the problem, but here is how I tried to find out; first, I used $20. I took half—which made $10. I could see from there I was not going to have enough. Then I tried $30. I took half—which made $15. I took $6 away and got $9. It isn't enough. Next I used $100 and I took half, and it made $50. I took $6 away, and it made $44.

I was happy to see that David was attempting to describe his thought processes, even though he had not been successful in finding an answer. He seemed to grasp the idea that working on mathematics problems is not just about having the correct answer. This realization was progress.

As the project continued, I noticed a huge decrease in complaints regarding someone's not doing his or her part. Students knew that they would each have to write a letter to their partner about how they arrived at their answer and why their solution worked.

As the experience progressed, I witnessed students' spending much more time analyzing why a solution works the way it does and striving for a deeper understanding of the mathematics. In her journal, Karen wrote, "By explaining it, I understood what happens, more than just calculating it." In a letter to her pen pal, Emily noted, "I really like this program. First of all, it is fun, and second of all, it makes you think about why answers are the way they are instead of just there." Libby wrote, "I have to think really hard before I write anything." This statement was gratifying because my main goal was to get students to think hard, at deeper levels. This partnership seemed to be doing just that—it was motivating students to really think about things, really analyze problems.

I also observed that some students were becoming much more reluctant to give up when they struggled; they were motivated to figure things out to please their partners and feel good about what they wrote. The IUPUI pen pals provided them with a real audience. Karen wrote, "They seemed like they really cared about what we said." Having partners to whom to write gave purpose to their writing. The interaction between partners was a vital part of increasing learning and motivation.

I noticed, too, that questions from their partners seemed to boost the sixth graders' motivation to be more detailed in their writing. In one of Libby's letters to her partner, she wrote, "I don't remember how I did the locker problem—sorry. This time I am writing about the checkerboard problem, and I will try to explain it better so you can understand."

I have finally found a way to get my students animated about problem solving and to strive for clear mathematical writing and a deep understanding of mathematical ideas. After witnessing the enthusiasm and learning this project generated among my students, I strongly recommend it to other interested teachers.

CHAPTER 10

Addressing the Needs of Exceptional Students through Problem Solving

Carmel M. Diezmann
Carol A. Thornton
James J. Watters

A CENTRAL theme of this volume is that learning with understanding occurs when problems are posed that are just within students' reach, allowing them to struggle to find solutions. To provide worthwhile problem-solving experiences for all students in the classroom, we teachers should pay particular attention to the needs of exceptional students, those with learning difficulties as well as those who are gifted in mathematics. To achieve this goal, we need to understand the characteristics of exceptional students and employ strategies that will engage them productively in problem-solving tasks.

In the following section, we briefly describe those characteristics that define exceptionality. We then address the prime aim of this chapter: how to tailor mathematics instruction to meet the needs of exceptional students. For students with learning difficulties, this approach involves teaching students compensatory strategies and making instructional modifications. For gifted students, teachers should employ strategies that extend students' learning beyond the regular curriculum for their age.

Characteristics of Exceptional Students

What are the specific characteristics of exceptional students that affect learning mathematics through problem solving?

Most classrooms contain students who have serious learning difficulties that impede their mathematical learning. Many of these students cannot attend to, or stay on, a task. They often learn at a slower pace and may be seriously distracted by the noise or the number of students in a regular classroom. Some have difficulty with retention, whereas others have abstract-reasoning, visual- or auditory-processing, or perceptual deficits that make learning difficult for them. Furthermore, students with memory or processing difficulties do not readily retrieve or employ appropriate solution strategies in new problem contexts (Montague 1998). Such students are mathematically "at risk" because they have never learned accessible, effective cognitive strategies, such as visualizing, paraphrasing, or generalizing, for approaching problem solving (Bley and Thornton 2001; Montague 1998).

Other students are distinguished by the high quality of their mathematical thinking. These gifted students are usually passionate about mathematics and have an extraordinary capacity for learning it (House 1987). Naturally, the extent to which gifted students display these characteristics varies. Often, mathematically gifted students are referred to as "mathematically talented," "highly able," having "a mathematical cast of mind," or "mathematically promising." Although gifted students are predisposed toward high performance and creative achievement, they are "at risk" and may underachieve when boredom or lack of challenge affects their interest in, enjoyment of, and long-term commitment to learning mathematics (Sheffield 1999).

To ensure that both groups of exceptional students engage in optimal and enjoyable learning experiences, their instruction should include rich, well-constructed tasks (Stenmark 1991; Van de Walle, this volume) that problematize mathematics (Russell et al., this volume), deepen their mathematical understanding (Lambdin, this volume), and create interest (Russell et al., this volume).

Optimizing Instructional Opportunities for Exceptional Students

Which instructional strategies are particularly appropriate for exceptional students?

Although students vary in their capacity to learn through problem solving, students with learning difficulties and those who are gifted have markedly different learning trajectories from each other and from regular students. Thus, in addition to instructional strategies that benefit all students (Lambdin, this volume), teachers should adopt specific strategies that address the considerable differences in exceptional students' knowledge and skills, their capacity for learning, and the time they require to complete tasks successfully. Students with learning difficulties benefit from compensatory strategies and instructional modifications; gifted students benefit from extension strategies. In the following sections, we discuss several strategies and modifications that we have found to be especially useful for helping all students achieve deep, rich understanding of mathematics.

Compensatory Strategies and Instructional Modifications

Compensatory strategies. Students with learning disabilities or other serious learning difficulties need to learn and use strategies that enable them to better understand and retain important mathematical concepts and apply mathematical skills. Teachers should (1) strategize with individual students to help them recognize how they learn best, and (2) encourage students to use their learning strengths to compensate for specific learning difficulties.

Although compensatory strategies needed by individuals are as different as their specific learning needs, several powerful strategies can benefit virtually all students with identified learning needs (Bley and Thornton 2001; Montague 1998). Research has shown, and our own experiences have demonstrated, that these strategies include, but are not limited to, opportunity and time for students to do the following:

- Use the learning approach that best suits their unique *learning needs* in problem situations—visual (color highlighting, drawing a simple diagram), auditory (verbalizing to internalize learning), or kinesthetic-tactile (finger tracing, using manipulatives).

- Communicate and record their thinking and solution approaches in a way that suits their idiosyncratic *learning style and strengths,* using actions, symbols, words, or manipulatives. In some way, perhaps by using a buddy system, specific links must be made between what is said, manipulated, and written during a task.

- Rephrase a task or problem *in their own words* or summarize what others have reported, because virtually all these students need to *hear themselves speak* so they can understand and retain ideas.

In addition, the following compensatory strategies accommodate specific learning needs that are very common in mathematics classrooms in prekindergarten through sixth grade today:

- Students who have attention deficits, especially those who are hyperactive, need legitimate excuses for moving about. These students benefit from more active learning and response strategies. As teachers we should accommodate students with attention deficits, for example, when we ask for hand signals as part of a response (e.g., "Use your hands to show whether we add or multiply: + or ×"; "Finger trace the answer in the air"; "Show thumbs up if you agree"). In severe cases, providing a soft rubber sponge for these students to squeeze while they wait for, or listen to, others is helpful.

- Students with sequential or short-term memory difficulties benefit when teachers help them create an indexed, annotated journal of "Types of math problems I can solve" as a reference for future work and review.

- Students with abstract reasoning or reading difficulties need to simplify and personalize written problems and tasks so that they clearly understand the meaning. Allowing extra time for these students to make "shorthand" notes that summarize *what I know* about this problem or task and *what I want to find out or do* is extremely helpful. Assigning a buddy to read the problem enables the student to make notes during the reading. The idea is to isolate relevant information from what may be, from the student's perspective, a complicated written statement so that the meaning is clear. Understanding is the stepping-stone to formulating a solution strategy or successfully carrying out the task.

Instructional modifications. Teachers can modify their instruction to accommodate specific learning differences among students in their classrooms (Bley and Thornton 2001; Goldman, Hasselbring, and the Cognition and Technology Group at Vanderbilt 1998; Thornton and Jones, 1996). Such modifications are essential for complementing and supporting compensatory strategies that students use to enhance their learning of mathematics. These modifications are as numerous and idiosyncratic as the creativity of dedicated teachers. Unless otherwise noted, such strategies include, but are not limited to, the following, which have proved useful for virtually all students with serious learning needs:

- Assigning fewer but more carefully selected problems
- Selecting problems and tasks that different students can approach in ways that suit their learning strengths
- Providing more time or different materials, to which a child might better relate, for completing a task
- Routinely calling on individual students to use their own words to rephrase the gist of a problem or task
- Asking students to share responses or explain solutions with a partner, then calling on the special education student to share what was heard
- Allowing students to write on a slate or at the board instead of on paper (especially those with vision, visual perception, or spatial-motor deficits)
- Using the buddy system, (especially for students with reading, memory, physical, or sensory difficulties)
- Breaking tasks into smaller parts and requiring students to report in as each part is finished (especially for children with memory, organization, or attention deficits)
- Allowing students to work in a secluded workspace (especially for those with auditory perception or attention deficits)

Many of these ideas—whether compensatory strategies used by students or instructional modifications employed by teachers—do in fact "work" for other students. Although these strategies and modifications are *helpful* to many students, they are *essential* for the student with a specially identified learning difficulty. Furthermore, while making full use of compensatory strategies and instructional modifications, only by engaging these special needs students in mathematical problem tasks *just beyond* their immediate grasp will we provide the stretch that allows these students to reach their learning potential.

This notion of "stretch" precisely defines making mathematics problematic for students and highlights the fact that, in a very real sense, important learning goals are the same for special education students as for all students. Because many students with learning disabilities or other serious learning difficulties have experienced only procedural rather than problem-centered instructional approaches in mathematics (Thornton and Jones 1996), they do not expect to learn mathematics any other way than through imitation. More than with other students, if we want to nurture mathematical thinking in special education students, we should repeatedly challenge these students to think and provide them with strategies that enable them to think. For all students, learning is a struggle, but compensatory strategies and instructional modifications can help students with learning difficulties learn important mathematics within the limits of their specific abilities.

For example, one third-grade inclusion teacher we have worked with reflected on her lesson that involved reviewing and redeveloping the basic concept of fractions. She noted,

> Initially, my students modeled and discussed situations involving equal shares of food, and they verbally identified or wrote matching fractions for each situation. Some students responded by using a finger to trace fractions in the air, after which I recorded their tracings on the chalkboard. Other times I wrote words (3 out of 4 equal pieces) while recording verbal responses. I then posed such problems as "3/4 of the dozen eggs were brown; the rest were white. How many were white?" The special education teacher had asked some students near her to *restate the problem* verbally and prompted others to write their own "shorthand" version of the problem. Most students intuitively understood and, using counters, demonstrated their recognition that the problem called for 4 equal-sized groups, and 3 of these groups were brown—so 1 group (3 eggs) was white. Because I knew that students needed to verbalize their thinking, I asked the children to explain to their partner how they solved the problem. I then asked them to use sentences to write their solutions, compare solutions with their partner, and then work together to create (and write an answer key for) similar problems for sharing the next day.

In this example, which used a teaching-mathematics-through-problem-solving approach, special education students with memory and abstract-reasoning difficulties benefited when they were asked to restate the problem in their own words. These students and others with reading, figure-ground, and other visual-perception difficulties also benefited when challenged to make their own shorthand notes of the important facts in the problem—what was known and what they were to find out. The visual-tactile and active-learning approaches embedded in the lesson (e.g., finger tracing, using counters to model, verbalizing solutions, and creating similar problems) addressed the needs of ADHD (attention deficit hyperactivity disorder) students and others with attention deficits.

Note that in the example, the teacher engaged the students by working with fraction problems similar to the dozen-eggs problem. The power of using similar problems emerged again during a recent seminar conducted by one of the coauthors for second-grade teachers in a teacher enhancement project. In this seminar, several teachers reported that they had based lessons on the following two types of place-value problems:

- Mom made 36 doughnuts and packed them, 10 to a box. How many boxes did she fill? Were there any extra ones? (This type of problem starts with a two-digit number and asks students to partition the number into 10's and 1's.)

- Erica's dad bought candy bars for her birthday party. He got 6 bags and put 10 candy bars in each bag. There were 2 extras, so he gave them to Erica. How many candy bars did Dad buy? (This type of problem starts with 10's and 1's and asks for a two-digit number.)

One teacher explained that she had revisited place value using these types of problems because she realized that many students in her inclusion class did not have a good understanding of two-digit numbers. She further commented that her earlier teaching had been more traditional and she wanted to try a problem-based approach.

The lesson that the teacher focused on involved problems similar to the doughnut problem previously described. During the lesson, the teacher presented the students with several problems of this type, and students created and shared other similar problems. In all instances, the children solved problems using cubes (10-trains and 1's), recorded their solutions, then compared and discussed their solutions with a partner. During the lesson wrap-up, students' solutions to four problems were placed on the board and shared more broadly. When the teacher (pointing to 36 in the doughnut problem) asked, "Where are the three boxes of ten doughnuts in this number?" Aisha, a child with abstract-reasoning difficulties, called out, "Oh! The 3 is the tens and the 6 are the extra ones." The teacher then showed Aisha's daily mathematics log entry, in which Aisha had written about the tens and ones in "36," her solution to the doughnut problem.

Aisha, like several of her peers, had not previously internalized any real understanding of the tens or ones places in two-digit numbers. The problems posed in class that day had repeatedly provided a context to which Aisha could relate. They challenged her to think deeply about tens and ones to solve each problem, provided time and opportunity for her to use materials to illustrate the similar story lines, and required her to compare and discuss her written solutions with a carefully selected buddy. In other words, within the context of meaningful, similar problems, the structure of the lesson allowed students like Aisha to use compensatory strategies necessary for learning while making specific links among what they *did* (with manipulatives), what they *said*, and what they *wrote*. By the end of this lesson, for the first time, Aisha demonstrated real understanding of place value in two-digit numbers.

A further example of the effectiveness of compensatory strategies emerged during a seminar with fourth-grade teachers led by one of the coauthors. One team of teachers from an inclusion classroom reported how they had targeted ten students in their class, none of whom were consistently able to determine when to add, subtract, multiply, or divide in a problem situation. Five of these students had abstract-reasoning, visual-perception, or memory disabilities; two had attention deficits; and the other three had done quite poorly in mathematics even though their psychological screening scores were too high to qualify them for special education intervention.

The teachers reported how they had started with part-total problems and used the approach suggested by figure 10.1. The students were asked to make their own shorthand notes as they read each problem, so as to isolate the important information, then to complete a part-total box to match their notes. They then counted, used manipulatives or a calculator to solve the problem, and recorded the matching number sentence. When students did not know which operation to use, they tried several operations and reenacted the problem to see which one made sense.

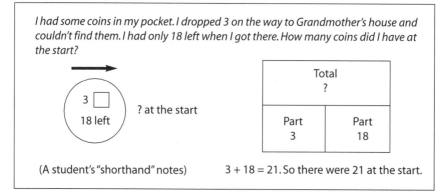

Fig. 10.1. The coin problem with "shorthand" notes, and part-total box

The students were then asked to sort the problems into two piles, those in which the part was needed and those in which the total was needed; examine the matching number sentence for each; discuss patterns they noted; and record these patterns on a class poster. Dealing with just addition or subtraction problems, students noted the patterns boxed in figure 10.2. On subsequent days, the think bubbles were added to the poster to account for the multiplication or division patterns that students noted in these types of problems. The teachers shared several students' mathematics logs that had personal versions of the class posters. Rafel, who had visual-perception problems, and Mei, who had short-term-memory deficits, had both been encouraged to use color to highlight important parts of their posters.

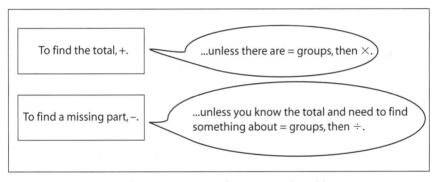

Fig. 10.2. Students' classroom poster for part-total problems

The teachers reported that within two weeks, six of the ten students were consistently successful with all types of part-total problems. The teachers believed that with added experience, the others would soon come around. They believed that the focus on similar examples and the challenge to articulate recurring patterns—coupled with other modifications and compensatory strategies—were helping these ten students internalize and retain the basic patterns in part-total problems, regardless of the operation. The teachers intended to use a similar approach to address "compare" problems.

The strategies displayed in these examples involving inclusion classrooms are idiosyncratic to the requirements of the special needs students in these classes. Similar strategies, employed in every classroom in which students struggle to learn, are characteristic of problem-centered teaching and go a long way toward making learning through problem solving an effective reality for these students.

Extension Strategies

Gifted students can often complete regular classroom tasks with ease because of their exceptional capacity for learning mathematics and their rapidity of learning. Hence, teachers should implement *extension* strategies with these students to provide them with opportunities to "stretch" their thinking and efforts beyond the level at which they are currently working. Extension strategies take into account gifted students' relatively advanced knowledge and rapid learning by modifying the content and pacing of the curriculum (Rogers 2002). Successful extension strategies for the mathematically gifted include curriculum compacting, acceleration, and enrichment (Johnson 1994).

Curriculum compacting. This strategy involves a variation in the pacing of the curriculum that recognizes students' prior knowledge and learning capacity (Reis and Purcell 1993). As gifted students will generally achieve the desired curriculum outcomes faster than their same-age peers, the time saved enables these students to do more productive work, thereby fostering their creative interest in mathematics. This "free time" can be used particularly effectively when clusters of gifted students work at a level beyond that of their same-age peers to share and critique one another's problem-solving methods (Benbow 1998). Clustering gifted children is important because these students often complain that their ideas are neither understood nor valued by nongifted classmates.

For example, when a group of six gifted students selected from sixth-grade and seventh-grade classes worked together in their free time, they were able to apply and integrate knowledge in a problem about a power outage (Diezmann and Watters 2001). After all students had attempted the problem with various degrees of success, Rachel shared an elegant solution (see fig. 10.3), which became the subject of much discussion at a sophisticated level.

Rachel did this problem in three steps. First she converted the actual time (5:21) on the wind-up clock to twenty-four-hour time (17:21). Then she worked out what time the power came back on again by subtracting the six hours and three minutes the power was off from 17:21. Rachel knew that the power had been off for six hours and three minutes because the digital electric clock, which resets to midnight when the power goes off, showed 6:03. Next Rachel worked out what time the power went off. She calculated this time by subtracting the six hours and three minutes the power was off from the time on the analog electric clock of 3:50, which she also converted to twenty-four-hour time (15:50). Unlike

One day while I was at school, the electricity went out at home. When I left for swim practice that morning, all the clocks were working and agreed that the time was 6:30. When I got home they all said different times. The wind-up clock, which was unaffected by the electricity, read 5:21. The analog electric clock stops running when you unplug it from the wall, and it starts up where it left off when you plug it back in. The clock said it was 3:50. My digital electric clock, which resets itself to midnight when the electricity goes out, flashes until you correct the time. It was flashing 6:03 a.m. Assuming the electricity went out just once, what time did it go out, and how long was it off? (The Math Forum @Drexel, 2001)

17.21	15.50	11.18
− 6.03	− 6.03	− 9.47
11.18	9.47	1.31

The power went off at 9:47 a.m. and came back on at 11:18 a.m. It was off for 1 hour 31 minutes.

Fig. 10.3. Rachael's solution to the power-outage problem

the digital clock, the analog electric clock did not reset itself but recommenced functioning when power was restored. Finally, Rachel had worked out that the power came on at 11:18 and went off at 9:47, she subtracted these times and determined that the power had been off for one hour and thirty-one minutes. Rather than be deterred by the challenge of this task, the students agreed that the problem was enjoyable *because it was difficult.*

Thus, in this example, the special needs of the gifted children were met in a number of ways. First, having completed the tasks set for the regular classroom, the students had achieved an understanding of the current topic. Instead of wasting time and becoming bored or frustrated while the teacher assisted other students, the gifted students responded to the challenge of a new task that was problematic. These students also had opportunities to share their strategies with peers who were capable of contributing crucial input to the discussion. Finally, the new task generated intense interest and motivation among the gifted students.

Acceleration. This strategy involves providing gifted students with advanced tasks that are commensurate with their capability. Gifted students often commence a topic with more advanced conceptual knowledge than their nongifted peers. Individual gifted students or groups can work on an accelerated program within a grade level, or gifted students might work with nongifted students from a higher grade level. In the following example (see fig. 10.4), the teacher realized that although division with remainders was challenging for most students in this grade, it was too easy for the gifted students. Once the students had agreed that in the regular task Justin would also get a share of the sweets, they had no difficulty with the calculations. Because of the students' ease in completing the regular task, the teacher problematized the division task by replacing the wording "4 of his friends" with "up to 5 friends," omitting the numerical parameters for the solution of "between 10 and 20 sweets," and including the wording "least number" to focus students' attention on finding a particular number to suit the specification. The students were told that the packet could contain any number of sweets. This change in wording from the regular task to the problematized task had two implications. First, the students had to find a number that was divisible by 2, 3, 4, 5, and 6 to accommodate the possibility that Justin might have to share the sweets with between 1 and 5 friends. Thus the students were no longer working on a relatively simple division problem involving a small remainder but on a more advanced division problem that involved the divisibility of a set of numbers. Second, because the students had to find the lowest number that was divisible by the numbers between 2 and 6 inclusive, they had to explore patterns and relationships in numbers. Most of these gifted students initially attempted this task by guessing numbers and then checking their guesses. Some students focused on the wording "least number" and started by guessing low numbers, whereas others started by guessing three-digit numbers that they knew were multiples of each of the numbers in the range, such as 120. Irrespective of their initial approach, all students quickly realized that they needed to work systematically, record the outcomes of their trials, and use their knowledge of divisibility. For example, after a few unsuccessful guesses, one pair of girls realized that the answer had to be a multiple of 10 to be divisible by both 2 and 5. They then systematically tested the multiples of 10 in ascending order and checked whether they were divisible by 3, 4, and 6, recording their findings as they went until they reached the solution of sixty sweets.

Problematizing a task shifts a regular task just out of the reach of gifted students and makes the students *think* (Diezmann and Watters 2000). Thus, instead of the regular division task, which was quite straightforward for gifted students, the problematized division task engaged these students in an exploration of the divisibility of various numbers and the creation of a recording format to keep track of their investigations. Although these students were gifted, none of them realized that they could check whether a number was divisible by 2, 3 and 6 by simply checking

Regular task: Justin has between 10 and 20 sweets. If he shares all of them among **4 of his friends,** he will have 2 left over. How many sweets could he have had?	Problematized task: What would be the **least number** of sweets in a bag if Justin could share his sweets exactly with **up to 5 friends**?

Fig. 10.4. The regular sweets task and the modified sweets task

whether it was divisible by 6. Hence, the problematized task offered additional scope for more sophisticated mathematical thinking.

Enrichment. A third extension strategy, enrichment, provides an opportunity for gifted students to engage in mathematically rich problems that are beyond the scope of the regular curriculum. These problems may be based on students' interests, or they may provide students with an opportunity to explore a variety of mathematically oriented topics, such as famous mathematicians, mathematical discoveries, mathematics in other cultures, or applications of mathematics in other subjects. For example, a group of six- to eight-year-old gifted students who were interested in space travel were having difficulty understanding the distance of the stars from the earth because of the large numbers involved and the unfamiliar term light years that was used in books and multimedia materials. Understanding large distances in space is quite mathematically complex and requires a sound understanding of place value; an appreciation that time—namely, light years—is used as the measure of distance; and an awareness of the speed of light. Although these topics are generally beyond the curriculum for young children, the gifted students' interest in space travel provided the incentive for them to learn about large numbers.

The teacher capitalized on these students' interest in space through an enrichment activity about the relative position of stars in space. She created a number line on the floor with masking tape and marked off hundreds of light years. The teacher also attached the names and distances of the ten brightest stars to upturned paper cups that the students could easily move about. The teacher challenged the students to work together and place these stars in the correct location on the number line. Although the students could easily count by hundreds, some students had difficulty determining where stars marked with particular distances should be placed on the number line. This task was problematic because the number line was marked only in hundreds of light years, whereas the numbers on the stars included tens and ones. This difference meant that students had to decide which pair of consecutive hundreds each star lay between and then determine exactly where to place the star to reflect its proximity to the closest hundred. For example, a star marked with 231 light years should be placed closest to the 200 and approximately one-third of the distance between 200 and 300. Students also had to compare and order numbers that were between the same pair of hundreds on the number line. The children were very interested in this problem and worked hard to solve it. After completing a series of large-number problems, including this number-line task, the students were able to use large numbers more meaningfully in their discussions about space travel. Although this task would be too challenging for most students of this age, the gifted students' learning from these problems bridged the gap between the mathematics that they already knew and the mathematics that they needed to know to gain some understanding of distances in space. Thus, these experiences enhanced the students' capacity to reason mathematically within the context of space travel.

Concluding Comments

Exceptional children have special needs that must be accommodated in planning and implementing the curriculum. A problem-solving approach provides exceptional students with learning opportunities for thinking and reasoning mathematically. This approach contributes to the development of mathematical literacy in students with learning difficulties and provides the foundation for gifted students to become creative mathematical thinkers. In both groups of students, problem solving provides the mathematical stretch for these students to reach their learning potential more readily.

Meeting the needs of exceptional students in the regular classroom is challenging. Teaching and learning through problem solving, however, is a powerful medium for responding to this challenge—one that must be met if we are to achieve a mathematically literate society and support those with an orientation toward mathematical careers.

Supporting Second-Language Learners in the Mathematics Classroom

Jan Rook, fourth-grade teacher

Working on significant mathematical problems requires a great deal from young students. If teachers take seriously the charge of the NCTM *Principles and Standards for School Mathematics* (2000) that "reasonable and appropriate accommodations be made as needed to promote access and attainment for all students" (p. 12), then creating a class in which all students participate in problem solving requires a great deal from teachers as well. Developing general pedagogical strategies that help students learn mathematics is not sufficient. As Diezmann and her colleagues point out in chapter 10, teachers must reflect on the particular students and groups represented in the classroom and develop approaches to support the range of learners' needs. This range almost certainly includes students who are struggling with mathematics as well as students who are strong problem solvers. The class may also include students with special needs and students from a variety of cultural and language groups. As Jan Rook focuses her attention on the bilingual students in her classroom, she finds that helping her students and herself articulate ideas about responsibility and support benefits the learning of all her students.

—Susan Jo Russell

O NE OF the issues that I have been thinking about a great deal this year is how to support second-language learners in my mathematics class. This year, for the first time, our school has opted to integrate all bilingual students in the fourth and fifth grade into the English-speaking classes. In the past, students who had achieved a certain level of expertise in English were gradually integrated into the monolingual (English) classes. So this year, more than half my class is made up of students coming directly from the third-grade bilingual class. These students return each day to the bilingual fourth-grade teacher for a two-hour literacy block in which they receive instruction in both English and Spanish. However, they are in my class for the rest of the day, including for mathematics.

In my classroom, I expect students to become serious mathematical thinkers. They are not spoon-fed a series of algorithms and asked to memorize them—the approach through which I was taught and by which I taught for many years. The students are required to be thoughtful, to work with peers, and to develop their own ideas through the problems they are working on. They are required to respect one another's work, to try to understand the thinking of their peers, to question, and to participate fully. In establishing these expectations, I am asking a lot of nine- and ten-year-olds.

Students whose primary language is not English can work in this type of environment, but their needs must be recognized for them to work successfully. Think of the difficulty faced by students, especially in the beginning of the year, in tackling difficult concepts involving number when they are constantly translating what they hear in English back into Spanish, trying to make sense of it in Spanish, and then translating it back again into English so that they can be part of the group discussion. No wonder that for the first few months of this year, less than half my class seemed to participate. It took me a while to realize what was going on. When I asked some of the bilingual students what language they were thinking in, most said Spanish. Sometimes we assume that because second-language learners can speak English, they also think in English. Much of the time, they do not. The transition takes a long, long time.

So how did I adjust? First, we talked about the situation as a class. We talked about the responsibilities of the students and came to the following agreements:

1. To be respectful to everyone—our number-1 rule

2. To listen to one another—and listen hard

3. To be sure that everyone in the group is involved, and if they are not, to try to help them get and stay involved

4. To respect themselves enough to say they do not understand a concept when they do not, to take responsibility for their own understanding, and to be sure that they are heard

5. If someone's, anyone's, idea is not clear to the class, to help the presenter by asking for further explanation, a rewording, or some other means of clarification

6. To have the courage to speak up, especially when they may not be totally clear about their ideas, and to know that when they do, their ideas will be respected

7. To not be hard on themselves if they do make a mistake, because mistakes are part of learning

This discussion also made me think hard about my responsibilities to the class—what I need to do to support the bilingual students and other students who have a difficult time processing in English. As I made a list of my own responsibilities, I realized that some of the things on my list are what I should be doing for all the students in my class. For example, I want to make sure that the environment of the class is one of acceptance and respect, to bring the group together physically when having a group discussion to help focus students' attention, to use concrete representations and drawings more often, and to walk around the room more so as to stay in touch with the students as they work.

Also on the list are ideas that I thought would particularly support the bilingual students. I need to continually express my understanding that learning in another language is hard, especially when the concepts and ideas are difficult. I need to be clear and specific in my directions and to go over the vocabulary in a problem so that everyone understands it, asking the students to reword the problem to check their understanding. Recently I talked about a "case of soda," and many students did not know the word *case*. I should speak clearly and slowly, summarize and review more frequently, and allow a much longer wait time before accepting answers, thus allowing students who are thinking in Spanish or who take longer to process the problem an equal opportunity to respond. I have tried having students not raise their hands when they are ready to respond but to signal me with their eyes or their hands. This method has helped because often when the faster students raise their hands, the rest of the class stops thinking.

Finally, I need to be willing to laugh at myself when I make a mistake—which happens all too often!—and should allow the students to do the same. And, maybe most important, I want to work at being sure that I understand a student's thinking and, if I do not—which also happens often!—that I respect them enough to try to get at the root of what they are saying, even if it is a long and gnarled root.

CHAPTER 11

Engaging Students in Problem Posing in an Inquiry-Oriented Mathematics Classroom

Lyn D. English

PROBLEM posing—like its companion, problem solving—is a fundamental part of learning and doing mathematics. It is involved in creating new problems from old ones, as well as in reformulating given problems. Also like problem solving, problem posing is a natural part of our everyday lives. Each day, we face situations in which we need to interpret what is happening, question why and how it has happened, decide which of several options to take, and think through possible consequences of our actions. One can view the role of problem posing in the mathematics classroom from two perspectives: the perspective of the teacher and the perspective of the student.

The first perspective is that of the teacher who endeavors to teach mathematics through problem solving. Fundamental to teaching mathematics through problem solving are two assumptions: (1) deep, rich understanding of mathematics is the primary goal of instruction, and (2) understanding is best fostered through solving problems (see Lambdin, chapter 1, this volume). In practice, acceptance of these two assumptions means that teachers must design or choose truly problematic tasks for their students; that is, a primary role of the teacher is one of problem poser. The teacher-as-problem-poser perspective is nicely articulated in this volume in chapters by Van de Walle (chapter 5) and by Russell and her colleagues (chapter 6). Consequently, in this chapter, I focus on the other perspective, namely, the student-as-problem-poser.

The Student-as-Problem-Poser Perspective

We see problem posing in children's play when they create and respond to "what-if" scenarios and when they construct various questions and conjectures in their efforts to make sense of mathematics. Although problem posing occurs in many facets of students' lives, its use in the mathematics classroom continues to receive inadequate recognition and emphasis in spite of the fact that its partner—problem solving—is accepted as integral to children's mathematical growth (NCTM 2000). Traditionally, problem posing has been defined as the creation of a new problem from a given situation or experience, with this creation taking place before, during, or after solving a problem (Brown and Walter 1993; Silver 1994). These days, the nature and role of problem posing within the mathematics classroom is seen in broader terms, with problem-posing processes taking place when children participate in investigative activities of all kinds.

Problem posing is not confined to any single topic area, nor is it a "special event" activity. Rather, problem posing contributes directly to students' learning of important mathematical ideas and structures with a "deep, rich understanding" (Hiebert, this volume, p. 53). As such, problem posing is a fundamental component of the curriculum and goes hand-in-hand with problem solving. The challenge that we as teachers face is determining how to foster in the classroom a disposition toward problem posing that promotes children's ability to think mathematically. In this chapter, I offer some suggestions for meeting this challenge. I begin by considering the nature of classroom learning environments that foster problem posing. I then consider how the act of problem posing (a) promotes students' conceptual development, (b) plays a crucial role in students' understanding of problem structure and design, and (c) enhances students' access to important mathematics.

Inquiry-Oriented Learning Communities

In establishing inquiry-oriented classrooms, many educators emphasize the importance of "environments for collaborative mathematical thinking" (Stein, Silver, and Smith [1998, p. 19]; see also Cobb and Bowers [1999]). In particular, the authors of two other chapters in this volume discuss issues associated with establishing a classroom environment that is conducive to collaborative inquiry (Russell et al., chapter 6; Stephan and Whitenack, chapter 9). In such environments, situations that are problematic for students are the norm. Both the children and the teachers ask important mathematical questions as they explore these situations. Children participate in constructive dialogue and debate and readily explain, clarify, and revise their mathematical ideas and constructions.

Learning communities of this nature invite children to express their perceptions of, and dispositions toward, mathematics, mathematical problems, and problem solving and posing. As part of their discussions, children can identify some problem situations that they have met in familiar places, such as at the school canteen, at sporting events, and in their homes. They can describe their problems, explain why they were problems, and tell what they did in their efforts to solve them. As a consequence, children become more aware of different types of problems, how they arise, and approaches to solving them. They also gain confidence in dealing with a wider range of problem types (Brown and Walter 1993). Furthermore, as children express their thoughts, teachers gain valuable insights into their students' mathematical development.

Promoting Conceptual Development

In a curriculum in which problem posing is a natural learning tool, children are more likely to generate interesting and varied responses to open-ended statements. For example, in one fifth-grade class in which problem posing was emphasized, I asked the students, "Is 498 – 247 a problem?" Their answers varied, with some children saying, "It would be if it had an equals sign." When I asked why, one student explained, "Because that could be '498 to 247,' but if you put an equals sign on the end, that would probably make it a minus." The student subsequently created a problem using this interpretation: "If you take that as 498 to 247, say if the police searched rooms 247 to 498 (I just swapped the numbers around to make them work) and there was an average of three people per room, how many people did they search?"

Problem posing with open-ended statements that comprise numerical and nonnumerical information is also effective in fostering conceptual and computational flexibility. Asking children to convert such statements into mathematical problems provides them with many opportunities to create a wide range of situations, as well as incorporate further mathematical ideas. For example, I presented the following example to a sixth-grade class:

> At the end of the day, Crusty Bakehouse had 27 fruit loaves, 15 bread rolls, and 10 sliced loaves on its shelves.

When I asked children if these statements were problems, some children related them to real life, explaining, "Yes, they are, because obviously Crusty Bakehouse wants to make some money. And if they have 27 fruit loaves, 15 bread rolls, and 10 sliced loaves left on their shelves, they probably aren't making business that well." Given the concern for the financial state of the bakehouse, one child created this multistep problem:

> If Crusty Bakehouse usually sold 40 fruit loaves, 20 bread rolls, and 100 sliced loaves a day, and the fruit loaves were sold for $6 each and bread rolls were sold for $3 each and sliced loaves sold for $2.50 each, how much money did they lose on an average day?

Exploring travel advertisements and mathematical or scientific reports that comprise interesting mathematical information is also an enjoyable and effective way of enriching students' understanding of important mathematics concepts. One advertisement, taken from a daily newspaper that I have used successfully with children, appears in figure 11.1. Children love to investigate these real-world situations as they pose questions about the various travel options, compare the costs involved, consider the time durations, and create appealing questions and problems for their peers to try.

Understanding Problem Structure and Design

New problem experiences, whether they draw on number, geometry, measurement, or other core domains, initially require children to interpret and construct meaning from the information presented. Problem-posing processes come into play as children try to *(a)* distinguish the important from the unimportant data, and *(b)* detect the mathematical structure, or what Walter and Goldenberg (2003) refer to as the "anatomy" of the problem, that is, the important facts and relationships embedded in the problem situation.

Children need assistance in recognizing the mathematical structure of a given problem and also require guidance in detecting corresponding structures in related problems. This guidance enables them to use their understanding of one problem to help them formulate and solve new problems, a process that involves reasoning by analogy (English 1999). Although children reason analogically in everyday activities (English, in press), they need guidance in doing so in classroom problem solving and problem posing. Much research shows that children have difficulty identifying problems with similar structures or similar solution proce-

Sit back and relax on a luxurious coach tour of the great sights and sounds of the real AUSTRALIA!

OUTBACK QUEENSLAND

18 Day Beef, Reef & Rainforest Accommodated Adventure, July 2	$2943
21 Day Cape York Safari to "The Top of Australia", July 22	$2489
21 Day Cape York Accommodated Explorer, Aug 14	$3798
7 Day Birdsville Races, Sep 4	$ 714
4 Day Camarvon Gorge, Aug 9, Nov 15	$ 436

EASTCOAST SPRINGTIME

19 Day Red Centre & Outback New South Wales, Aug 24	$2998
14 Day Land of Contrast. White Cliffs, Woomera & Lake Eyre, Sep 14	$1866
15 Day Southern Springtime Garden Festivals, Victoria, Oct 1	$2080
12 Day Opals, Broken Hill & the Riverlands, Oct 21	$1765
16 Day Flinders Ranges, Kangaroo Island & Great Ocean Road, Oct 26	$2488

OUTBACK AUSTRALIA

38 Day Grand Australian Explorer, July 19	$6884
16 Day Red Centre and Top End Adventure, July 19	$3337
25 Day Grand West Coaster, Aug 1	$4539

ADVENTURE SAFARIS

32 Day Round Australia & Bungle Bungle Safari, July 8, Aug 10	$6884
27 Day Best of the West & Bungle Bungle Safari, July 13, Aug 15	$3337
16 Day Red Centre Walkabout & Lake Eyre, July 22, Sept 21	$4539
23 Day Best of the Territory Safari, July 13, Sept 14	$2685
21 Day Outback Highways Safari, Aug 17	$1892

• Free pick-up   **Kangaroo**   • Courteous staff
• Quality accommodation   • Air-conditioned comfort
• No hidden extras   **Tours**   • See your local travel agent

FREE CALL 1 800 555 1234

Fig. 11.1 Travel advertisement in a newspaper

dures (e.g., English [1999]; Hegarty, Mayer, and Monk [1995]). Instead, students frequently sort problems according to similar contexts—they focus their attention on surface features of the problem statement. For example, children would claim that the problems "Penny has collected 11 stickers. Jane has collected 8 more stickers than Penny. How many stickers has Jane collected?" and "Suzie has collected 20 stickers. She has collected 5 more than Robyn. How many stickers has Robyn collected?" go together because they "are about collecting more and they both have 'has' at the end." Children who are able to detect similar problem structures focus on the relationships between the mathematical ideas in the problems, not simply on the problem's story line. They give such explanations as "With these two problems, the friend has more than the person, and with these two, the person has more than the friend."

Tied in with this structural understanding is an understanding of problem design, that is, knowing the components that make up a problem, such as the known and unknown information, the goal to be attained, and any imposed constraints or conditions on achieving the goal (Moses, Bjork, and Goldenberg 1990). This understanding of problem design enables children to differentiate mathematical problems from nonmathematical problems, good problems from poor, and solvable from nonsolvable problems. Understanding problem design is essential to children's creation of their own problems and promotes the ability to provide quality feedback on their peers' problems. I have found that children need many opportunities to critically analyze various problems, those found in their textbooks as well as problems they create themselves. They can consider such issues as whether the problem is a mathematical one, whether it is solvable, whether the mathematics is challenging or too easy, whether the problem is appealing, and, of high importance, how the problem could be improved, enriched, and extended.

Finding Important Mathematics in Complex Situations

One method that seems to be successful in increasing our students' access to rich mathematical ideas is using what Lesh and his colleagues call "thought-revealing activities" (Lesh et al. 2000). These activities engage students in challenging but meaningful problem situations that encourage problem posing, diverse reasoning processes, multiple solution approaches, and multifaceted products. The nature of the products that children have to construct is such that we gain rich insights into their ways of thinking in creating them. What is especially important about these activities, though, is that they can be solved at many different levels of sophistication, and hence, that every child has access to the mathematical content contained in the problem.

One example of a thought-revealing activity appears in figure 11.2. This activity requires students to mathematize (i.e., make mathematical interpretations of) real-world situations (Lesh and Doerr 2002). The activity promotes students' development of mathematical models, which are used to construct, describe, explain, or make intelligible interpretations of real-world situations. In the Green Thumb Gardens problem, students have to select four employees for a lawn-mowing company to rehire, on the basis of information about the individual employees' number of hours worked, number of kilometers driven, dollar amount of products sold, and number of lawns mowed. The students' end product (i.e., their mathematical model) must be applicable to other, similar situations.

Many important mathematical ideas and processes are addressed in this problem, including the quantification of qualitative data, such as determining what makes a "good" employee. Some students address this issue by calculating averages for each of the employees and deciding that a person with high averages (e.g., average number of hours worked, average number of lawn-mowing jobs completed) is a worthwhile employee.

The problem also entails aggregating data with mixed units (e.g., dollars and job size), leading to a consideration of rate, such as the number of lawn-mowing jobs per hour. However, because the jobs are of different sizes, the notion of weighted factors arises. For example, students might decide to increase the value of the small and medium jobs by factors of 3 and 2, respectively, to make them equivalent to the number of big jobs. In deciding whether to do so, students must consider the information given about the nature of the different jobs and pose some hypotheses about their relative worth (e.g., Is a big job equivalent to 3 small jobs? To 2 medium jobs?). Questions regarding relative importance of the tables of information also arise, for example, is the number of kilometers driven important compared with the other data presented? Furthermore, what does "kilometers driven" really mean? Is the number of kilometers driven related to the number of lawns mowed or products sold? I have found these issues to generate much discussion among students as they repeatedly revise or refine their interpretations and conceptions of the problem.

We see evidence of this discussion in the following excerpt of a group of fifth graders in the early stages of working the Green Thumb Gardens problem. Notice how Gill is trying to make sense of the information given but is forming some inappropriate assumptions as he scans across the tables of data. Anna challenges him on his assumptions and suggests a more systematic approach to working the problems. She suggests calculating average amounts because the hours worked varied across the months. In the meantime, Sue has been misinterpreting one of the tables of data (money from products sold), and so Gill and Anna do their best to point out her error.

Background Information

At Green Thumb Gardens, James Sullivan will provide lawn-mowing service for his customers. Another local landscaping service has closed, so he has offered to hire four of their former employees in addition to taking on some of their former clients. He has received information from the other landscaping business about the employee schedules during December, January, and February of last year. The employees were responsible for mowing lawns and selling other yard products, such as fertilizer, weed killer, and bug spray.

The other business recorded how many hours each employee worked each month, the number of lawns each employee mowed, and how much money they made selling other products. The lawns mowed are divided into big, medium, and small jobs. Big jobs may have larger lawns or require more work than medium or small jobs. Some lawns may be small but may have many obstacles for the mower to get around, or they may require different kinds of edging or trimming to be done; all these factors determine the size of the job. The business had also recorded the kilometers driven to clients in one of the green-and-white company trucks during each month.

Problem

James needs to decide which four employees he wants to hire from the old business for this summer. Using the information provided, help him decide which four people he should hire. Write him a letter explaining the method you used to make your decision so that he can use your method for hiring new employees each summer.

Hours Worked					**Kilometers Driven**			
Employee	Dec.	Jan.	Feb.		Employee	Dec.	Jan.	Feb.
Jonathan	80	80	80		Jonathan	198	200	201
Cynthia	75	65	70		Cynthia	199	201	198
Jack	66	64	63		Jack	197	199	198
Kayla	45	50	55		Kayla	201	203	199
Tim	67	70	79		Tim	200	199	200
Aaron	65	70	78		Aaron	198	196	195
Matthew	80	79	78		Matthew	200	204	202
Julie	40	42	46		Julie	196	198	197
Travis	80	75	80		Travis	201	203	204
Kim	78	76	79		Kim	195	199	198

Total Number of Lawns Mowed

	December			January			February		
Employee	Big	Medium	Small	Big	Medium	Small	Big	Medium	Small
Jonathan	15	12	30	16	14	34	16	15	35
Cynthia	18	10	35	19	12	35	14	16	36
Jack	14	16	22	15	16	22	13	16	22
Kayla	15	13	15	14	13	17	15	12	18
Tim	20	12	14	22	14	16	20	13	25
Aaron	16	27	32	14	18	33	15	19	42
Matthew	32	12	9	30	11	10	30	10	13
Julie	9	22	12	12	15	16	8	10	12
Travis	13	34	32	13	33	31	15	35	12
Kim	12	11	25	11	10	26	13	14	30

(Continued on next page)

(Continued from previous page)

Average Money Per Week from Products Sold

Employee	December	January	February
Jonathan	$ 150	$ 175	$ 170
Cynthia	$ 75	$ 80	$ 80
Jack	$ 125	$ 150	$ 150
Kayla	$ 80	$ 72	$ 65
Tim	$ 135	$ 130	$ 125
Aaron	$ 127	$ 153	$ 165
Matthew	$ 110	$ 115	$ 120
Julie	$ 55	$ 54	$ 60
Travis	$ 300	$ 255	$ 275
Kim	$ 200	$ 250	$ 265

Fig. 11.2. The Green Thumb Gardens problem

Gill: You have to think about kilometers driven. Kilometers driven isn't all that relevant, but you have to spend money for gas to go places. But then Travis, if you look at him, he has 201 in June, 203 in July, August 204. And he's good.... Also I think Jonathan is good because he works top hours and doesn't drive much. Also mows quite a lot of lawns and makes a bit of money. Also I thought Aaron was good. Hours aren't very high; doesn't drive that much; he mows the most lawns I think.... Yeah, he does. And he doesn't make that bad at money.

Anna: Gill, *not necessarily* he mows the most lawns.

Gill: Yeah, his average is about 30 of big, medium, and small. Some of them are low, but let's look at ... Travis is not that bad. He's got a lot.

Anna: How about we work out the hours they worked? How about we work out their average?

Gill: Yes, because you want to have quite a good amount of hours because if they don't have too much hours, then they don't work as much, but if they make a lot of money, then it's not that bad. But still you want them to work a lot of hours so the customers are happier.

Anna: Well, I'm working out the average of the hours they worked. It's kind of difficult working [out] how much they worked each month. Sometimes they worked less and sometimes more.

Gill: So what do you think—which people would you choose, Anna?

Anna: I haven't chosen yet, but I'd choose Travis.

Gill: Yeah, Travis is good.

Sue: I'd choose Jonathan, Aaron, Travis, and Kim.

Gill: He doesn't work that many lawns but ... I had them, too. But I'm not sure about Kim. What are other good hours for people? Just check. I think Cynthia's pretty good. Doesn't get any money: 80, 80, 75. That is poor. No, not Cynthia. What is good money?

Sue: $300.

Gill: Yeah. Travis is good. He's one of the best people.

Sue: Yeah, but they don't want to give them more money. The business....

Gill: No. They make that money.

Anna: They *made* the money.

Gill: Average money per week from products *sold*. They don't *give* them this.

Sue: They do, they do, yes, they do.

Gill: Well, how come it's "products sold"?

As the group continued working this problem, Gill and Sue persisted with their unsystematic ways of working, despite challenges from Mary, another group member.

Mary: But what if we don't want them?

Sue: Well, Matthew is one of the best.

Gill: Yes, he is pretty good.

Mary: Sue, *how do you know that?*

Gill: Look at all the stats!

Sue: Hours worked, 80; kilometers driven, 200.... Matthew...

Gill: Pretty good at lawns ...his money's not that bad....

Mary: So just on that information you can't just say, "Okay, we want him."

Gill: He's pretty high.

Mary: This is pulling people out of the hat again.

Sue: We're not pulling them out of the hat. We're just compromising. (Argument ensues.)

Mary: What's the structure for that?

None of the group members at that stage had considered the notion of rate, let alone the weighting of factors. Nevertheless, all the students were engaged fully in the problem and could apply their existing knowledge to consider different pathways to a solution. Problem posing plays a central role in working these problems. Because the given information and the desired model are open to interpretation, students naturally pose many questions, conjectures, and hypotheses while working the problem. In doing so, they often display unwarranted assumptions, misinterpretations, and inadequate or inappropriate reasoning. Students come to revise and refine their thinking as their peers challenge their statements and pose alternative scenarios for them to consider. Without these problem-posing actions, students would make limited progress toward a solution.

Concluding Points

Problem posing—like its companion, problem solving—should be an integral component of the mathematics curriculum across all content domains. Although problem posing occurs naturally in everyday life, it does not receive due attention in the mathematics classroom. Problem posing is more than just constructing problems. Children apply problem-posing processes when they are actively engaged in challenging situations that involve them in exploring, questioning, constructing, and refining mathematical ideas and relationships.

In this chapter, I have addressed, in part, the challenge of making problem posing a regular part of the curriculum. I have considered the importance of building inquiry-oriented learning communities that foster problem posing. In such communities, students participate in constructive dialogue and debate, share their mathematical constructions with others, work productively as a community of learners, and exchange constructive feedback on one another's creations.

I have also addressed some ways in which problem posing promotes students' conceptual development, with an emphasis on conceptual and computational flexibility. Open-ended mathematical situations provide many opportunities for students to experience multiple meanings and approaches to basic computational ideas. In particular, authentic resources, such as newspaper advertisements and scientific reports, offer motivating and meaningful opportunities for enriching core understandings.

This chapter emphasizes the importance of interpreting and constructing meaning from new problem experiences. Problem-posing processes come into play as children distinguish the important information from the unimportant and as they try to detect the mathematical structure, or "anatomy," of the problems. The ability to detect corresponding structures in related problems is an essential problem-posing process and is fundamental to successful problem solving. Likewise, recognizing the design of a problem is a necessary process in differentiating mathematical problems from nonmathematical problems, good problems from poor, and solvable from nonsolvable problems. This process is essential to children's creation of their own problems, as well as to their skills in providing quality feedback on one another's problem constructions.

Finally, teachers need to increase all students' access to powerful mathematics through activities that promote the development of models for dealing with complex, real-world systems. Thought-revealing activities, which engage students in both problem-posing and problem-solving processes, provide ideal opportunities for accessing significant mathematical ideas and representational systems.

This chapter has explored only a few of the many ways in which problem posing underpins students' mathematical learning. Irrespective of the topic being studied or the grade level attained, children's mathematical learning experiences must involve them in questioning, describing, constructing, justifying, and explaining—that is, the fundamentals of problem posing.

Job Tickets: Collecting and Analyzing Data

Jan Szymaszek, third-grade teacher

"Good problem solvers tend naturally to analyze situations carefully in mathematical terms and to pose problems based on situations they see" (NCTM 2000, p. 53). As Lyn English points out in chapter 11, "[L]ike problem solving, problem posing is a natural part of our everyday lives. Each day, we face situations in which we need to interpret what is happening, question why and how it has happened, decide which of several options to take, and think through possible consequences of our actions" (p. 187). Data collection can provide a rich source for problem posing related to students' own experiences and context. In this third-grade class, a common occurrence—students' forgetting to record their completion of classroom jobs—is the impetus for collecting and analyzing data. Jan Szymaszek recognizes that the questions posed by her students offer the opportunity to dig into fundamental ideas about summarizing and comparing data.

—Susan Jo Russell

IN MY class, students have daily jobs to do, and after completing their jobs, they are supposed to turn over their "job tickets," which hang on a board in the classroom, as a confirmation of a job well done. I have twenty-one students in my class, and each day I write on the board the fraction that shows how many students out of twenty-one remembered to turn over their job tickets the day before. In the depths of winter, although the jobs were getting done, the number of tickets turned over was running low. One day, only nine of twenty-one students remembered to turn them over. The students made some suggestions for improving our record, and one was that we should keep a daily record of the number of tickets that were turned over. The students liked the fact that they would be able to see whether they were making improvements, and I loved the potential set of data that such a record would generate. We collected data for several weeks and organized them into the following table:

Date	Weekday	Tickets Turned Over	Date	Weekday	Tickets Turned Over
2/24	Thursday	9	3/8*	Wednesday	17
2/25	Friday	21	3/9*	Thursday	19
2/28	Monday	20	3/10*	Friday	16
2/29	Tuesday	21	3/20	Monday	17
3/1	Wednesday	19	3/21	Tuesday	21
3/2	Thursday	20	3/22	Wednesday	18
3/3	Friday	16	3/23	Thursday	21
3/6*	Monday	15	3/24	Friday	15
3/7*	Tuesday	14			

* A day Ms. Szymaszek was on safety duty

One day, Justin looked at the table and said, "I think 17 happens a lot." In fact, it only came up twice in the days recorded, whereas 21 occurred four times, but this opening was just what I had been waiting for! I asked the class what questions they thought this set of data could help us answer. I mentioned to them that people who use data like these might start with a question or something they are wondering about and then collect data to help them understand that thing or answer their questions. In this situation, we would be doing something different. We already had the set of data, and now we were going to use it to help us learn something about our job-ticket record by posing some questions that we thought the data might help us answer. The questions they came up with included the following:

- Did we do better in the first half or the second half?
- Did we do better when Ms. Szymaszek was on safety duty [when I had to leave earlier and left them with other teachers] or when she wasn't?
- On which day of the week did we do the best?

The next day, students worked with partners to choose a question, either from our group-generated list or another one they had come up with overnight. Then they were asked to represent the data in a way that would help them answer the question they chose to investigate. Because this context led naturally to the comparison of two or more groups (e.g., first half/second half; on safety duty/off safety duty; Monday/Tuesday), I knew that the students would have to grapple with how to characterize a group of data values as a whole set to compare it with another set of values, and I looked forward to seeing how they would work with this idea. Although I was not planning to formally introduce calculations for finding an average, I realized that the students would need to think about a crucial underlying idea—that one can summarize a data set that contains many different values rather than simply list all the separate values. The questions posed by the group led to an activity that spanned several days of pair work and whole-group discussions that focused on how to summarize and compare data sets.

Hannah and Lucia investigated the question "Did we do better when Ms. S. was on safety duty or not on safety duty?" In their written work, they described their findings:

> When we had 20s, it was when Ms. Szymaszek was not on safety duty. So that shows that everyone tried to do their best with her in the room. 14, 15, and 16 are numbers that we are not satisfied with. . . . There weren't any 20s or 21s when Ms. Szymaszek was on safety duty.

Another group who had investigated the same question agreed with Hannah and Lucia's findings. They had divided the data into three groups: "before safety," "safety week," and "after safety." They concluded,

> We did worse when Ms. Szymaszek was on safety. Before safety, we had in the teens and twenties. On safety, we got in the teens only. After safety, we got teens and twenties.

Because we had data for seventeen school days, the partner pairs who were interested in the question about the first half of the data as compared with the second half faced an immediate dilemma: Where did the first half end and the second half begin? Some pairs decided to use the first eight and the last nine, whereas others did the first nine and the second eight. One pair of students who counted the extra piece of data in the second half accounted for it when they reported the answer to their question.

They wrote, "We found out that if you took the 14 [the data for the ninth day] out of the second half it would only be 3 tickets better." Another pair of students counted the 14 in both the top half and the bottom half. They concluded, "The top half and the bottom half were only 3 apart. We did better in the second half." A third pair of students included the 14 in the first half, but they talked together for a long time about what to do about the unevenness of the groups. They later told me that another group working on this same question "could have more in the second half if they did it eight days in the first and nine in the second."

Kevin, Justin, and James, who were trying to find the "best day of the week," realized that two of the days had four values and that three days only had three values. They also realized that they could not simply add the values for each group. They said, "You can't just add, because there's three or four values. You can't just take the first three each time, so we tried to find the average." They worked on a definition for *average:* "We think the average is the number most common, but if the most is more than one number [if no single number is most common], we look for the middle of the range." The following is their chart; the last number in each row is the value they have chosen to represent the average for that day:

Thursday	9	20	19	21	—	15
Friday	21	16	16	15	—	16
Wednesday	19	17	18		—	18
Monday	20	15	17		—	17
Tuesday	21	14	21		—	21

When they explained their ideas to the class, they "walked us through" each day of the week. For example, for Thursday's values, which were the first on their chart, they said, "Since there is no number most common, we had to find the average or middle. We thought of how many numbers from 9 to 21. There were twelve numbers. We did 9 + 6 = 15, then 21 – 6 = 15. We got 15 for the average because the middle of the range would be closest to all of the numbers." Their explanation generated much discussion. No one in the class disputed their decisions for Friday and Wednesday. For Monday's values, they had chosen 17 "because if there are three numbers, you pick the middle one, not the high or the low." Lindsey commented that it would actually be 17 and a half "because that would be between 15 and 20."

Tuesday's average was the most problematic, which may have explained why they saved it for last. Using their definition, they arrived at 21 as the average. Many students objected to this number because 21 seemed too high, unlike Friday's average of 16, which was in the middle of the range. Arthur said, "Why not 17?" Justin replied, "Because we said that if it was most common, we would pick it." The values for Tuesday did more than those for any other day to stir up the debate. Students really did not like arriving at an extreme for the average when the other number seemed so far away from it. For all the other days, they said, "The average seemed pretty close to the other numbers, but this one is too far away from the 14."

The problems the class posed about our job tickets led them to think about how to summarize and compare groups of data. Some students were able to see the big picture of their data by dividing the range of values into chunks, as Hannah and Lucia had done when they used "teens" and "twenties" in their analysis of "on safety duty" versus "off safety duty." Interestingly, they did not report any dilemma about the imbalance in the number of pieces of data in each group (e.g., five days on safety duty, twelve days not on safety duty). Many students realized that comparing by adding the values in each group would not work when the groups contained different numbers of pieces of data. This realization led to a class discussion in which students pushed themselves to find a reasonable value to represent the number of tickets usually or typically turned over on a specific day of the week.

Spring vacation arrived, and we temporarily stopped our work on the job-ticket data. I think, however, that the issues that came up during that work will surface again as we continue to explore ways of working with data.

CHAPTER 12

Problem Solving as a Vehicle for Teaching Mathematics:
A Japanese Perspective

Yoshinori Shimizu

THE FINDINGS of the video component of the Third International Mathematics and Science Study (TIMSS) suggest that mathematics instruction in Japanese classrooms is very different from mathematics instruction in U.S. classrooms (Stigler et al. 1999). One difference is the way in which lessons are structured and delivered. Specifically, U.S. lessons tend to have two phases: an initial acquisition phase, followed by an application phase. During the acquisition phase, the teacher demonstrates or explains how to solve a sample problem. During the application phase, students practice solving examples on their own while the teacher helps individual students who are experiencing difficulty. In Japanese lessons, by contrast, the teacher first poses a complex, thought-provoking problem for the students to solve, then various students present their ideas or solutions to the class. After the teacher summarizes the class's conclusions, students work on similar problems (Stigler et al. 1999, p.136).

As the Stigler study suggests, Japanese teachers often organize an entire lesson around just a few problems, with a focus on the students' various solutions. They seem to share a belief that the best opportunities for learning arise when the students engage in solving a challenging problem. In this chapter, I address two basic questions related to this approach: Why do teachers in Japan consider teaching mathematics through problem solving beneficial? and How do they achieve their goal of teaching mathematics content through the process of problem solving?

To answer these questions, I first provide an overview of the Japanese approach to teaching mathematics through problem solving and describe a typical organization of mathematics lessons in Japanese elementary schools. Next I present a specific problem that is typically found in Japanese textbooks and the corresponding anticipated students' solutions to it to show how students share and analyze their solutions during whole-class discussion. Finally, I present some practical ideas for the classroom that I have gleaned from my work with Japanese teachers.

The Japanese Approach to Teaching Mathematics through Problem Solving

In this section, I describe the organization of a typical mathematics lesson in a Japanese elementary school classroom. I then discuss a fundamental assumption about the nature of learning that underlies this organization.

The Organization of a Typical Mathematics Lesson

Japanese teachers in elementary schools often organize an entire mathematics lesson around multiple solutions to a single problem in a whole-class instructional mode. This organization is particularly useful when introducing a new concept or a new procedure during the initial phase of a teaching unit. Even during the middle or final phases of the unit, teachers often organize lessons by posing a few problems with a focus on the various solutions students come up with.

A typical mathematics lesson in Japan, which lasts forty-five minutes in the elementary schools, can be divided into several segments (e.g., Becker et al. [1990]; Stigler, Fernandez, and Yoshida [1996]). These segments serve as the steps or stages in both the teachers' planning and the actual teaching-learning processes in the classroom (Shimizu 1999):

- Posing a problem
- Students' problem solving on their own
- Whole-class discussion
- Summing up
- Exercises or extension, which are optional depending on time available and students' facility in solving the original problem

Lessons usually begin with a word problem in the textbook or a practical problem that is posed on the chalkboard by the teacher. After the problem is presented and read by the students, the teacher asks questions to determine whether the students understand the problem. If some students do not understand some aspect of the problem, the teacher may ask those students to read the problem again, or the teacher may ask questions to help clarify the problem. Also, in some instances, the teacher may ask a few students to share their initial ideas of how to approach the problem or to make a guess at the answer. The intent of this initial stage is to help students develop a clear understanding of what the problem is about and what all the terms mean.

The students are usually given about ten to fifteen minutes to solve the problem on their own. Then teachers often encourage their students to work with classmates in pairs or in small groups. While the students work on the problem, the teacher moves around the classroom to observe their work, making suggestions or giving individual help to students who are having difficulty approaching the problem. The teacher also notes the students who have good ideas, with the intention of calling on them in a certain order during the subsequent whole-class discussion. If time allows, the teacher encourages the students who have arrived at a solution to find an alternative method for solving the problem.

For Japanese teachers, a lesson is regarded as a drama, which leads up to at least one climax, or *yamaba*. In fact, a central characteristic of Japanese teachers' lesson planning is their deliberate structuring of their lessons around the yamaba. Thus, when a whole-class discussion begins, students listen carefully to the solutions proposed by their classmates and present their own ideas, because during this discussion, the lesson highlights, or yamaba, appear.

Finally, the teacher reviews and sums up the lesson and, if necessary and if time allows, poses an exercise or an extension task that applies what the students have just learned from the lesson.

Learning Opportunities

Japanese teachers consider teaching mathematics through problem solving—with the organization of lessons as just described—to be beneficial because they believe that learning opportunities for students are best raised while they are working on a challenging problem and reflecting on their solutions. They believe that deep understanding of a mathematical concept comes about in the process of problem solving when students must invent their own methods to solve the problem by applying their previous learning. Also, Japanese teachers believe that their students need opportunities to learn different ways of thinking about how to solve problems and that students should be challenged to look for the best solutions they can find in terms of efficiency and elegance.

The vision shared by most Japanese teachers is consistent with statements by U.S. mathematics educators on the role of problem solving in mathematics; for example, "the most important role for problem solving is to develop students' understanding of mathematics" (Schroeder and Lester 1989, p. 31), and "problem solving is an integral part of all mathematics learning" (NCTM 2000, p. 52). From a Japanese perspective, the extent to which this vision becomes a reality depends on how well the teacher does two things: (1) ensures that students have sufficient time to work on the problem on their own, and (2) incorporates students' solution methods into the process of helping them learn the important mathematical ideas in the problem. In this regard, Japanese teachers carefully select the problem to be posed and anticipate the solution approaches that students are most likely to use. Because Van de Walle discusses the importance of choosing appropriate problems in chapter 5 of this volume, here I focus my attention on the second of these two requirements.

Anticipating Students' Responses to a Problem

As I have noted, Japanese teachers organize their lessons around the multiple solution methods presented by students, so the discussion stage depends on the solution methods that students actually use. For this lesson structure to work effectively and naturally, teachers must have not only a deep understanding of the mathematics content but also a keen awareness of the possible solution methods that students will use. Having a very clear sense of the ways in which students are likely to think about and solve a problem, prior to the start of a lesson, enables teachers to know what to look for when they are observing students working on the problem.

Teachers should anticipate students' responses for all types of problems—even for simple calculation problems—because students will come up with multiple approaches to problems that reflect their prior learning experiences. For example, given the problem "$15 - 7 = ?$" first graders will come up with such ideas as

$$15 - 7 = (10 + 5) - 7 = 10 - 7 + 5,$$
$$15 - 7 = 15 - (5 + 2) = 15 - 5 - 2,$$
$$15 - 7 = (15 - 5) - (7 - 5) = 10 - 2,$$

and so on.

For a lesson to be successful, teachers should know both the mathematics content in, and what their students have already learned about, the problem to be posed. In Japan, suggestions about students' possible solutions to the problems in the mathematics textbook are provided in a teacher's edition in the form of a lesson plan. Such information is extremely helpful for teachers in planning lessons that capitalize on students' thinking. Thus, knowing students' possible responses to a problem prior to the start of the lesson is important in the Japanese approach to teaching mathematics through problem solving.

Students' Methods for Solving a Proportion Problem

Let me use a particular problem to illustrate the described approach as it would be used in an actual classroom. Suppose that the following proportion problem is going to be presented in a fifth-grade class to teach the meaning of proportion and how to use it.

Who Is the Better Free-Throw Shooter?

Ken and Yoko shot several free throws in their basketball games. The result of their shooting is shown in the table. Who is better at shooting free throws?

	Goals	Free Throws
Ken	12	20
Yoko	16	25

For this problem to be effective in helping students understand basic proportion concepts, the teacher must anticipate how the students are likely to attempt to solve it. This step is crucial in the preparation for a successful lesson because the Japanese approach relies heavily on having the teacher build on students' thinking. To illustrate, figure 12.1 describes seven anticipated student solution methods; perhaps the reader can think of others.

The methods the students used—both those the teacher had anticipated and any others—are displayed on the chalkboard. Then, during the whole-class discussion, the teacher asks students to present their solution methods at the chalkboard in an order based on the teacher's intentions and observations. For example, in the free-throw-shooting problem, suppose that several students used method G and that the teacher has decided to eliminate this method first because it is incorrect. The teacher might

A. Determining how many free throws are needed to get one goal

Ken: 20 ÷ 12 = 1.666... Yoko: 25 ÷ 16 = 1.5625

Yoko is better because she can get one goal with fewer free throws.

B. Determining the number of goals made if each player shoots only 1 free throw

Ken: 12 ÷ 20 = 0.6   Yoko: 16 ÷ 25 = 0.64

Yoko is better because she can get more goals with one free throw.

C. Determining the number of goals per free throw (rate of success)

Ken: 12 ÷ 20 = 0.6   Yoko: 16 ÷ 25 = 0.64

Yoko is better because her rate for getting a goal is higher than Ken's rate.

D. Comparing the number of goals if each player shoots the same number of free throws.

	Goals	Free Throws
Ken	60	100
Yoko	64	100

Yoko is better because she would get more goals if they each shot one hundred free throws.

E. Comparing the number of free throws if each player makes the same number of goals

	Goals	Free Throws
Ken	48	80
Yoko	48	75

Yoko is better because she would need fewer free throws to get the same number of goals.

(Continued on next page)

(Continued from previous page)

F. Counting by 5s

Ken shot 20 free throws; if he shot 5 more, he would have shot the same number as Yoko. But since he would have made only 3 more goals, he would then have a total of 15 goals. Thus, Yoko, who got 16 goals, is a better free-throw shooter.

G. Comparing the players by using the difference between the number of free throws and the number of goals

Ken: 20 – 12 = 8   Yoko: 25 – 16 = 9

Ken is better because he missed fewer times than Yoko.

Figure 12.1. Several possible student solution methods to the free-throw-shooting problem

ask the students to think about the appropriateness of considering who is the better free-throw shooter on the basis of only the number of failures. The teacher might then ask the students to use method G to determine the winner if Ken makes 0 goals out of 4 free throws and Yoko makes 5 goals out of 10; would it make sense to say that Ken is a better free-throw shooter when he did not make any goals? Once this method has been eliminated, the teacher then turns the students' attention to the other solution methods.

On the basis of observation of the students' work on the problem, the teacher carefully calls on students, asking them to present their solution methods at the chalkboard. The order of selecting students is important for both encouraging those students who used naive methods and highlighting students' ideas in relation to the mathematical connections among the methods that will be discussed. Presenting an idea, even a wrong one, is strongly encouraged and praised by the teacher. The teacher's role is not to point out the best solution method but to guide the discussion toward an integrated idea or a more sophisticated method.

As individual students present their methods, the class as a whole compares several solution methods with the same correct answer. (In the instance of this problem, methods A–F all resulted in the same answer.) After eliminating method G, the teacher might decide to call on students who used methods A or B, after making sure that they are determining free-throw success, not simply using the difference between the goals and free throws. Then methods D and E might be presented and discussed, followed by method C.

Having confirmed that Yoko is a better player than Ken by looking at the methods presented, the class next discusses commonalties and differences among the methods. Students may notice that, for example, one similarity among methods A through E is that each of these methods includes a step for comparing free-throw-shooting success by fixing a number as a reference point for the two players in various ways. They may also notice that the same calculations are carried out in methods B and C.

Students next compare the solution methods from the mathematical viewpoints of simplicity, efficiency, and applicability to other problem situations. Students should notice that finding a least common multiple, methods D and E, would become troublesome when the number of free throws attempted is bigger than that in the original problem, whereas methods A, B, and C do not become as difficult to use when the numbers are made larger. Also, in comparing methods A and B, the teacher should point out that method B is more natural because we can represent a better free-throw shooter with a bigger number. Method F, counting by 5s, will not work if the difference between Ken's and Yoko's total number of free throws is not a multiple of 5.

According to the goal of the lesson, the focus should shift to method C. The teacher might ask the students the meaning of quotients of the divisions in methods B and C to clarify the difference between them. Then she or he might introduce the word *proportion* with an explanation of its meaning in method C and use it in another, similar situation.

The proposed methods are compared with regard to their simplicity, efficiency, applicability to other problems, and so on. The teacher hopes that through the experience the students have had with the free-throw problem, they will be developing a disposition for seeking a better method in other problem situations as well. Finally, if no student used a specific anticipated method, the teacher may proceed with only those that were presented, or may present to the class a missing a method that was not brought up. The expected norms of behavior in the classroom are carefully developed by the teacher over time. (Refer to Stephan and Whitenack [chapter 9 of this volume] for their discussion of establishing appropriate social and sociomathematical norms.)

Some Practical Ideas Shared by Japanese Teachers

Various teachers with whom I have worked over the past several years have made numerous suggestions to me regarding the Japanese approach to teaching mathematics. Among these suggestions, five are especially pertinent to the focus of this chapter.

Suggestion 1: Label students' methods with their names. During the whole-class discussion of students' solution methods, each method is labeled with the name of the student who originally presented it. Thereafter, each solution method is referred to by the name of student in the discussion. This practical technique may seem trivial, but it is very important to ensure the student's ownership of the presented method and makes the whole-class discussion more captivating and interesting for students.

Suggestion 2: Use the chalkboard effectively. Another important technique used by the teacher relates to using of the chalkboard, which is called *bansho* by Japanese teachers. Whenever possible, teachers put everything written during the lesson on the chalkboard without erasing. By not erasing anything the students have done and by placing their work on the chalkboard in a logical, organized manner, the teacher and students can more easily compare multiple solution methods. Also, the chalkboard can be a written record of the entire lesson, giving both the students and the teacher a bird's-eye view of what has happened during the lesson.

Suggestion 3: Use the whole-class discussion to polish students' ideas. The Japanese word *neriage* describes the dynamic and collaborative nature of a whole-class discussion in the lesson. This word, which can be translated as "polishing up," works as a metaphor for the process of polishing students' ideas and constructing an integrated mathematical idea through a dynamic whole-class discussion. Japanese teachers regard neriage as crucial to the success or failure of the entire lesson.

Suggestion 4: Choose the numbers in, and the context of, the problem carefully. The specific nature of the problem presented to the students is very important. In particular, the numbers in the proportion problem, as well as those in the free-throws context, were carefully selected for eliciting a wide variety of responses from students. For example, using 20 and 25 as the shots taken by Ken and Yoko in the problem was likely to result in such solution methods as "equalizing the number of free throws taken" (method D) or "counting by 5s" (method F). Also, choosing 12 and 16 for the number of goals makes finding the least common multiple (method E) relatively easy for students. Thus, careful selection of the problem is the starting point for getting a variety of responses from students.

Suggestion 5: Consider how to encourage a variety of solution methods. Suppose the students had used only methods D and E, as well as the incorrect method G. In this situation, the teacher could mention that finding a least common multiple (method D and E) might be troublesome if the number of free throws was, for example, 24 and 35. Making this observation would implicitly encourage the students to think of other, more efficient methods— including methods A, B, and C—that are related to the goal of the lesson. The teacher should encourage students to find alternative solution methods in addition to their initial approaches.

Conclusion

The Japanese approach to teaching mathematics through problem solving usually involves posing one or two problems and focuses on the subsequent discussion of various solution methods generated by the students. The students' ideas are incorporated into the classroom process of discussing multiple solution methods to the problem. In this approach, problem solving is an essential vehicle for teaching mathematics. This instructional approach is used not only on special occasions or once a week; rather, it is the standard approach followed for teaching all mathematics content.

For lessons to be successful, teachers need to fully understand the relationship between the mathematics content to be taught and students' possible thinking about the problem to be posed. Anticipating students' responses to a problem is the crucial aspect of lesson planning in the Japanese approach to teaching mathematics through problem solving.

Section 3

The Role of Technology

CHAPTER 13

Using Technology to Enhance a Problem-Based Approach to Teaching:

What Will and What Will Not Work

Warren D. Crown

THE TECHNOLOGY *Principle in Principles and Standards for School Mathematics* suggests that "technology is essential in teaching and learning mathematics; it influences the mathematics that is taught and enhances students' learning" (NCTM 2000, p. 7). The accompanying narrative in the *Overview* goes on to address issues of excellence, equity, and access in the use of technology:

> Calculators and computers are reshaping the mathematical landscape, and school mathematics should reflect those changes. Students can learn more mathematics more deeply with the appropriate and responsible use of technology. They can make and test conjectures. They can work at higher levels of generalization or abstraction. In the mathematics classrooms envisioned in *Principles and Standards*, every student has access to technology to facilitate his or her mathematics learning. (NCTM 2000, p. 7)

But how do teachers achieve these lofty goals with their students? What is the teacher's role beyond selecting appropriate software and hardware? What can technology do for us that is harder to achieve without it? In this chapter, I consider the role that technology can play and the role that it cannot play in helping teachers implement a problem-based approach in their mathematics teaching. I discuss several of the kinds of technology available for use in elementary school classrooms and examine their strengths and weaknesses in supporting problem-based instructional approaches.

Technology and Problem-Based Instruction

Calculators and computers have been shown to be effective in helping students achieve a wide variety of skills and understandings in many disparate settings. The purpose of this chapter, however, is to see how technology can best serve the goal of this book—to enhance a problem-based approach to the teaching of elementary mathematics—and to give several examples.

In chapter 4 of this volume, Hiebert talks about students' developing a deep, rich understanding of mathematics. How can the technology be used to support their attainment of that understanding? And in chapter 5, Van de Walle discusses the processes of selecting and designing problematic tasks around which to build discussion and instruction. How can technology support these processes? In brief, technology best serves as an environment in which problems can come alive for students, helping them build representations and problem solutions and aiding them in their attempts to construct explanations and justifications. In the following sections, I separately discuss how calculators and computers can enhance learning mathematics through problem solving.

Calculators

Calculators most creatively support problem-based learning when their special functions can be used to help children explore mathematical objects and operations. As a simple example, consider a group of fourth or fifth graders who are beginning to feel comfortable with decimals but need to further explore the notions of decimal comparisons and "betweenness." Most simple, four-function calculators have a function that allows any input number to be multiplied by itself by simply pressing the × and = keys in succession. The teacher could introduce this key-press sequence to students and ask them to enter "5 × =" to show that, indeed, the calculator gives 25 as the product. The challenge could then be "Find the number that, when multiplied by itself, gives 19 as the product." Students will quickly verify that 4 is smaller than the answer and that 5 is larger. As students try first one-place, then two-place, and then three-place decimals between 4 and 5, they create a series of successive approximations, arriving at more and more accurate estimates of the square root of 19. The process of deciding how to increase or decrease the trial numbers involves the students in just the kind of discussion about decimal comparison and betweenness that the teacher desires, whether he or she wants to discuss and name the concept of square root at this point or defer these considerations for another lesson.

Another popular calculator activity that focuses students' attention on properties of operations and numbers is the "broken key" activity. Even though this setting is terribly contrived, younger elementary school students love it because it lets them demonstrate their flexibility in thinking about arithmetic. The teacher assigns a piece of computation to be done on a calculator but says that the calculators in use have one or more "broken" keys. Those keys cannot be used, and the students have to work around them. For example, one problem reads, "Find a way to do '5 × 29' if the '2' key is broken." Students are encouraged to develop a variety of solutions, such as the following:

$(5 \times 19) + (5 \times 10) =$

$(5 \times 30) - 5$

$30 + 30 + 30 + 30 + 30 - 5$

$5 + = = = =$ (29 times)

The ensuing class discussion would focus not only on the correctness of these suggestions but also on their similarities and differences, the other operations that are used in the process of discovering the multiplication product, and, with older students, the formal properties of multiplication that are evident in the solutions—commutativity and distributivity.

These two examples of the creative uses of calculators in classrooms demonstrate that they can be valuable tools to support a problem-based approach to instruction as children attempt to reach genuine understanding of essential mathematics. Calculators provide an environment in which students can seek real problem solutions. This view is radically different from the one that considers calculators merely as tools for checking students' pencil-and-paper computation or for reducing the computational burden while solving word problems.

Computers

Computers can do a tremendous variety of things, depending entirely on the software being run and that software author's intent. When asked to imagine a student using a computer in an elementary school classroom, a knowledgeable adult might see the student practicing basic addition facts with electronic flash cards, playing an arcade game that requires solving mathematical puzzles to proceed, building a geometric construction, working through a set of online instructions for finding the circumference of a circle, or any of thousands of other possible scenarios. One cannot talk generically about using computers in elementary mathematics classrooms. Some specification and definition of the various types of software are essential for us to address the question of support for problem-based instruction. As a result, the remainder of this section describes the six types of educational software typically found in elementary mathematics classrooms and potential uses of each type in a problem-oriented setting.

Drill-and-Practice Software

The first type of mathematics educational software developed for personal computers was drill-and-practice software. First appearing in the late 1970s, this software focuses on low-level skills, offering students practice and feedback about the accuracy of their work. Screen design and program sophistication have been greatly improved since the earliest incarnations of such software, but the educational goals remain the same: mastery of low-level procedural skills, mostly basic arithmetic facts and multi-digit computational algorithms. Whether students are using the very popular Math Blaster (from Vivendi Universal) or a Web site that offers electronic flash cards, the dominant activity is students' response to a computation exercise posed by the computer. Because feedback is immediate and because exercises can be tailored to a student's ability level, these programs usually prove very successful at achieving their goals.

Although among the most demonstrably effective educational software in the marketplace, and certainly among the most commercially successful, drill-and-practice programs do not offer very much to the teacher interested in creating and conducting a problem-based approach to mathematics instruction. Concerned primarily with developing automaticity in students—the ability to quickly and reflexively complete algorithmic procedures and recall basic arithmetic facts—these programs' educational objectives are quite different from those espoused in this book. The programs do not allow students' engagement with the deeper meanings of these exercises, and students do not typically find an opportunity to discuss their work with others in these settings. This software is not bad; it is just inappropriate for supporting a problem-based instructional approach.

Tutorial Software

As a response to the narrow objectives of the then-available drill-and-practice software, teachers in the early 1980s started demanding a new kind of mathematics software: tutorial software. Tutorial software attempts to teach new knowledge and skills to children rather than simply offer an environment for practicing old ones. This software, too, has seen tremendous development and increasing levels of sophistication over the past two decades. In fact, some of the most sophisticated computer software currently being developed is a subclass of this category called *intelligent tutoring systems*. The following are three examples of the kind of elementary mathematics tutorial programs that currently populate the World Wide Web:

- http://www.themathpage.com/ARITH/decimals.htm
- http://pittsford.monroe.edu/jefferson/calfieri/algebra/ AddSubPosNeg.html
- http://www.arcytech.org/java/pi/preface.html

The first tutorial program is a text-based introduction to decimal notation, the second models operations on integers with animated number lines, and the third is a technology-based exploration of the relationship between the diameter and the circumference of a circle.

Tutorial programs take a piece of mathematics curriculum and try to "teach" it, frequently trying to mimic the way a human teacher would teach the same content. This software commonly includes screen after screen of information and explanation, much like an electronic textbook, with little opportunity for students' involvement or input—just many consecutive presses of the Enter key. As a result, a lot of tutorial software is boring and fails to hold students' interest. Some of the best tutorial software is very good, though, and does, indeed, offer students an opportunity for independent learning. However, the teacher must take care to choose tutorial software that provides just the right sort of guidance and support to students. One of the most frequent errors made by teachers who are trying to implement a problem-based mathematics teaching approach is to present their own generalizations or summaries before students are ready for them. As Van de Walle notes in this volume,

> [E]ven the best students need multiple opportunities to acquire difficult concepts or develop difficult skills. If a conceptual activity is followed too closely with a proce-

dural skill or rule, all too often the rule becomes the focus and the poorly developed underpinnings are lost. For the inefficient learner, the danger of premature introduction of rules or procedures is even greater. (p. 76)

Premature rule giving and generalizing are especially likely to occur when tutorial software is used. Even though much of this software starts out conceptually, even posing interesting problems and situations for students to think about, the software almost always jumps, at some point, to the rule or procedure to be mastered, and then frequently to some test items.

Hiebert, in chapter 4 of this volume, says that "[u]nderstanding is best supported through a delicate balance among engaging students in solving challenging problems, examining increasingly better solution methods, and providing information for students at just the right time" (p. 53). Although some tutorial software programs manage the first task well, they rarely are able to do either of the other two. Well-intentioned teachers sometimes use tutorial software as a replacement for themselves; they place students in front of computers with a tutorial and expect deep learning to take place.

Simulation Software

The problems used in a teaching-through-problem-solving approach need not be "real world" problems. Sometimes, though, the additional motivation offered by real and engaging situations is an advantage. Some of the most creative and attractive educational software programs commercially available allow students to simulate real-life settings and act in mathematically intelligent ways. Simulation software challenges students to formulate strategies to deal with complex mathematical systems to achieve a desired goal.

One of the first popular simulation programs, and one that is now available on the Internet, is Lemonade Stand (www.lemonadegame .com). In this program, students run a lemonade stand, making day-to-day decisions about how much lemonade to make, what price to sell it for, what to spend on advertising, and how to alter decisions on the basis of the weather. Students receive feedback about their decisions in the form of the number of cups of lemonade sold that day. Strategies for maximizing profits within this relatively simple system can be the focus of stimulating discussions among middle school children. The impact of price increases on number of cups sold, for instance, is a mathematical relationship that can be studied through direct experimentation within the software's setting. More-complex systems involving the same themes are evident in SimCity, SimTown, (both from Electronic Arts, Inc.) and Roller Coaster Tycoon (from Atari), all very engaging programs with a great deal of embedded mathematics that can be isolated and investigated.

A simpler use of simulation software is the generation of random data. Frequently, software is used effectively in problem-based classrooms to simulate multiple trials of simple experiments. A thousand tosses of a pair of dice, 500 spins of a multicolored spinner, or 10,000 flips of a coin can all be accomplished in a matter of seconds and the results shown in a table or on a graph with the right simulation software. Certainly, giving students the experience of producing a small amount of data by themselves with the actual materials has its advantages, but having a large amount of data available in classes that do not have an effective means of producing it has obvious educational benefits. One such piece of simulation software is a Web site called The Birthday Problem (www.mste.uiuc.edu/reese/birthday/intro.html). It randomly generates as large a set of dates of the year as the user desires, then checks for the number of matches within the set. It is a wonderful tool for investigating the likelihood that two people in a class have the same birthday, a popular upper elementary or secondary school problem.

Simulation software can contribute a great deal to the problem-solving orientation in a classroom. However, the teacher should carefully plan its use and carefully orchestrate students' activity and discussion if students are to achieve valuable mathematical outcomes, not just success in the games.

Problem-Solving Software

A great many pieces of commercial software promote themselves as problem-solving software. It is by far the most diverse category of software because of the variety of definitions and meanings of *problem solving,* and some of the software is creatively done. Such software would seem to be perfect for a problem-based classroom, but it may not be so.

Some problem-solving software, and a great many Web sites, are simply collections of problems. To the extent that these problems are amenable to the kind of mathematics teaching being addressed here, they may be useful to a teacher in fashioning a problem-based approach. Two noteworthy Web sites in this group are MegaMath (www.c3.lanl.gov/mega-math/), a very nice collection of discrete mathematics problems for elementary school students, and Math Forum Problem of the Week (mathforum.com/

elempow/), a well-administered site that posts a new challenging problem each week for elementary school students.

Another type of problem-solving software takes the student through an "adventure," in which a variety of mathematical situations arise that require the student's action to resolve. Probably the best known and best researched of this software is the Adventures of Jasper Woodbury series (see peabody.vanderbilt.edu/ projects/funded/jasper). Jasper is a student who, during the course of a video-based adventure, needs to solve a variety of "real life" mathematical problems. These programs certainly engage students in solving multistep application problems, and the best of them have been effective in improving students' performance in standard problem-solving tasks. But such programs are so focused on the tasks that they cannot and do not constitute a problem-based approach to teaching everyday mathematical skills and concepts. Teachers who use this type of software should provide a good deal of structure and support to allow students to focus adequately on the underlying mathematical relations, meanings, and understandings embedded in the contexts and problems.

Game Software

A common sight in computer-using elementary classrooms is students playing games on the machines, either in pairs against each other or against the computer. These programs foster high interest on the part of students and usually require either basic skills or logic to win the games. They are wonderful environments for practicing skills and for developing strategies and logical reasoning. Good examples here include strategy games, such as mankala (www.elf.org/mankala/ Mankala.html); computer games devised specifically for mathematics skill practice, such as How the West Was $1 + 3 \times 4$ (from Sunburst Technology); and online collections of old favorites, such as Connect 4 and ticktacktoe (www2.allmixedup.com/).

Games can be used to support a problem-based approach in a classroom, but only when the games themselves become objects of study. When students playing tickackoe, nim, or mankala engage in discussions about the best strategies to use in the next move, about which move will bring them closer to their goal of winning the game, about what their opponent is likely to do next, then a good deal of mathematics can be discovered and formulated. Playing against a machine that will respond in the same way every time it is presented with the same situation offers useful advantages in trying to reach generalizations about strategy. This content, although important and playing an increasingly larger role in elementary school mathematics, is still not what most teachers would consider the core of elementary mathematics—it is not the numbers and operations and measurement and geometry that students need to master.

Tool Software

Tool software is ultimately the most useful computer software for supporting a problem-based mathematics teaching approach. In a tool-software environment, students build and explore their own representations of mathematical objects and relationships. The environment is both open ended and student controlled. At least two types of tool software are used extensively in elementary school classrooms: standard adult tools used in an educational setting and mathematics education–specific tools built only for that purpose.

The best examples of adult tools are spreadsheets and graphing programs. Like all good tool software, a spreadsheet or a graphing program does nothing when started up. It just waits for the user—adult or student—to use it to represent some ideas or relationships. The user enters data and uses the tool to help make sense of the data or to better represent some embedded relationships or trends in the data.   Students can use such tools in much the same way that adults do. These programs can help bring order to a "problematic" situation and help students make discoveries about and see number relationships and properties.

Many good examples of the mathematics education–specific type of tool software also exist. Some older examples are Logo (see el.media.mit.edu/logo-foundation) and The Geometer's Sketchpad (from Key Curriculum Press). Logo is a programming language in which students can solve a variety of interesting geometry problems by directing the movements of a "turtle" on the computer screen. The Geometer's Sketchpad is also primarily a geometry drawing tool but one that takes the user's perspective of the screen rather than the turtle's. In chapter 14 of this volume, Battista describes some recently developed tool software that can be used to teach elementary geometry concepts through problem solving.

Some of the most recent additions to the software choices available to elementary-grades mathematics teachers are called *virtual manipulatives*. They are computer-based versions of the most popular concrete materials used to help children learn mathematics: pattern blocks, base-ten blocks, money, fraction strips, geoboards, and the like. The best of these electronic tools have properties and abilities that their concrete counterparts do not have.

Consider, for example, the base-ten blocks in the Scott Foresman suite of "eTools" (Crown, Caldwell, & Schielack, in press). The student can hit an electronic "hundred block" with an electronic hammer to break it into 10 "ten blocks." One of these can then be hit to break it into 10 "one blocks." The student can use a special electronic glue to build larger blocks from groups of smaller blocks. And of course, the program has an unlimited number of each type of block for the student to use on his or her "desktop." Many of the tools also have symbolic readouts that help the student relate the pictorial image of the blocks on the screen to several different symbolic versions of the number represented. For example, with 3 hundreds, 4 tens, and 5 ones on the screen, the student might cycle through a standard symbolic readout (345), an expanded form (300 + 40 + 5), or a verbal one (3 hundreds, 4 tens, 5 ones).

Imagine the power of such a tool in allowing a first grader to explore all the ways to show "34." Many first graders see "34" as a collection of 34 ones, not as 3 tens and 4 ones. Such a child might build a representation of "34" by putting 34 "one" blocks on the screen. One symbolic readout would show "34"; another would show "34 ones." But then, prompted by the teacher to "show '34' as many ways as you can," the student might glue ten of the blocks together (34 = 1 ten and 24 ones), then another ten (34 = 2 tens and 14 ones), and then another ten (34 = 3 tens and 4 ones). Another child, who initially made the "34" as 3 tens and 4 ones, could use the hammer to reverse the process. To see another example of tool software that allows children to explore place-value ideas, visit acrytech.org/java/b10blocks.

Similar examples could be given for any mathematics problem for which concrete representations have helped children develop understanding. Electronic versions of those materials can frequently help children in the same ways and even more. The constraints built into the environments and the available ties to standard symbolic representations provide a new dimension to the usefulness of the tools.

An additional advantage of the tools is the ease with which they can be used as an "electronic chalkboard" on a large display at the front of the room, as the teacher engages the class in a discussion about a mathematical topic. Suppose, for example, the class was exploring the relationship between the area and the perimeter of a rectangle. A large electronic geoboard for the whole class to see could serve to record all the rectangles the students could think of that have a perimeter of 16. The discussion could focus on the different dimensions of the rectangles, the ones with the largest and the smallest areas, and the students could make predictions about the set of rectangles that could be made with perimeters of 20.

One of the tenets of problem-based teaching is that we, as teachers, should allow everyday problems to be problems. We need not search high and low for the extravagant, the special, the "nonroutine" problems, but rather, we can use the routine problems; these are the meat-and-potatoes of the elementary-grades mathematics curriculum, and we can ask children to deal with them day after day. For this reason, tool software is probably the ideal class of software to handle routine problems. Good tool software embodies all the best representational devices we have invented for helping learners make sense of mathematics over the past three thousand years. If we allow sufficient time and give sufficient support, then elementary school students in this kind of environment can truly develop a deep understanding of the mathematics we expect them to learn.

Conclusion

Technology offers tremendous opportunities to teachers who want to orient their mathematics teaching around a problem-based approach. Its abilities to focus students' attention on the problems at hand, to provide an effective method of building meaningful representations and solutions for those problems, and to allow easy and targeted student discussion of those products are all potentially useful to teachers. But not all educational computer software and not all classroom uses of calculators meet these criteria. Teachers must find software and calculator activities that fit into an already well conceived problem-based-teaching approach to maximize the potential of the technology.

Software resources

Adventures of Jasper Woodbury. Nashville, Tenn.: Vanderbilt University. Available at http://peabody.vanderbilt.edu/projects/funded/jasper as of July 2003.

Geometer's Sketchpad. Berkeley, Calif.: Key Curriculum Press. Available at http://www.keycurriculumpress.com/ as of July 2003.

How the West Was 1 + 3 × 4. Pleasantville, N.Y.: Sunburst Technology. Available at http://www.sunburst.com/ as of July 2003.

Math Blaster. New York: Vivendi Universal Games. Available at http://www.vugames.com/vug/ as of July 2003.

RollerCoaster Tycoon. New York: Atari. Available at http://us.atari.com as of July 2003

SimCity, SimTown. Redwood City, Calif: Electronic Arts. Available at http://www.ea.com/ as of July 2003.

CHAPTER 14

Computer Technologies and Teaching Geometry through Problem Solving

Michael T. Battista

A S STUDENTS study mathematics in a spirit of inquiry and sense making, they invent, reflect on, and refine ideas in ways that make their mathematical thinking more complex, abstract, and powerful. Computer technology can support this problem-based learning by providing representations that enable students to more productively manipulate, investigate, and make sense of mathematical ideas.

In this chapter, I illustrate ways that special computer software can be used to support problem-based learning of geometry. I give examples of sequences of problems that carefully stimulate and guide students' construction of geometric concepts. I illustrate the nature of students' reasoning as they work on these problems. And I show how mathematics learning occurs as students construct increasingly sophisticated and abstract mathematical conceptualizations in response to well-chosen sets of problems.

Problem-Based Inquiry in Geometry

A major goal of elementary school geometry is for students to progress through increasingly sophisticated levels of understanding of geometric concepts (Battista 2001; NCTM 2000). At the lowest level of understanding, students recognize shapes as visual wholes and think intuitively and imprecisely about shapes. At the next level, students use geometric concepts, such as angles, sides, angle measure, and length, to describe and analyze properties of shapes—that is, spatial relationships among the components of shapes. At the highest level, students interrelate properties of shapes, form abstract definitions for shapes, classify shapes hierarchically, and give logical arguments to justify their classifications. The remainder of this chapter has two foci: (1) to illustrate how computer-based problem solving can be used to help students progress to deeper levels of understanding of two-dimensional shapes, and (2) to demonstrate how dynamically interactive shape software can enhance students' geometric understanding.

Helping Students Develop Deep Understanding of Two-dimensional Shapes

To help students develop deeper understanding of shapes, instructional problems should encourage students to move away from holistic conceptions to conceptions that are based on analyses of the parts of shapes and relationships among those parts. At first, students' componential analyses are informal, but later, with encouragement from teachers and curricula, these analyses become framed in formal geometric language.

Investigations of Line Symmetry

Manipulating figures on a computer screen can help students analyze the components of figures that are symmetric about a line and observe how these components are related, increasing the level of sophistication in students' understanding of the concept of symmetry.

Problems for the primary grades

In the sketch in figure 14.1, drawn with The Geometer's Sketchpad, each square on the right of the vertical symmetry line has a mirror image on the left side of the line. As squares on the right are moved to various grid positions with a computer mouse, the mirror-image squares move simultaneously to their positions. (The special file, or "sketch," that must be read into The Geometer's Sketchpad's application program for this activity and the symmetry activity shown subsequently for the intermediate grades are available from the author. For similar stand-alone computer environments for investigating symmetry with pattern blocks, see Akers and others. [1998].)

Introduction. Students make three different designs with Symmetry Design Maker 1. They draw each of their designs with crayons on dot paper or make them with plastic squares and grid paper. This activity introduces students to the environment.

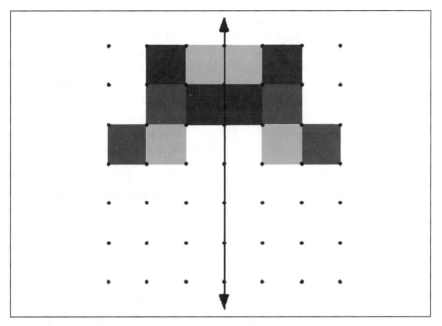

Fig.14.1. Design produced with the Symmetry Design Maker 1 tool using The Geometer's Sketchpad

Problem 1. Students predict which designs in figure 14.2 can be made with Symmetry Design Maker 1. Ask them how they know whether a design can or cannot be made. After each prediction, students check their answers on the computer. Note that the first design is not line-symmetric; the second one is. However, the third and fourth designs have regularities that students often mistake for line symmetry, with the last design having rotational instead of line symmetry. Additional problems like these should be posed.

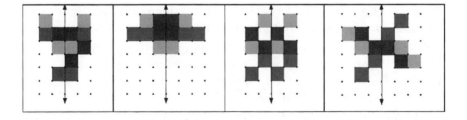

Fig.14.2. Primary-grades activity: Which designs can be made with Symmetry Design Maker 1?

Problem 2. By using plastic squares or drawings on grid paper, students make four different designs that they think can be made with Symmetry Design Maker 1. After students check their work on the computer, they should describe criteria for deciding which designs can and cannot be made with Symmetry Design Maker 1. They should discuss their criteria and test them on the computer.

Problems for the intermediate grades

In the sketch in figure 14.3, drawn with The Geometer's Sketchpad, the three segments on the left are reflections of the segments on the right. Students solve problems by manipulating the segments on the right using the circled points.

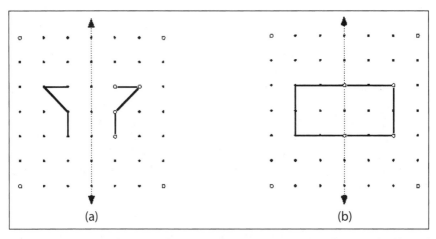

(a)   (b)

Fig. 14.3. Intermediate-grades symmetry activity using designs produced with the Symmetry Design Maker 2 tool using The Geometer's Sketchpad

Problem set 1. The same type of problems given for Symmetry Design Maker 1 can be given for Symmetry Design Maker 2. Show designs, and ask students whether they can be made with Symmetry Design Maker 2. Or have students use grid paper to make different designs that they think can be made with Symmetry Design Maker 2, then check their answers on the computer.

Problem set 2. Students use Symmetry Design Maker 2 to make a design that consists of a single rectangle (see fig. 14.3b), square, isosceles triangle, nonrectangular parallelogram, scalene triangle, nonsquare rhombus, and trapezoid.

Comments. The most important component of these computer representations of symmetry is the controllable and coordinated motion of shape components with their reflected images. Because the human perceptual system is especially attentive to motion, and because the computer environment allows precise control over movement of shape components, this environment is especially useful in helping students properly relate the components on one side of a symmetric figure to the corresponding components on the other side. This conceptualization is essential in moving students to property-based thought because it helps them understand symmetry in terms of spatial relationships between parts of a shape.

Computer Environments for Exploring Shapes as Paths

A mathematical path can be thought of as the visual record of the continuous movement of a point in a plane; for instance, one might think of drawing a curve with a pencil, or walking through new-fallen snow. Because children initially understand spatial notions in terms of action, investigating paths is a natural and interesting pursuit for them in their beginning study of geometry. Creating paths in such computer-graphics environments as Logo can help students abstract, reflect on, and analyze geometric ideas from a path perspective. In such environments, students issue commands that direct the movement of a screen object—a turtle in Logo, a ladybug in E-example 4.3 of *Principles and Standards for School Mathematics* (NCTM 2002) (Battista and Clements 1991; Clements et al. 1998). As the turtle or ladybug moves according to these commands, it draws a path of its movement. The interconnected representations of this movement—the commands and path—offer a powerful way for students to reflect on shape components and their interrelationships, helping students progress to property-based thinking.

Using commands to make geometric figures

Using a computer connected to a screen that all students can see, illustrate the basic movement commands by directing the turtle or ladybug to make a figure consisting of two line segments. For instance, in Logo, you could issue the commands FORWARD 50, RIGHT 90, FORWARD 70; this sequence of commands can be abbreviated as FD 50 RT 90 FD 70.

Problem set 1. Have students maneuver the turtle or ladybug through mazes (see Clements et al. [1998] or NCTM [2002] E-example 4.3).

Problem set 2. Have students issue commands that make the turtle or ladybug draw (*a*) a path that ends at the same point at which it begins, (b) a path that crosses itself three times, (c) a path that ends where it begins but does not cross itself, (d) a square, (e) a rectangle, and (f) a rectangle that is two times as tall as it is wide.

Problem set 3. After learning to command the turtle or ladybug to draw squares and rectangles with horizontal and vertical sides, students attempt to issue commands for the turtle or ladybug to draw "tilted" squares and rectangles—those with sides that are not vertical and horizontal.

Comment. The tasks in problem set 3 can be quite perplexing to students, causing them to construct new ways of thinking about the shapes. For instance, to solve the rectangle problem, students must first conceptualize that the "tilted" shape is in fact the same rectangular shape they are familiar with, just rotated; this realization is a major breakthrough for many young students. Second, students must conceptualize the defining properties of rectangles—opposite sides have equal lengths, all angles are 90 degrees. Students often have to be questioned about the commands they used to make the shapes, so that they become explicitly aware of these properties. Prior to doing such problems, students usually create squares and rectangles using strictly visual strategies, often with much trial and error; they use no explicit knowledge of properties of the figures. Thus, this activity encourages students to abstract and make explicit the properties of those shapes.

Predicting the results of groups of symbolized commands

Teachers can further encourage students to move to more sophisticated thinking by asking them to predict the commands needed to make shapes. Two methods for representing commands in these predictions are shown in figure 14.4. Making such predictions requires students to imagine the turtle actions that make a shape, forcing their thinking about actions and shapes to become more abstract and powerful.

Comments. Giving students appropriate problems in computer-based path environments encourages them to analyze the visual aspects of figures and the way in which their component parts are put together. Such analysis can facilitate students' transition from visual, intuitive thinking to property-based, analytic geometric thinking. Problems of this type also help students understand elements of the property-based reasoning used to analyze shapes geometrically.

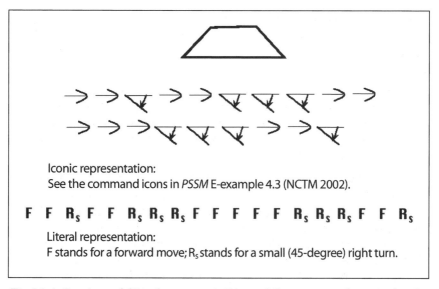

Iconic representation:
See the command icons in *PSSM* E-example 4.3 (NCTM 2002).

F F R_s F F R_s R_s R_s F F F F F R_s R_s R_s F F R_s

Literal representation:
F stands for a forward move; R_s stands for a small (45-degree) right turn.

Fig.14.4. Iconic and literal representations of the commands to make the ladybug draw the trapezoid shown

Dynamically Interactive Computer Shapes

To illustrate the power of technology in problem-based teaching, in this final example I show the type of student thinking that can be engendered in students' study of two-dimensional shapes in computerized dynamically interactive shape environments.

The Shape Makers™ Environment

The Shape Makers microworld (Battista 1998), a special add-on set of files for the dynamically interactive shape program The Geometer's Sketchpad (Jackiw 1995), furnishes screen manipulable objects for making common geometric shapes. For instance, the Parallelogram Maker makes any parallelogram that fits on the computer screen, no matter what its shape, size, or orientation—but only parallelograms. The parallelogram's shape is changed by dragging its vertices with the mouse (see fig. 14.5).

The Parallelogram Maker enables students not only to feel the constraints that maintain the parallelogram shape but also to clearly see continuous transformations of one parallelogram into another. Indeed, the Shape Makers environment takes advantage of students' natural proclivity to reason about shapes by transforming them in various ways. Such transformations are essential to the basic cognitive apparatus for perception of shape.

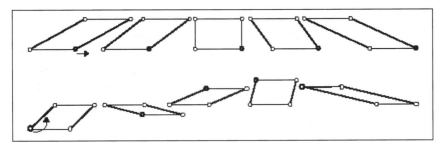

Fig.14.5. Dragging the vertices using the Shape Makers software tool Parallelogram Maker changes the shape of the parallelogram.

An Example of the Development of Students Geometric Thinking

In a classroom in which I was working, fifth graders were asked to use the seven quadrilateral Shape Makers to make the design shown in figure 14.6. As she worked on this task, Natalie posed for herself the problem of trying to make shape C with the Rhombus Maker.

Natalie: [After finding that she could not make shape B with the Rhombus Maker] I think I might have to change the Rhombus Maker to shape C.

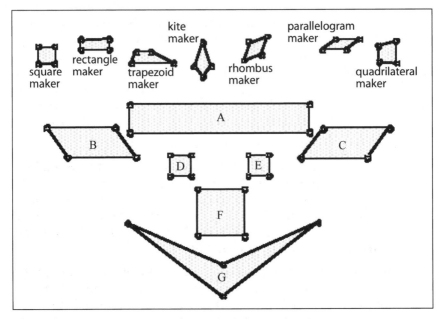

Fig.14.6. Design to be made with Shape Makers tools

Teacher: Why C?

Natalie: The Rhombus Maker is, like, leaning to the right. On B, the shape is leaning to the left. I couldn't get the Rhombus Maker to lean to the left, and C leans to the right, so I'm going to try it. [After her initial attempts to get the Rhombus Maker to fit on shape C] I don't think that is going to work.

Teacher: Why are you thinking that?

Natalie: When I try to fit it on the shape, and I try to make it bigger or smaller, the whole thing moves. It will never get exactly the right size. [As she tries to make shape C with the Rhombus Maker, she makes a shape that resembles a square.] Let's see if I can make the square with this. [Manipulates] Here's a square. I guess it could maybe be a square....

Teacher: When you tried to fit it on C, did you notice anything about shape C or the Rhombus Maker?

Natalie: The Rhombus Maker could make the same shape as shape C pretty much, but if you tried to make it small enough to fit on C, it would make the whole thing smaller or it would move the shape down....

Teacher: You said the Rhombus Maker could make the same shape as shape C, what do you mean by that?

Natalie: It could make the same shape. It could make this shape, the one with two diagonal sides and two straight sides that are parallel. I don't really know. [Natalie manipulates the Rhombus Maker in various ways, finally making a rhombus that is "slanted" the same as shape C.] See, it could make the same shape as that. [Pause] Oh, I see why it didn't work, because the four sides are even and this [shape C] is more of a rectangle....

Teacher: So what made you just notice that?

Natalie: Well, I was just thinking about it. If the Rhombus Maker was the same shape, then there is no reason it couldn't fit in to C. But I saw when I was playing with it to see how you could move it and things like that, that whenever I made it bigger or smaller, it was always like a square, but sometimes it would be leaning up, but the sides are always equal.

Comments. Natalie began this problem-solving episode thinking about shapes holistically and vaguely. As she worked on the task, her attention shifted to focusing on the lengths of the sides of shape C. This new focus, along with her self-directed manipulations of the Rhombus Maker, enabled her to abstract the property that the shapes drawn by Rhombus Makers must have sides that are all the same length. This property-based conception of the Rhombus Maker output enabled Natalie to understand why the Rhombus Maker could not make shape C—a limitation that had truly puzzled her.

This episode clearly demonstrates how the combination of well-chosen problematic tasks together with the appropriately constrained dynamic manipulation capabilities of Shape Makers is a powerful instructional tool for helping students progress from intuitive, often inaccurate, geometric ideas to more precise and powerful property-based conceptualizations.

Conclusion

The activities described in this chapter illustrate how computer software can be used pedagogically to provide sequences of problematic tasks that stimulate and support students' construction of increasingly sophisticated geometric ideas. These problem-based instructional-task sequences were carefully chosen to stimulate and support students' step-by-step construction of specific geometric conceptualizations and reasoning. They were carefully crafted on the basis of detailed analysis of both the geometric topics and research on students' learning of the topics.

The activities also illustrate the critical notion of "problem solving as conceptualization." During appropriate problem-solving activities, students create conceptualizations that enable them to "see" situations in new ways. The process of conceptualization during problem solving not only produces learning, it is itself an essential mathematical skill. To become powerful users of mathematics, students must learn to construct and use mathematical concepts to analyze and solve complex and often ill-posed problems, just as Natalie did in the foregoing classroom episode. Indeed, a major portion of the genuine problem-solving activity that takes place both within mathematics and in real-world applications involves creating and using appropriate mathematical conceptualizations.

Section 4

Research

CHAPTER 15

What Research Tells Us about Teaching Mathematics through Problem Solving

Jinfa Cai

THE TEACHING of problem solving has a long history in school mathematics (D'Ambrosio this volume; Stanic and Kilpatrick 1988). The past several decades have seen significant advances in our understanding of the complex processes involved in problem solving (Lester 1994; Schoenfeld 1992; Silver 1985). Also, considerable discussion has taken place about teaching mathematics with a focus on problem solving (e.g., Hembree and Marsh [1993]; Henningsen and Stein [1997]; Hiebert et al. [1997]; Kroll and Miller [1993]; Stein, Smith, and Silver [1999]). However, teaching mathematics through problem solving is a relatively new idea in the history of problem solving in the mathematics curriculum (Lester 1994). In fact, because teaching mathematics through problem solving is a rather new concept, it has not been the subject of much research.

Although less is known about the actual mechanisms that students use to learn and make sense of mathematics through problem solving, researchers widely agree that teaching through problem solving holds the promise of fostering students' learning

The author thanks Vic Cifarelli, Jim Hiebert, Frank Lester, and Judi Zawojewski for extremely helpful discussions, suggestions, and support in the process of preparing this chapter. The preparation of this chapter was partially supported by grant no. ESI-0114768 from the National Science Foundation (NSF). However, any opinions expressed herein are those of the author and do not necessarily represent the views of NSF.

(Schroeder and Lester 1989). Many of the ideas typically associated with this approach (e.g., changing the teacher's roles, designing and selecting problems for instruction, collaborative learning, problematizing the curriculum) have been studied extensively, resulting in research-based answers to various frequently asked questions about problem-solving instruction.

Issues and Concerns Related to Teaching through Problem Solving

This chapter discusses four common issues and concerns related to teaching through problem solving: (1) Are young children really able to explore problems on their own and arrive at sensible solutions? (2) How can teachers learn to teach through problem solving? (3) What are students' beliefs about teaching through problem solving? and (4) Will students sacrifice basic skills if they are taught mathematics through problem solving? In the discussion of each issue, I review the available research evidence that addresses the issue, then suggest what research is needed to address the issue more completely.

Issue 1: Are Young Children Really Able to Explore Problems on Their Own and Arrive at Sensible Solutions?

Teaching through problem solving starts with a problem. Students learn and understand important aspects of the concept or idea by exploring the problem situation. The problems used tend to be more open-ended and allow for multiple correct answers and multiple solution approaches. In teaching through problem solving, problems not only form the organizational focus and stimulus for students' learning but also serve as a vehicle for mathematical exploration. Students play a very active role in their learning—exploring problem situations with the teacher's guidance and "inventing" their own solution strategies. In fact, the students' own exploration of the problem is an essential component in teaching through problem solving. For example, in curriculum projects designed to help students in the primary grades learn and understand number concepts and operations with understanding, such learning is perceived as a "conceptual problem-solving activity" in which teachers support students' efforts to work out their own procedures and rules related to addition and subtraction (Fuson et al. 1997). However, a fundamental question arises: Are students really capable of exploring problem situations and inventing strategies to solve the problems?

Many researchers (e.g., Carpenter et al. [1998]; Kamii [1989]; Maher and Martino [1996]; Resnick [1989]) have investigated students' mathematical thinking and indicated that young children can explore problem situations and "invent" ways to solve the problems. For example, traditionally, to find the sum 38 + 26, students are expected to add the ones (8 + 6 = 14), write down 4 for the unit place of the sum, and carry over 1 to the tens place. Carpenter and his colleagues (1998) found that many first-, second-, and third-grade students were able to use the following invented strategies to solve the problem: (1) "Thirty and twenty is fifty, and the eight makes fifty-eight. Then six more is sixty-four"; (2) "Thirty and twenty is fifty, and eight and six is fourteen. The ten from the fourteen makes sixty, so it is sixty-four"; (3) "Thirty-eight plus twenty-six is like forty and twenty-four, which is sixty-four." In their study, Carpenter and others (1998) found that 65 percent of the students in their sample had used an invented strategy before standard algorithms were taught. By the end of this study, 88 percent of students in the sample had used invented strategies at some point during their first three years of school. The researchers also found that students who used invented strategies before they learned standard algorithms demonstrated better knowledge of base-ten number concepts and were more successful in extending their knowledge to new situations than were students who initially learned standard algorithms.

Recently, some researchers (e.g., Ben-Chaim et al. 1998; Cai 2000) have also found evidence that middle school students are able to use invented strategies to solve problems. For example, when U.S. and Chinese sixth-grade students were asked to determine whether each girl or each boy gets more pizza when seven girls share two pizzas equally and three boys share one pizza equally, they used eight different correct ways to justify that each boy gets more than each girl (Cai 2000).

Collectively, the aforementioned studies not only demonstrate that students are capable of inventing their own strategies to solve problems but also show that students' invented strategies can be used to enhance their understanding of mathematics. Thus, students in elementary and middle schools clearly are capable of inventing their own strategies to solve problems. However, at least two questions remain unanswered.

How Do Students Learn to Use Invented Strategies Before Any Instruction Takes Place?

This first question has to do with students' invented strategies. In classrooms using problem-based inquiry (e.g., Carpenter et al.

[1998]; Cobb et al. [1991]), students have opportunities to use and discuss alternative strategies for solving problems before being taught any specific strategies. What kinds of experiences and knowledge do students draw on to create sensible strategies? Kamii (1989) has argued that "the procedures children invent are rooted in the depth of their intuition and their natural ways of thinking" (p. 14). Clearly, we need to learn much more about what students' "natural" ways of thinking in mathematics are. We also must determine whether these natural ways are content or grade-level dependent.

How Can Students Be Helped to Develop More Efficient Strategies?

When students develop inefficient strategies, how can they be helped to develop more efficient ones? Previous research has shown that students are capable of inventing problem-solving strategies or mathematical procedures, but research has also revealed that invented strategies are not necessarily efficient ones (Cai, Moyer, and Grochowski 1999; Carpenter et al. 1998; Resnick 1989). For example, in a study by Cai, Moyer, and Grochowski (1999), a group of middle school students was asked to solve the following problem involving arithmetic average.

Problem. The average of Ed's ten test scores is 87. The teacher throws out the top and bottom scores, which are 55 and 95. What is the average of the remaining set of scores?

Description of the solution. The student first used one of the properties of average and determined that the average for the remaining eight scores must be between 55 and 95. Then the student drew a row of ten circles and put 95 in the first and 55 in the last, leaving eight empty circles. Using a modified sharing approach, the student realized that 55 and 95 contributed 15 to the average [(95 + 55) ÷ 10 = 15]. So the student said that each of the eight blank spaces should get 15. But since 15 is 72 less than 87, which is the average for the ten scores, the student then multiplied 10 by 72 and got 720 and then divided 720 by 8 to get 90. Thus, 90 became the average of the remaining eight scores after the top and bottom scores were thrown away.

One student came up with an unusual solution strategy in which he viewed throwing away the top and bottom scores as taking 15 away from each of the other scores. By inventing this approach, the student demonstrated an incredible understanding of averaging. However, his approach is somewhat inefficient. Clearly, invented strategies can serve as a basis for students' understanding of mathematical ideas and procedures, but students also should be guided to develop efficient strategies on the basis of their level of understanding.

Issue 2: How Can Teachers Learn to Teach through Problem Solving?

In chapter 8 of this volume, Curcio and Artzt discuss the various roles that teachers play in teaching through problem solving. Unfortunately, little research is available about how teachers learn these roles, although it does inform us in some important ways. It indicates that teachers' success in teaching through problem solving is related to the encouragement and support they receive from their fellow teachers and other resource partners as they begin to change their approach to teaching (Cobb et al. 1991; Cohen 1990; Greeno and Goldman 1998; Ma 1999; Stein, Smith, and Silver 1999; Stigler and Hiebert 1999). Teachers learn their new roles through teaching and self-reflection rather than merely from taking courses (Ball 1993; Borko and Putnam 1996; Bransford, Brown, and Cocking 1999; Shimahara and Sakai 1995). After a series of studies of elementary-level and secondary-level preservice teachers, Ball (1993) concluded that requiring teachers to take more courses would not improve their understanding of school mathematics and enhance their teaching. Instead, teachers need opportunities to analyze mathematical ideas and make connections in instructional situations. Also, teachers learn to play their roles in teaching through participating in daily collegial activities in school (Paine and Ma 1993; Stein, Smith, and Silver 1999). Shimahara and Sakai (1995) found that both U.S. and Japanese new teachers learn more about teaching from daily conversations with other teachers than from formally organized workshops or from student teaching. Everyday conversation about teaching in the school setting is important because the conversation is concrete and contextual rather than abstract and context free.

Two new roles that teachers are asked to play in a learning environment based on teaching through problem solving are selecting appropriate tasks and organizing classroom discourse, and research suggests that both roles are important for fostering students' mathematical understanding. Research also offers some insights about the factors that influence teachers in these efforts.

Selecting Appropriate Problems

As Van de Walle points out in chapter 5 of this volume, when teachers teach through problem solving, students actively participate in the process of constructing knowledge and, therefore, make sense of mathematics in their own terms. In other words, they become active participants in the creation of knowledge rather than passive receivers of rules and procedures. Although teaching through problem solving starts with problems, only worthwhile problems give students the chance both to solidify and extend what they know and to stimulate their learning. One of the teacher's roles is to select or develop such worthwhile problems.

Doyle (1988) argues that problems with different cognitive demands are likely to induce different kinds of learning. Problems govern not only students' attention to specific aspects of content but also their ways of processing information. Regardless of the context, worthwhile tasks should be intriguing, with a level of challenge that invites exploration, speculation, and hard work (NCTM 2000, p. 19). Mathematical problems that are truly problematic and involve significant mathematics have the potential to provide intellectual contexts for students' mathematical development.

What is a worthwhile problem? Lappan and Phillips (1998) developed a set of criteria useful for choosing problems for middle-grades mathematics instruction. These criteria can also be applied to selecting problems for instruction in earlier grades. Of course, the most important criterion of a worthwhile mathematical problem is that it should serve as a means for students to learn important mathematics. Such a problem does not have to be complicated with a fancy format. As Hiebert and his colleagues (1996) noted, a problem as simple as finding the difference in heights between two children, one sixty-two inches tall and the other thirty-seven inches tall, can be worthwhile if teachers use it appropriately to teach students multidigit addition.

Organizing Classroom Discourse

Although using worthwhile problems is an important feature of effective problem-based mathematics instruction, a worthwhile problem may not be implemented appropriately. For example, Stein, Grover, and Henningsen (1996) found that only about 50 percent of tasks that were set up to require the application of procedures with meaningful connections were implemented in a way that resulted in meaningful connections. Therefore, another role that teachers play is deciding how to use worthwhile problems to maximize students' learning opportunities in the classroom. In addition to engaging students in good problem-solving activities, the type of engagement is vitally important. Put another way, the nature of the classroom discourse—involving both students and teacher—is a very important consideration. In learning through problem solving, students not only have more opportunity to express their ideas and justify their answers verbally but also have more opportunity to pose and respond to cognitively demanding questions (Hiebert and Wearne 1993; Lampert 1990).

A number of factors may influence the implementation of worthwhile problems in the classroom. One of the predominant factors is the amount of time allocated to solving problems and discussing solution efforts (Henningsen and Stein 1997; Perry, Vanderstoep, and Yu 1993; Stigler and Hiebert 1999). In teaching through problem solving, discussing a problem and its alternative solutions usually takes longer than demonstrating a routine classroom activity. Hiebert and Wearne (1993) found that class-rooms with a primary focus on teaching through problem solving used fewer problems and spent more time on each of them com-pared with classrooms without a primary focus on problem solv-ing. Moreover, in problem-solving classrooms, teachers ask more conceptually oriented questions (e.g., ones that describe a strate-gy or explain the underlying reasoning that led to an answer) and fewer recall-based questions than teachers do in classrooms with-out a primary focus on problem solving. These findings are con-sistent with those in cross-cultural comparative studies (Perry, Vanderstoep, and Yu 1993; Stigler and Hiebert 1999).

In teaching through problem solving, the teacher's role in guiding mathematical discourse is a highly complex activity. Besides devoting an appropriate amount of time to the discussion of problems, "teachers must also decide what aspects of a task to highlight, how to organize and orchestrate the work of the stu-dents, what questions to ask to challenge those with varied levels of expertise, and how to support students without taking over the process of thinking for them and thus eliminating the challenge" (NCTM 2000, p. 19). In other words, teachers must provide ade-quate support for students' mathematical exploration but not so much that they take over the process of thinking for their students (e.g., Ball [1993]; Hiebert et al. [1997]; Lampert [1985]). No specif-ic, research-based guidelines exist that teachers can use to achieve the appropriate balance of teacher-directed and teacher-guided instruction, and research will not likely ever be able to pro-vide such guidelines.

Not only do teachers need specific ideas about how they learn to play their roles, they also need concrete examples to guide their practice. Educators must document more cases and describe what is involved in teaching through problem solving, how appro-priate mathematical problems are selected, and how classroom discourse is organized to appropriately guide students engaging in the mathematical problem (Ball and Bass 2000).

Issue 3: What Are Students' Beliefs about Problem Solving?

All too often, students hold the belief that only one "right" way exists to approach and solve a problem. The results from both national (Lindquist 1989) and international (Lapointe, Mead, and Askew 1992) assessments show that many students view mathematics not as a creative and intellectually engaging activity but rather as a set of rules and procedures that they must memorize to follow the single correct way rapidly to obtain the single correct answer. For example, nearly 50 percent of U.S. students reported that learning mathematics is mostly memorizing, and about one-fifth of students disagreed with the statement that a mathematical problem can be solved in different ways (Lindquist 1989).

Students' beliefs about the nature of problem solving are not restricted to how problems are supposed to be solved. Many students also have firmly held beliefs about what is expected of them when their teachers give them problems to solve. For example, in solving the absurd problem "There are 26 sheep and 10 goats in a ship. How old is the captain?" 10 percent of Belgian kindergartners and first graders "solved" this problem by adding the numbers to get the captain's age (Verschaffel and De Corte 1997). The percents of students who "solved" the problem in this way increased to 60 percent for the third and fourth graders and 45 percent for the fifth graders. Although they had had more formal education, the third-, fourth-, and fifth-grade students paid less attention to making sense of the problem and their solutions than the first graders did. A similar problem was administered to a group of Chinese fourth graders, seventh graders, eighth graders, and twelfth graders. About 90 percent of the Chinese fourth graders, 82 percent of the seventh and eighth graders, and 34 percent of the twelfth graders "solved" this problem by combining the numbers in it without realizing the absurd nature of the problem (Lee, Zhang, and Zheng 1997). When asked why they did not realize that the problem was meaningless, many of these students responded that "any problem assigned by a teacher always has a solution." Similar results have been documented consistently by other researchers (e.g., Lester, Garofalo, and Kroll [1989]).

Students' beliefs about problem solving may also be revealed when they are asked to solve a problem using alternative strategies. For example, in a study by Silver, Leung, and Cai (1995), Japanese and U.S. fourth-grade students were asked to find multiple ways to determine the total number of marbles that had been arranged in a certain way. Some students obtained different answers when they used alternative solution strategies; surprisingly, the discrepancies in their answers did not seem to bother them.

Studies by a number of researchers (e.g., Carpenter et al. [1998]; Cobb et al. [1991]; Verschaffel and De Corte [1997]) suggest that teachers can change students' beliefs about mathematics and problem solving by using alternative instructional practices, such as teaching through problem solving. For example, Cobb and his colleagues (1991) found that in contrast with students in a control group, students in their problem-centered project held more positive beliefs about the importance of understanding the mathematics. Teaching through problem solving may provide the kind of healthy learning environment that students need to form positive beliefs about mathematics and problem solving before they have a chance to develop any negative dispositions. Some questions regarding students' beliefs about problem solving remain unanswered.

How Do Students' Beliefs about Problem Solving Affect Their Learning?

The finding that teachers' beliefs about mathematics affect their teaching is well documented (Thompson 1992). Teachers who hold different beliefs about mathematics teach differently. What about students? How do students' beliefs about problem solving affect their learning through problem solving? Research clearly shows that some students do not believe that a mathematical problem can be solved in different ways, and they think that learning mathematics is mostly memorizing (Lester, Garofalo, and Kroll 1989; Schoenfeld 1992). How would students who hold such negative beliefs about problem solving learn mathematics differently from those who have more positive beliefs?

What Difficulties Do Students Face When Switched to a Problem-Based Classroom?

Another unanswered question regards students' internal struggles when they go from traditional to problem-based classrooms. Research shows that when teachers shift from their usual ways of teaching to problem-based teaching, they face a number of dilemmas and internal struggles (Smith 2000a). If students have already become used to one way of instruction and suddenly experience a very different form of instruction in which they are expected to explore mathematics rather than follow procedures, what dilemmas do they face?

Issue 4: Will Students Sacrifice Basic Skills If They Are Taught Mathematics through Problem Solving?

In learning through problem solving, students have opportunities to explore problem situations and solve problems, and they are encouraged to use whatever solution strategies they wish. Students also have opportunities to share their various strategies with one another. Thus, students' learning and understanding of mathematics can be enhanced through considering one another's ideas and debating the validity of alternative approaches. In teaching through problem solving, the focus is on conceptual understanding rather than on procedural knowledge; students are expected to learn algorithms and master basic skills as they engage in explorations of worthwhile problems. However, many people, parents and teachers alike, worry that developing students' higher-order thinking skills in teaching through problem solving comes at the expense of developing basic mathematical skills. Obviously, both basic skills and higher-order thinking skills in mathematics are important, but having one does not ensure having the other. These concerns, therefore, are reasonable (Battista 1999; Schoenfeld 2002).

Several studies involving elementary-grades students (Carpenter et al. 1998; Cobb et al. 1991; Fuson, Carroll, and Drueck 2000; Hiebert and Wearne 1993) have consistently shown that in comparison with students in control groups, students experiencing problem-based instruction usually have higher levels of mathematical understanding and problem-solving skills and have at least comparable basic numerical skills. For example, Fuson, Carroll, and Drueck (2000) found that students using a problem-based curriculum outperformed students using a traditional curriculum on a computation test. On a ten-task number-sense test, students using the problem-based curriculum scored higher than traditional students on two tasks, lower on one task, and the same on the remaining seven tasks.

In another study, Cobb and others (1991) examined the performance on a standardized mathematics achievement test of ten classes, whose students had participated in a yearlong, problem-centered mathematics project, and compared the results with those of students in eight non–project classes. The researchers also compared the students' performance on instruments designed to assess students' computational proficiency and conceptual development in arithmetic. They found that levels of computational performance between project-class and non-project-class students were comparable, but the former had higher levels of conceptual understanding in mathematics than the latter did.

Other studies involving elementary school students (e.g., Carpenter et al. [1998]; Hiebert and Wearne [1993]) have obtained similar results: Students learning mathematics through problem solving do at least as well as those students receiving traditional instruction on both basic computation and conceptual understanding.

Similarly, the few existing studies involving middle school students (Ridgeway et al. 2002; Romberg and Shafer 2002) have shown that students with problem-based instruction have higher levels of mathematical understanding than students with more traditional instruction, and students in the two groups display comparable basic number skills. Results from the study by Romberg and Shafer (2002) suggest that students using problem-centered curricular materials can maintain basic number skills while developing higher-order thinking skills. Ridgeway and his colleagues (2002) obtained similar results when they compared the performance of middle school students who had received problem-based instruction with that of students who had used more traditional middle school mathematics curricula. Specifically, they compared the two groups' performance on two tests: the Iowa Test of Basic Skills (ITBS) to assess basic skills, and a test designed by the Balanced Assessment Project to assess students' performance in mathematical reasoning, communication, connections, and problem solving. They found that the students who had experienced problem-based instruction showed significantly more growth in mathematical reasoning, communication, making connections, and problem solving than did students receiving traditional instruction, whereas the growth of basic skills in the two groups was the same as in the ITBS national sample.

Research involving elementary and middle school students indicates that students will not sacrifice basic skills if they are taught mathematics through problem solving[1]. However, one would be premature to make hard-and-fast claims with absolute

---

[1] The results from research involving high school students are not consistent. For example, in a comparative study of the effects of the high school Core-Plus Mathematics Project (CPMP) curriculum and more conventional curricula on the growth of students' understanding, skill, and problem-solving ability in algebra, Huntley et al. (2000) found that the CPMP curriculum is more effective than conventional curricula in developing students' ability to solve algebraic problems when those problems are presented in realistic contexts and when students are allowed to use graphing calculators. Conventional curricula are more effective than the CPMP curriculum in developing students' skills in manipulating symbolic expressions in algebra when those expressions are presented free of application context and when students are not allowed to use graphing calculators.

confidence about the computational proficiency of students in a learning environment that focuses on teaching through problem solving. A number of unanswered questions must still be explored.

How Can Teachers Teach Basic Skills in a Problem-Based Classroom?

First, how can we develop students' basic mathematical skills in a problem-based classroom? Research makes clear that meaningless, rote memorization is not an appropriate way for students to learn basic facts and develop computational proficiency (Hiebert 1999). Students seem to develop sound basic mathematical skills when taught through problem solving, but adequate descriptions of such teaching and its effect should be studied and documented.

Should Students Acquire Basic Skills More Quickly in a Problem-Based Setting?

Another unanswered question is related to the expectation of students' level of proficiency with basic mathematical skills. Research has shown that elementary and middle school students who have learned mathematics through problem-based instruction outperform their counterparts in traditional programs on tasks assessing higher-order thinking skills, without sacrificing basic mathematical skills. Apparently, however, the growth in higher-order thinking skills is greater than that in the basic skills. Should we be satisfied with this level of proficiency? Although this question is decided by value judgments rather than merely by empirical research, the issue is still worth exploration and discussion because of the importance of basic skills in school mathematics. Cross-national studies have consistently shown that U.S. students have inadequate knowledge of basic number facts and computational proficiency, especially when compared with Asian students (Cai 1995; Stigler, Lee, and Stevenson 1990; U.S. Department of Education 1997). Could we reasonably expect students to develop basic facts and operation skills with numbers and symbols at the same level as higher-order thinking skills when they are taught through problem solving?

Final Thoughts

What does research tell us about teaching mathematics through problem solving? This chapter clearly shows that some aspects of the approach have considerable support from empirical research, but some important issues require additional research. In spite of the absence of research, teaching through problem solving is receiving increasingly strong support from researchers and educators. This support might be related to the unsatisfactory findings from national and international assessments of U.S. students' mathematical performance, which indicate the urgent need for developing more ambitious learning goals and reforming instructional practices. Traditional ways of teaching—which involve memorizing and reciting facts, rules, and procedures, with an emphasis on applying well-rehearsed procedures to solve routine problems—are often inadequate. Researchers and educators are eager to reform instructional practices to emphasize the development of students' thinking, understanding, reasoning, and problem solving.

Based on careful analysis of theoretical perspectives and empirical results on teaching mathematics through problem solving, consensus is growing among researchers and educators that this method of teaching offers considerable promise. Theoretically, this approach makes sense. In problem-based classrooms, learning takes place during the process of problem solving. As students solve problems, they may use any approach they can think of, draw on any piece of knowledge they have learned, and justify their ideas in ways they believe are convincing. The learning environment of a problem-based classroom provides a natural setting for students to present various solutions to their group or class and learn mathematics through social interactions, meaning negotiation, and shared understanding. Such activities help students clarify their ideas and acquire different perspectives of the concept they are learning. Increasing amounts of research data confirm the promise of teaching through problem solving. However, to realize this promise, much more effort, research and development, and refinement of practice must take place. We need to systematically explore issues raised in this chapter as well as issues related to the mechanisms and effectiveness of teaching through problem solving to make the promise a reality.

Section 5

References

References

Akers, Joan, Michael T. Battista, Anne Goodrow, Douglas H. Clements, and Julie Sarama. *Shapes, Halves, and Symmetry.* Unit in Investigations in Number, Data, and Space curriculum. Glenview, Ill.: Scott, Foresman & Co., 1998.

Artzt, Alice F., and Eleanor Armour-Thomas. "Development of a Cognitive-Metacognitive Framework for Protocol Analysis of Mathematical Problem Solving in Small Groups." *Cognition and Instruction* 9 (1992): 137–75.

———. "Mathematics Teaching as Problem Solving: A Framework for Studying Teacher Metacognition Underlying Instructional Practice in Mathematics." *Instructional Science* 26 (March 1998): 5–25.

———. *Becoming a Reflective Mathematics Teacher: A Guide for Observations and Self-Assessment.* Mahwah, N.J.: Lawrence Erlbaum Associates, 2002.

Ball, Deborah L. "With an Eye on the Mathematical Horizon: Dilemmas of Teaching Elementary School Mathematics." *Elementary School Journal* 93 (March 1993): 373–97.

Ball, Deborah L., and Hyman Bass. "Interweaving Content and Pedagogy in Teaching and Learning to Teach: Knowing and Using Mathematics." In *Multiple Perspectives on the Teaching and Learning of Mathematics,* edited by Jo Boaler, pp. 83–104. Westport, Conn.: Ablex Publishing Corp., 2000.

Battista, Michael T. *Shape Makers: Developing Geometric Reasoning with The Geometer's Sketchpad.* Berkeley, Calif.: Key Curriculum Press, 1998.

———. "The Mathematical Miseducation of America's Youth." *Phi Delta Kappan* 80 (1999): 424–33.

———. "A Research-Based Perspective on Teaching School Geometry." In *Advances in Research on Teaching: Subject-Specific Instructional Methods and Activities,* edited by Jere Brophy, pp. 145–85. New York: JAI Press, 2001.

Battista, Michael T., and Douglas H. Clements. *Logo Geometry.* Morristown, N.J.: Silver Burdett & Ginn, 1991.

Becker, Jerry P., Edward A. Silver, Mary Grace Kantowski, Kenneth J. Travers, and James W. Wilson. "Some Observations of Mathematics Teaching in Japanese Elementary and Junior High Schools." *Arithmetic Teacher* 38 (October 1990): 12–21.

Benbow, Camilla P. "Grouping Intellectually Advanced Students for Instruction." In *Excellence in Educating Gifted and Talented Learners,* edited by Joyce Van-Tassel-Baska, pp. 261–78. Denver, Colo.: Love Publishing Co., 1998.

Ben-Chaim, David, James T. Fey, William M. Fitzgerald, Catherine, Benedetto, and Jane Miller. "Proportional Reasoning among Seventh-Grade Students with Different Curricular Experiences." *Educational Studies in Mathematics* 36 (1998): 247–73.

Bley, Nancy, and Carol A. Thornton. *Teaching Mathematics to Students with Learning Disabilities.* Austin, Tex.: Pro Ed, 2001.

Borasi, Raffaella and Judith Fonzi. "Introducing Math Teachers to Inquiry: A Framework and Supporting Materials for Teacher Educators." Unpublished multimedia materials.

Borko, Hilda, and Ralph T. Putnam. "Learning to Teach." In *Handbook of Educational Psychology,* edited by David C. Berliner and Robert C. Calfee, pp. 673–708. New York: Macmillan, 1996.

Bransford, John D., Ann L. Brown, and Rodney R. Cocking, eds. *How People Learn: Brain, Mind, Experience, and School.* Washington, D.C.: National Academy Press, 1999.

Brooks, Edward. *The Normal Elementary Algebra: Containing the First Principles of the Science, Developed with Conciseness and Simplicity, for Common Schools, Academies, Seminaries and Normal Schools.* Philadelphia: Sower, Potts, 1871.

Brown, Stephen I., and Marion I. Walter. *The Art of Problem Posing.* 2d ed. Hillsdale, N.J.: Lawrence Erlbaum Associates, 1990.

———. *Problem Posing: Reflections and Applications.* Hillsdale, N.J.: Lawrence Erlbaum Associates, 1993.

Brownell, William. A. "The Place of Meaning in the Teaching of Arithmetic." *Elementary School Journal* 47 (January 1947): 256–65.

Brownell, William A., and Verner M. Sims. "The Nature of Understanding." In *Forty-fifth Yearbook of the National Society for the Study of Education, Part I: The Measurement of Understanding,* edited by Nelson B. Henry, pp. 27–43. Chicago: University of Chicago, 1946.

Cai, Jinfa. *A Cognitive Analysis of U.S. and Chinese Students' Mathematical Performance on Tasks Involving Computation, Simple Problem Solving, and Complex Problem Solving.* Monograph 7 of the *Journal for Research in Mathematics Education.* Reston, Va.: National Council of Teachers of Mathematics, 1995.

———. "Mathematical Thinking Involved in U.S. and Chinese Students' Solving Process-Constrained and Process-Open Problems." *Mathematical Thinking and Learning: An International Journal* 2 (2000): 309–40.

Cai, Jinfa., John. C. Moyer, and Nancy. J. Grochowski. "Making the Mean Meaningful: An Instructional Study." *Research in Middle Level Education* 22 (1999): 1–24.

Carpenter, Thomas P. "Learning to Add and Subtract: An Exercise in Problem Solving." In *Teaching and Learning Mathematical Problem Solving: Multiple Research Perspectives* edited by Edward A. Silver, pp. 17–40. Hillsdale, N.J.: Lawrence Erlbaum Associates, 1985.

———. "Teaching as Problem Solving." In *The Teaching and Assessing of Mathematical Problem Solving,* edited by Randall I. Charles and Edward A. Silver, pp. 187–202. Reston, Va.: National Council of Teachers of Mathematics, and Hillsdale, N.J.: Lawrence Erlbaum Associates, 1988.

Carpenter, Thomas P., Megan L. Franke, Victoria R. Jacobs, Elizabeth Fennema, and Susan B. Empson. "A Longitudinal Study of Invention and Understanding in Children's Multidigit Addition and Subtraction." *Journal for Research in Mathematics Education* 29 (January 1998): 3–20.

Case, Adam. *Who Tells the Truth?* Stradbroke, England: Tarquin Publications, 1991.

Cauley, Kathleen M. "Construction of Logical Knowledge: Study of Borrowing in Subtraction." *Journal of Educational Psychology* 80 (June 1988): 202–5.

Clements, Douglas. H., Michael T. Battista, Joan Akers, Virginia Woolley, Julie S. Meredith, and Sue McMillen. *Turtle Paths.* Unit in Investigations in Number, Data, and Space curriculum. White Plains, N.Y.: Dale Seymour Publications, 1998.

Cobb, Paul, and Janet Bowers. "Cognitive and +− Situated Learning Perspectives in Theory and Practice." *Educational Researcher* 28 (March 1999): 4–15.

Cobb, Paul, Erna Yackel, and Terry Wood. "Curriculum and Teacher Development: Psychological and Anthropological Perspectives." In *Integrating Research on Teaching and Learning Mathematics,* edited by Elizabeth Fennema, Thomas P. Carpenter, and Susan J. Lamon, pp. 92–130. Madison: Wisconsin Center for Education Research, University of Wisconsin—Madison, 1988.

Cobb, Paul, Terry Wood, and Erna Yackel. "Discourse, Mathematical Thinking, and Classroom Practice." In *Contexts for Learning: Sociocultural Dynamics in Children's Development,* edited by Ellice A. Forman, Norris Minick, and C. Addison Stone, pp. 99–119. New York: Oxford University Press, 1993.

Cobb, Paul, Terry Wood, Erna Yackel, John Nicholls, Grayson Wheatley, Beatriz Trigatti, and Marcella Perlwitz. "Assessment of a Problem-Centered Second-Grade Mathematics Project." *Journal for Research in Mathematics Education* 22 (January 1991): 3–29.

Cohen, David K. "A Revolution in One Classroom: The Case of Mrs. Oublier." *Educational Evaluation and Policy Analysis* 12 (1990): 263–76.

Crown, Warren D., Janet Caldwell, and Jane Schielack. *eTools*. Glenview, Ill.: Scott Foresman, in press.

Davis, Robert. B. "Understanding 'Understanding.'" *Journal of Mathematical Behavior* 11 (1992): 225–41.

Dewey, John. *How We Think: A Restatement of the Relation of Reflective Thinking to the Educative Process*. Boston: D.C. Heath & Co., 1933.

Diezmann, Carmel M., and James J. Watters. "Catering for Mathematically Gifted Elementary Students: Learning from Challenging Tasks." *Gifted Child Today* 23, no. 4 (2000): 14–19, 52.

———. "The Collaboration of Mathematically Gifted Students on Challenging Tasks." *Journal for the Education of the Gifted* 25, no. 1 (2001): 7–31.

Doyle, Walter. "Work in Mathematics Classes: The Context of Students' Thinking during Instruction." *Educational Psychologist* 23 (1988): 167–80.

Economopoulos, Karen, and Susan Jo Russell. *Coins, Coupons, and Combinations: The Number System*. A grade-2 unit in Investigations in Number, Data, and Space curriculum. White Plains, N.Y.: Dale Seymour Publications, 1998.

English, Lyn. "Reasoning by Analogy: A Fundamental Process in Children's Mathematical Learning." In *Developing Mathematical Reasoning in Grades K–12*, 1999 Yearbook of the National Council of Teachers of Mathematics (NCTM), edited by Lee Stiff, pp. 22–36. Reston, Va.: NCTM, 1999.

———. "Mathematical and Analogical Reasoning of Young Learners." In *Mathematical and Analogical Reasoning of Young Learners*, edited by Lyn English. Mahwah, N.J.: Lawrence Erlbaum Associates, in press.

Fesler, Jane. *Problem of the Week*. Torrance, Calif.: Frank Schaffer Publications, 1995.

Fuson, Karen C., William M. Carroll, and Jane V. Drueck. "Achievement Results for Second and Third Graders Using the Standards-Based Curriculum Everyday Mathematics." *Journal for Research in Mathematics Education* 31 (May 2000): 277–95.

Fuson, Karen C., Diana Wearne, James C. Hiebert, Hanlie G. Murray, Pieter G. Human, Alwyn I. Olivier, Thomas P. Carpenter, and Elizabeth Fennema. "Children's Conceptual Structures for Multidigit

Numbers and Methods of Multidigit Addition and Subtraction." *Journal for Research in Mathematics Education* 28 (March 1997): 130–62.

Garofalo, Joseph, and Frank K. Lester, Jr. "Metacognition, Cognitive Monitoring, and Mathematical Performance." *Journal for Research in Mathematics Education* 16 (May 1985): 163–76.

Goldenberg, E. Paul, and Marion I. Walter. "Problem Posing as a Tool for Teaching Mathematics." In *Teaching Mathematics through Problem Solving: Grades 6–12,* edited by Harold L. Schoen and Randall I. Charles, pp. 69–84. Reston, Va.: National Council of Teachers of Mathematics, 2003.

Goldman, Susan R., Ted S. Hasselbring, and the Cognition and Technology Group at Vanderbilt. "Achieving Meaningful Mathematics Literacy for Students with Learning Disabilities." In *Mathematics Education for Students with Learning Disabilities: Theory to Practice,* edited by Diane Pedrotty Rivera, pp. 237–54. Austin, Tex.: Pro Ed, 1998.

Greeno, James. "Situative Research Relevant to Standards for School Mathematics." In *A Research Companion to "Principles and Standards for School Mathematics,"* edited by Jeremy Kilpatrick and W. Gary Martin, pp. 304–32. Reston, Va: National Council of Teachers of Mathematics, 2003.

Greeno, James G., and Shelley V. Goldman, eds, *Thinking Practice in Mathematics and Science Learning.* Mahwah, N.J.: Lawrence Erlbaum Associates, 1998.

Hegarty, Mary, Richard Mayer, and Christopher Monk. "Comprehension of Arithmetic Word Problems: A Comparison of Successful and Unsuccessful Problem Solvers." *Journal of Educational Psychology* 87 (March 1995): 18–32.

Hembree, Ray, and Harold Marsh. "Problem Solving in Early Childhood: Building Foundations." In *Research Ideas for the Classroom: Early Childhood Mathematics,* edited by Robert J. Jensen, pp. 151–70. Reston, Va.: National Council of Teachers of Mathematics, 1993.

Henningsen, Marjorie A., and Mary Kay Stein. "Mathematical Tasks and Students' Cognition: Classroom-Based Factors That Support and Inhibit High-Level Mathematical Thinking and Reasoning." *Journal for Research in Mathematics Education* 28 (November 1997): 524–49.

Hiebert, James. "Relationships between Research and the NCTM Standards." *Journal for Research in Mathematics Education* 30 (January 1999): 3–19.

Hiebert, James, and Thomas P. Carpenter. "Learning and Teaching with Understanding." In *Handbook of Research on Mathematics Teaching and Learning,* edited by Douglas A. Grouws, pp. 65–97. New York: Macmillan, 1992.

Hiebert, James, Thomas T. Carpenter, Elizabeth Fennema, Karen Fuson, Piet Human, Hanlie Murray, Alwyn Olivier, and Diana Wearne. "Problem Solving as a Basis for Reform in Curriculum and Instruction: The Case of Mathematics." *Educational Researcher* 25 (1996): 12–21.

Hiebert, James, Thomas P. Carpenter, Elizabeth Fennema, Karen Fuson, Diana Wearne, Hanlie Murray, Alwyn Olivier, and Piet Human. *Making Sense: Teaching and Learning Mathematics with Understanding.* Portsmouth, N.H.: Heinemann, 1997.

Hiebert, James, and James W. Stigler. "A Proposal for Improving Classroom Teaching: Lessons from the TIMSS Video Study." *Elementary School Journal* 101 (September 2000): 3–20.

Hiebert, James, and Diana Wearne. "Instructional Task, Classroom Discourse, and Students' Learning in Second Grade." *American Educational Research Journal* 30 (1993): 393–425.

Hong, Lily Toy. *Two of Everything.* Morton Grove, Ill.: Albert Whitman & Co., 1993.

House, Peggy, ed. *Providing Opportunities for the Mathematically Gifted K–12.* Reston, Va.: National Council of Teachers of Mathematics, 1987.

Huntley, Mary Ann, Chris L. Rasmussen, Roberto S. Villarubi, Jaruwan Sangtong, and James T. Fey. "Effects of Standards-Based Mathematics Education: A Study of the Core-Plus Mathematics Project Algebra and Functions Strand." *Journal for Research in Mathematics Education* 31 (May 2000): 328–61.

Jackiw, Nicholas. The Geometer's Sketchpad. Berkeley, Calif.: Key Curriculum Press, 1995. Software.

Johnson, Dana T. "Mathematics Curriculum for the Gifted." In *Comprehensive Curriculum for Gifted Learners,* edited by Joyce VanTassel-Baska, pp. 231–61. Needham Heights, Mass.: Longwood, 1994.

Kamii, Constance K., with Leslie Baker Housman. *Young Children Reinvent Arithmetic: Implications of Piaget's Theory.* New York: Teachers College Press, 1989.

Kroll, Diana Lambdin and Tammy Miller. "Insights from Research on Mathematical Problem Solving in the Middle Grades." In *Research Ideas for the Classroom: Middle Grades Mathematics,* edited by Douglas T. Owens, pp. 58–77. Reston, Va.: National Council of Teachers of Mathematics, 1993.

Labinowicz, Ed. *Learning from Children.* Menlo Park, Calif.: Addison-Wesley Publishing Co., 1985.

———. "Children's Right to Be Wrong." *Arithmetic Teacher* 35 (December 1987): 2.

Lampert, Magdalene. "How Do Teachers Manage to Teach?" *Harvard Educational Review* 55 (1985): 178–94.

————. "When the Problem Is Not the Question and the Solution Is Not the Answer: Mathematical Knowing and Teaching. *American Educational Research Journal* 27 (1990): 29–63.

————. *Teaching Problems and the Problems of Teaching.* New Haven, Conn.: Yale University Press, 2001.

Lampert, Magdalene, Peggy Rittenhouse, and Carol Crumbaugh. "Agreeing to Disagree: Developing Sociable Mathematical Discourse." In *Handbook of Education and Human Development: New Models of Learning, Teaching, and Schooling,* edited by David R. Olson and Nancy Torrance, pp. 731–64. Cambridge, Mass.: Blackwell Publishers, 1996.

Lapointe, Archie E., Nancy A. Mead, and Janice M. Askew. *Learning Mathematics.* Princeton, N.J.: Educational Testing Service, 1992.

Lappan, Glenda, and Elizabeth Phillips. "Teaching and Learning in the Connected Mathematics Project." In *Mathematics in the Middle,* edited by Larry Leutzinger, pp. 83–92. Reston, Va.: National Council of Teachers of Mathematics, 1998.

Lee, Binyi, Danzhou Zhang, and Zheng Zhengyao. "Examination Culture and Mathematics Education." *EduMath* 4 (1997): 96–103.

Lesh, Richard, and Helen Doerr. *Beyond Constructivism: A Models and Modeling Perspective on Mathematical Problem Solving, Learning, and Teaching.* Mahwah, N.J.: Lawrence Erlbaum Associates, 2002.

Lesh, Richard, Mark Hoover, Bonnie Hole, Anthony Kelly, and Tom Post. "Principles for Developing Thought-Revealing Activities for Students and Teachers." In *Handbook of Research Design in Mathematics and Science Education,* edited by Anthony Kelly and Richard Lesh, pp. 591–646. Mahwah, N.J.: Lawrence Erlbaum Associates, 2000.

Lester, Frank K. Jr. "Musings about Mathematical Problem Solving Research: 1970–1994." Special 25th-anniversary issue, *Journal for Research in Mathematics Education* 25 (December 1994): 660–75.

Lester, Frank K., Joe Garofalo, and Diana L. Kroll. "Self-Confidence, Interest, Beliefs and Metacognition: Key Influences on Problem-Solving Behavior." In *Affect and Mathematical Problem Solving: A New Perspective,* edited by Douglas B. McLeod and Verna M. Adams, pp. 75–88. New York: Springer-Verlag, 1989.

Lindquist, Mary M. *Results from the Fourth Mathematics Assessment of the National Assessment of Educational Progress.* Reston, Va.: National Council of Teachers of Mathematics, 1989.

Ma, Liping. *Knowing and Teaching Elementary Mathematics: Teachers' Understanding of Fundamental Mathematics in China and the United States.* Mahwah, N.J.: Lawrence Erlbaum Associates, 1999.

Maher, Carolyn A., and Amy M. Martino. "The Development of the Idea of Mathematical Proof: A Five-Year Case Study." *Journal for Research in Mathematics Education* 27 (March 1996): 194–214.

Mason, John. "Researching from the Inside in Mathematics Education— Locating an I–You Relationship." In *Proceedings of the Eighteenth International Conference for the Psychology of Mathematics Education,* edited by João P. da Ponte and João F. Matos, pp. 176–94. Lisbon, Portugal: University of Lisbon, 1994.

Math Forum at Drexel. "The Math Forum Student Center, Middle School Problem of the Week." Available at mathforum.org/midpow/solutions/solution.ehtml?puzzle=25 as of May 2001

Milne, William J. *A Mental Arithmetic.* New York: American Book, 1897.

Montague, Marjorie. "Cognitive Strategy Instruction in Mathematics for Students with Learning Disabilities." In *Mathematics Education for Students with Learning Disabilities: Theory to Practice,* edited by Diane Pedrotty Rivera, pp. 177–200. Austin, Tex.: Pro Ed, 1998.

Moses, Barbara, Elizabeth Bjork, and E. Paul Goldenberg. "Beyond Problem Solving: Problem Posing." In *Teaching and Learning Mathematics in the 1990s,* 1990 Yearbook of the National Council of Teachers of Mathematics (NCTM), edited by Thomas J. Cooney, pp. 82–91. Reston, Va.: NCTM, 1990. Republished in *Problem Posing: Reflections and Applications,* edited by Stephen I. Brown and Marion I. Walter. Hillsdale, N.J.: Lawrence Erlbaum Associates, 1994.

National Center for Research in Mathematical Sciences Education and Freudenthal Institute. "Comparing Quantities." Middle-Grades Unit in Mathematics In Context curriculum. Chicago, Ill.: Encyclopaedia Britannica Educational Corp., 1998.

National Council of Teachers of Mathematics (NCTM). *Curriculum and Evaluation Standards for School Mathematics.* Reston, Va.: NCTM, 1989.

———. *Professional Standards for Teaching Mathematics.* Reston, Va.: NCTM, 1991.

———. *Assessment Standards for School Mathematics.* Reston, Va.: NCTM, 1995.

———. *Principles and Standards for School Mathematics.* Reston, Va.: NCTM, 2000.

———. "E-Examples." Available at standards.nctm.org/document/ eexamples/index.htm as of July 2002.

National Research Council. *Adding It Up: Helping Children Learn Mathematics.* Edited by Jeremy Kilpatrick, Jane Swafford, and Bradford Findell. Washington, D.C.: National Academy Press, 2001.

National Research Council, Mathematical Sciences Education Board. *Everybody Counts: A Report to the Nation on the Future of Mathematics Education.* Washington, D.C.: National Academy Press, 1989.

Paine, Lynn, and Liping Ma. "Teachers Working Together: A Dialogue on Organizational and Cultural Perspectives of Chinese Teachers." *International Journal of Educational Research* 19 (1993): 675–98.

Perry, Michelle, Scott W. Vanderstoep, and Shirley L. Yu. "Asking Questions in First-Grade Mathematics Classes: Potential Influences on Mathematical Thought." *Journal of Educational Psychology* 85 (1993): 31–40.

Pólya, George. *How to Solve It.* Garden City, N.Y.: Doubleday, 1945.

———. *Mathematical Discovery: On Understanding, Learning, and Teaching Problem Solving.* Combined ed. New York: John Wiley & Sons, 1981.

Ray, Joseph. *Practical Arithmetic.* Cincinnati, Ohio: Wilson, Hinkle & Co, 1857.

———. *Ray's Algebra: Part First.* Rev. ed. Cincinnati, Ohio: Van Antwerp, Bragg & Co., 1848.

Reis, Sally M., and Jeanne H. Purcell. "An Analysis of Content Elimination and Strategies Used by Elementary Classroom Teachers and the Curriculum Compacting Process. *Journal for the Education of the Gifted* 16 (1993): 147–70.

Resnick, Lauren B. "Developing Mathematical Knowledge." *American Psychologist* 44 (1989): 162–9.

Ridgway James, Judith S. Zawojewski, Mark N. Hoover, and Diana Lambdin. "Student Attainment in the Connected Mathematics Curriculum." In *Standards-Oriented School Mathematics Curricula: What Are They? What Do Students Learn?* edited by Sharon Senk and Denisse Thompson. Mahwah, N.J.: Lawrence Erlbaum Associates, 2002.

Rogers, Karen B. *Re-forming Gifted Education: Matching the Program to the Child.* Scottsdale, Ariz.: Great Potential Press, 2002.

Romberg, Thomas, A., and Mary Shafer. "Mathematics in Context (MiC): Preliminary Evidence about Student Outcomes." In *Standards-Oriented School Mathematics Curricula: What Are They? What Do Students Learn?* edited by Sharon Senk and Denisse Thompson. Mahwah, N.J.: Lawrence Erlbaum Associates, 2002.

Russell, Susan Jo. "Mathematical Reasoning in the Elementary Grades." In *Developing Mathematical Reasoning in Grades K–12,* edited by Lee V. Stiff, pp. 1–12. Reston, Va.: National Council of Teachers of Mathematics, 1999.

Schifter, Deborah, Virginia Bastable, and Susan Jo Russell. *Making Meaning for Operations.* Parsippany, N.J.: Dale Seymour Publications, 1999.

Schifter, Deborah, and Catherine T. Fosnot. *Reconstructing Mathematics Education: Stories of Teachers Meeting the Challenge of Reform.* New York: Teachers College Press, 1993.

Schoenfeld, Alan. H. "Learning to Think Mathematically: Problem Solving, Metacognition, and Sense Making in Mathematics." In *Handbook of Research on Mathematics Teaching and Learning,* edited by Douglas A. Grouws, pp. 334–70. New York: Macmillan, 1992.

———. "Making Mathematics Work for All Children: Issues of Standards, Testing, and Equity." *Educational Researcher* 31 (2002): 13–25.

Schroeder, Thomas L., and Frank K. Lester Jr. "Developing Understanding in Mathematics via Problem Solving." In *New Directions for Elementary School Mathematics,* 1989 Yearbook of the National Council of Teachers of Mathematics (NCTM), edited by Paul R. Trafton, pp. 31–42. Reston, Va.: NCTM, 1989.

Sfard, Anna. "Balancing the Unbalanceable: The NCTM Standards in Light of Theories of Learning Mathematics." In *A Research Companion to "Principles and Standards for School Mathematics,"* edited by Jeremy Kilpatrick and W. Gary Martin, pp. 353–92. Reston, Va.: National Council of Teachers of Mathematics, 2003.

Sheffield, Linda J. *Developing Mathematically Promising Students.* Reston, Va: National Council of Teachers of Mathematics, 1999.

Shimahara, Nobuo, and Akira Sakai. *Learning to Teach in Two Cultures: Japan and the United States.* New York: Garland, 1995.

Shimizu, Yoshinori. "Aspects of Mathematics Teacher Education in Japan: Focusing on Teachers' Roles." *Journal of Mathematics Teacher Education* 2 (January 1999): 107–16.

Siefert, H. O. R. *Principles of Arithmetic: Embracing Common Fractions, Decimal Fractions, Percentage, Proportion, Involution, Evolution and Mensuration: A Manual for Teachers and Normal Students.* Boston: D. C. Heath & Co., 1902.

Silver, Edward A. "Foundations of Cognitive Theory and Research for Mathematics Problem-Solving Instruction." In *Cognitive Science and Mathematics Education,* edited by Alan H. Schoenfeld, pp. 33–60. Hillsdale, N.J.: Lawrence Erlbaum Associates, 1987.

———. "On Mathematical Problem Posing." *For the Learning of Mathematics* 14 (February 1994): 19–28.

Silver, Edward A., ed. *Teaching and Learning Mathematical Problem Solving: Multiple Research Perspectives.* Mahwah, N.J.: Lawrence Erlbaum Associates, 1985.

Silver, Edward A., Susan S. Leung, and Jinfa Cai. "Generating Multiple Solutions for a Problem: A Comparison of the Responses of U.S. and Japanese Students." *Educational Studies in Mathematics* 28 (1995): 35–54.

Simon, Martin A. "Reconstructing Mathematics Pedagogy from a Constructivist Perspective." *Journal for Research in Mathematics Education* 26 (March 1995): 114–45.

Smith, Margaret S. "Balancing Old and New: An Experienced Middle School Teacher's Learning in the Context of Mathematics Instructional Reform." *Elementary School Journal* 100 (2000a): 351–75.

———. "A Comparison of the Types of Mathematics Tasks and How They Were Completed during Eighth-Grade Mathematics Instruction in Germany, Japan, and the United States." Unpublished doctoral dissertation, University of Delaware, 2000b.

———. "Life of a Mathematics Task: Secondary Analysis of the Data from the Third International Mathematics and Science Video Study." Forthcoming.

Stanic, George M. A., and Jeremy Kilpatrick. "Historical Perspectives on Problem Solving in the Mathematics Curriculum." In *The Teaching and Assessing of Mathematical Problem Solving,* edited by Randall I. Charles and Edward A. Silver, pp. 1–22. Reston, Va.: National Council of Teachers of Mathematics, 1988.

Steffe, Leslie P., Paul Cobb, and Ernst von Glasersfeld. *Construction of Arithmetical Meanings and Strategies.* New York: Springer-Verlag, 1988.

Steffe, Leslie P., and Thomas Kieren. "Radical Constructivism and Mathematics Education." *Journal for Research in Mathematics Education* 25 (December 1994): 711–33.

Stein, Mary Kay, Barbara W. Grover, and Marjorie A. Henningsen. "Building Student Capacity for Mathematical Thinking and Reasoning: An Analysis of Mathematical Tasks Used in Reform Classrooms." *American Educational Research Journal* 33 (1996): 455–88.

Stein, Mary Kay, Edward Silver, and Margaret Schwann Smith. "Mathematics Reform and Teacher Development: A Community of Practice Perspective." In *Thinking Practices in Mathematics and Science Learning,* edited by James Greeno and Shelley Goldman, pp. 17–52. Mahwah, N.J.: Lawrence Erlbaum Associates, 1998.

Stein, Mary Kay, Margaret S. Smith, and Edward A. Silver. "The Development of Professional Developers." *Harvard Educational Review* 69 (1999): 237–69.

Stenmark, Jean. *Mathematics Assessment: Myths, Models, Good Questions, and Practical Suggestions.* Reston, Va.: National Council of Teachers of Mathematics, 1991.

Stephan, Michelle, Paul Cobb, Koeno Gravemeijer, and Beth Estes. "The Role of Tools in Supporting Students' Development of Measurement Conceptions." In *The Roles of Representation in School Mathematics,*

2001 Yearbook of the National Council of Teachers of Mathematics (NCTM), edited by Al Cuoco, pp. 63–76. Reston, Va.: NCTM, 2001.

Stigler, James W., Clea Fernandez, and Makoto Yoshida. "Traditions of School Mathematics in Japanese and American Elementary Classrooms." In *Theories of Mathematical Learning*, edited by Leslie P. Steffe, Perla Nesher, Paul Cobb, Gerald A. Goldin, and Brian Greer, pp. 149–75. Mahwah, N.J.: Lawrence Erlbaum Associates, 1996.

Stigler, James W., Patrick Gonzales, Takako Kawanaka, Steffen Knoll, and Ana Serrano. The *TIMSS Videotape Classroom Study: Methods and Findings from an Exploratory Research Project on Eighth-Grade Mathematics Instruction in Germany, Japan, and the United States.* Washington, D.C.: U.S. Government Printing Office, 1999.

Stigler, James W., and James Hiebert. *The Teaching Gap: Best Ideas from the World's Teachers for Improving Education in the Classroom.* New York: The Free Press, 1999.

Stigler, James W., Shiying Lee, and Harold W. Stevenson. *Mathematical Knowledge of Japanese, Chinese, and American Elementary School Children.* Reston, Va.: National Council of Teachers of Mathematics, 1990.

Thompson, Alba G. "Teachers' Beliefs and Conceptions: A Synthesis of the Research." In *Handbook of Research on Mathematics Teaching and Learning*, edited by Douglas A. Grouws, pp. 127–46. New York: Macmillan, 1992.

Thompson, Alba, Randolph Philipp, Patrick Thompson, and Barbara Boyd. "Calculational and Conceptual Orientations in Teaching Mathematics." In *Professional Development for Teachers of Mathematics*, 1994 Yearbook of the National Council of Teachers of Mathematics (NCTM), edited by Douglas B. Aichele and Arthur F. Coxford, pp. 79–92. Reston, Va.: NCTM, 1994.

Thorndike, Edward L. *The Psychology of Arithmetic.* New York: Macmillan, 1922.

Thornton, Carol A., and Graham A. Jones. "Adapting Instruction for Students with Special Learning Needs, K–8," *Journal of Education* 178 (spring 1996): 59–69.

Tunc Pekkan, Zelha. "What Can We Know about Pre-service Teachers' Mathematical Content Knowledge through Their E-mail Discussions with Sixth Grade Students?" Proceedings of the Second International Conference on the Teaching of Mathematics at the Undergraduate Level, University of Crete, Rethymnon, Greece, July 2002.

Upton, C. B. *Social Utility Arithmetics—First Book.* New York: American Book, 1939.

U.S. Department of Education, National Center for Education Statistics. *Pursuing Excellence: A Study of U.S. Fourth-Grade Mathematics and Science Achievement in International Context.* Washington, D.C.: U.S. Government Printing Office, 1997. [NCES 97-255]

Van de Walle, John A. *Elementary and Middle School School Mathematics: Teaching Developmentally.* 4th ed. New York: Longman, 2001.

Verschaffel, Leuven, and Erik De Corte. "Teaching Realistic Mathematical Modeling in the Elementary School: A Teaching Experiments with Fifth Graders." *Journal for Research in Mathematics Education* 28 (November 1997): 577–601.

von Glasersfeld, Ernst. *Constructivism and How It Relates to Teaching and Learning.* Milton Keynes, U.K.: Open University, 1988. [Cassette Recording No. MKCM 1226 887M 9252 ME 234 AC1]

Wearne, Diana, and James Hiebert. "A Cognitive Approach to Meaningful Mathematics Instruction: Testing a Local Theory Using Decimal Numbers." *Journal for Research in Mathematics Education* 19 (November 1988): 371–84.

Wentworth, G. A. *Plane and Solid Geometry.* Boston: Ginn & Co., 1899.

———. *New School Algebra.* Boston: Athenaeum, 1900.

Wood, Terry, and Patricia Sellers. "Deepening the Analysis: Longitudinal Assessment of a Problem-Centered Mathematics Program." *Journal for Research in Mathematics Education* 28 (March 1997): 163–86.

Yackel, Erna, and Paul Cobb. "Sociomathematical Norms, Argumentation, and Autonomy in Mathematics." *Journal for Research in Mathematics Education* 27 (1996): 458–77.

Readers of *Teaching Mathematics through Problem Solving: Prekindergarten–Grade 6* might be interested in the following resources on problem solving from the National Council of Teachers of Mathematics:

➤ *Children Are Mathematical Problem Solvers,* edited by Lynae E. Sakshaug, Melfried Olson, and Judith Olson. Reston, Va.: National Council of Teachers of Mathematics, 2002.

> This engaging collection of problems from the "Problem Solvers" column of *Teaching Children Mathematics* helps children explore significant mathematical content through many problem-solving experiences that apply and strengthen their problem-solving abilities. The book also features solutions and children's work from children and teachers around the country. Please consult www.nctm.org/catalog for order and price information.

➤ Special Focus Issue: **Problem Solving.** *Mathematics Teacher* 96, no. 8 (November 2003).

This theme issue includes—

- teachers' reflections on their own development as providers of problem-solving environments;

- author-submitted problems that generate constructive problem-solving activities and lead to important learning outcomes;

- descriptions of insightful student approaches and ways to use these approaches to advance students' learning;

- teachers' shared classroom heuristics, including several supported by the use of technology.

Please consult www.nctm.org/catalog for order and price information.

For the most up-to-date listing of NCTM resources on topics of interest to mathematics educators, as well as information on membership benefits, conferences, and workshops, visit the NCTM Web site at www.nctm.org.